Economic Beginnings in
Colonial South Carolina

TRICENTENNIAL STUDIES, NUMBER 3

This volume is part of a series of *Tricentennial Studies,* published by the University of South Carolina Press on behalf of the South Carolina Tricentennial Commission, to commemorate the founding of South Carolina in 1670.

ECONOMIC BEGINNINGS IN COLONIAL SOUTH CAROLINA
1670–1730

Converse D. Clowse

Published for the
South Carolina Tricentennial Commission
by the
UNIVERSITY OF SOUTH CAROLINA PRESS
Columbia, South Carolina

To
B. BARK C.

PREFACE

I N WORKS ABOUT EARLY AMERICA, THE ECONOMY RECEIVES comparatively little attention. There is no comprehensive economic history of colonial America. Of the narrower studies, many are incomplete or otherwise unsatisfactory. Though most historians would agree that this deficiency seriously impairs our understanding of the process of colonial maturation, some gaps may never be filled.

The explanation lies mainly with the sources and the dilemmas they engender. Some unsolved problems trace to the lack of research materials surviving, if they ever existed. In other instances, available data on a given subject may consist solely of widely scattered bits and pieces. Under these handicaps, piecing the sources together requires drudgery, and interpreting them is perplexing.

Colonial South Carolina's economic history conforms to the basic pattern outlined above. No economic history of the colony has been published. Few monographs on economic topics have appeared. There are source materials, but the evidence is dispersed and the missing links are many.

Originally, the ambitious objective of this study was to survey the economic history of the colony, but the limited primary and secondary sources forced a narrowing. The result is an examination of the economic beginnings in this colony during its first phase, the proprietary era. Since economic concerns intermingled with politics, local and imperial, as well as other aspects of the settlers' lives, these connections have been established, generally in a more suggestive than definitive manner. Hopefully, this interpretation of events will help someone to write a complete economic history of colonial South Carolina, whose early development does not closely parallel that of any other English settlement.

For the benefit of readers, a few procedures and practices followed should be explained. Since their exactness is not of prime importance in this study, dates have been left "Old Style," except that double designations of years have been modernized (for example: March 10, 1717/8 became March 10, 1718). January 1 has been treated as the start of each new year, though that was not the contemporary practice. Where a word or name might have variant spellings, an arbitrary choice has been made. Quotations have not been altered except that some commonly contracted words have been expanded; capital letters have been left unchanged.

I could not begin to give credit to every person who has at some time given me help, but some deserve mention. I owe most to Professor Clarence L. Ver Steeg who first interested me in colonial South Carolina in his seminar at Northwestern University. Over almost a decade, I have spent many delightful days at the South Carolina Department of Archives and History. I particularly wish to thank Mr. Charles Lee, Director, and Mr. William McDowell, Associate Director, as well as Miss Ruth Green, Miss Wylma Wates, Mrs. Florence Law, and Mr. Francis M. Hutson (now retired) for their assistance and guidance. Mr. E. L. Inabinett, Director, and his staff, at the South Caroliniana Library have extended many courtesies to me.

Librarians at the University of North Carolina at Greensboro, the University of North Carolina at Chapel Hill, and Duke University obtained many essential reference works for me. I am also grateful to the University of North Carolina at

Greensboro for a semester's leave of absence so that work on this study might proceed. A grant from the University's Research Council was used to prepare the manuscript. My thanks go to Mr. Charles L. Hodgin for drawing the map, and to Miss Elizabeth Booker, who typed the final draft.

Last, but hardly least, I want to express my gratitude to my wife, Barbara. She read, revised, corrected, criticized, and suggested until every page bears some improvement she initiated.

January 1970   C. D. C.
Greensboro, North Carolina

CONTENTS

Economic Beginnings in
Colonial South Carolina

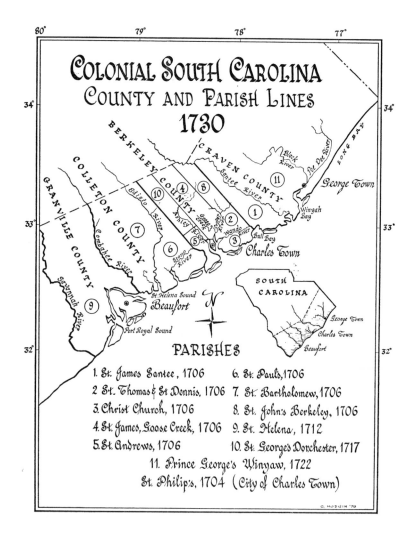

COLONIAL SOUTH CAROLINA
COUNTY AND PARISH LINES
1730

BERKELEY COUNTY
CRAVEN COUNTY
COLLETON COUNTY
GRANVILLE COUNTY

Black River
Pee Dee River
LONG BAY
Santee River
George Town
Winyah Bay
Edisto River
Ashley River
Goose Creek
Cooper River
Wando River
Bull Bay
Charles Town
Stono River
Combahee River
Savannah River
St. Helena Sound
Beaufort
Port Royal Sound

SOUTH CAROLINA
George Town
Charles Town
Beaufort

PARISHES

1. St. James Santee, 1706
2. St. Thomas & St Dennis, 1706
3. Christ Church, 1706
4. St. James, Goose Creek, 1706
5. St. Andrews, 1706
6. St. Pauls, 1706
7. St. Bartholomew, 1706
8. St. John's Berkeley, 1706
9. St. Helena, 1712
10. St. George's Dorchester, 1717
11. Prince George's Winyaw, 1722

St. Philip's, 1704 (City of Charles Town)

C. HODGIN '70

CHAPTER I

The Proprietors and Their Plans

WHEN CHARLES II RECOVERED HIS THRONE IN 1660, ENG-land's long-sublimated drive to start new colonies could be released. Though absorbed by internal events over the past twenty years, Englishmen of all political stripes had continued to regard commerce and colonies as vital as the passage of the first Navigation Acts and the first Dutch trade war attest. Despite the failure or unprofitableness of most colonizing ventures before 1640, many risk capitalists remained convinced of the potential of such projects. They believed that future failures would be avoided by learning from past mistakes. Their optimism was fed by the high returns being received from warm-climate colonies in the New World, and the slow but steady growth of the trade of the more northerly settlements. Such men were eager to take advantage of the new opportunities which the Restoration seemed to offer.

In 1660 English holdings on the North American mainland extended no farther south than Virginia. The weak Spanish mission system went no farther north than Guale, the Spaniard's name for what was to become Georgia. The area in between was attractive and had drawn interest for many decades. Those who had explored or lived there briefly had been impressed generally, and the unoccupied zone had strategic importance. Spain wanted it free from the control of any other European power since it was on the western and northern flanks of her treasure fleets which sailed north to near Bermuda before turning east. England eyed it for expansion and for protection of the southern border of her rapidly developing continental colonies.

From 1520 onward, Spain and France had made many "intrusions" into the region.[1] Though these thrusts were impermanent and limited in scope, they should not be dismissed lightly. The negative effect which the first European invaders had on the native peoples was important subsequently. Additionally, these Spaniards and Frenchmen produced literature describing the attributes and liabilities of the area. Such narratives provided basic information for everyone, for all Europeans concerned with the New World read the chronicles of their competitors as well as digested the evaluations of their own men. Some of the accounts were more misleading than helpful, but they were a start.[2]

[1] A convenient but brief summary of these episodes is by Paul Quattlebaum, *The Land Called Chicora: The Carolinas Under Spanish Rule with French Intrusions, 1520–1670* (Gainesville, 1956). More detailed works from the Spanish perspective include Woodbury Lowery, *The Spanish Settlements Within the Present Limits of the United States, 1513–1574*, 2 vols. (New York, 1901–1905); C. H. Haring, *The Spanish Empire in America* (New York, 1947); John Tate Lanning, *The Spanish Missions of Georgia* (Chapel Hill, 1935); Michael V. Gannon, *The Cross in the Sand: The Early Catholic Church in Florida, 1513–1870* (Gainesville, 1965). French attempts to make settlements in the area have been explained by Francis Parkman, *Pioneers of France in the New World*, Frontenac Edition (New York, 1915), I.

[2] For example, "Writers of Carolina," a list of French, Spanish, and English authors probably prepared in 1671, and noted by the editor as being in the handwriting of John Locke, in Langdon Cheves (ed.), *The Shaftesbury Papers and Other Records Relating to Carolina . . . prior to the Year 1676*, in *Collections of the South Carolina Historical Society*, V (Charleston, 1897), 265–266. Hereafter cited as Cheves (ed.), *Shaftesbury Papers*.

While Spain's contacts were more numerous and involved individuals pursuing a wider spectrum of objectives than those of France, sons of both nations left revealing details. Many of the Spaniards were interested in finding gold mines or the passage to the East, but missionaries and some adelantados and soldiers took time to determine the area's potential. Such a man was Pedro Menéndez de Aviles who in 1566 had gone to Chicora (the Spanish designation for South Carolina) to drive out the French. His extensive reports tell of his military operations, but they also place an emphasis on products such as wine, sugar, rice, silk, pitch, tar, timbers, and cattle which might be produced or grown there.[3] Jean Ribaut's efforts for France in the early 1560's centered on the hope that the Huguenots would find a haven where they could grow grapes and culture silk, economic activities supposedly fit for these latitudes.[4] Nearly every crop or industry tried in the English colonial era had been mentioned in some early report.

Since neither Spain nor France ever occupied the land permanently, England's colonizers seemed those most likely to move into this beckoning land. Long before 1660, Englishmen at home, to say nothing of Virginians, New Englanders, and Barbadians, had taken tentative steps toward making settlements there. Charles I had actually granted Sir Robert Heath the territory between the 31st and 36th parallels north latitude on October 30, 1629. Heath was charged with the usual responsibility of carrying the Christian religion to the Indians while increasing the trade and commerce of the kingdom.[5] Although the 1630's were boom years for English

[3] Quattlebaum, *Land Called Chicora*, 60. Lowery, *Spanish Settlements, 1562–1574*, 212–213.   [4] Quattlebaum, *Land Called Chicora*, 42–54.

[5] The Heath patent is included in numerous collections of documents including W. L. Saunders (ed.), *Colonial Records of North Carolina* (Raleigh, 1886–90), I, 5–13.

colonization, very little was done with Carolana (in subsequent charters the spelling was changed to Carolina).[6] A notable exception was at least the second attempt to transport a group of Huguenots to the area to start a silk industry. They never reached the projected place of settlement.[7]

While the Civil War and its aftermath kept Englishmen in England, English colonials were not stopped from investigating unoccupied lands, including the stretch of coast and the interior south of Virginia. Some New Englanders, concerned about agricultural conditions and the slow development of commerce in their area, were looking for lands with more promise. Carolina was one possibility. Some Virginians were curious about lands to the south. They furnished firsthand accounts which abounded in exciting details.[8]

Barbadians had more compelling reasons than New Englanders or Virginians for seeking new homes. First settled in 1627, Barbados had drawn thousands of Puritans during the Great Migration. The island, the most eastward of the West Indies, was not destined to become a Bible Commonwealth, however. In 1640 it had 35,000 whites and a few thousand slaves. By 1650 sugar plantations worked by African slaves had become the foundation of the island's wealth and shaper of its economic and social structure. By 1670 the number of white inhabitants had declined to about 20,000, with perhaps 40,000 slaves packed into an unexpandable 166 square

[6] For a discussion of the name, see A. S. Salley, *The Origin of Carolina* (Columbia, 1926).

[7] For documents pertaining to this attempted settlement, see W. Noel Sainsbury and others (eds.), *Calendar of State Papers, Colonial Series, America and West Indies, 1574– —* (London, 1862– —), I, 108–111, 190–191, 194, 197–198, 207.

[8] Edward Bland et al., *The Discovery of New Brittaine, 1650* (London, 1651), as reprinted by A. S. Salley (ed.), *Narratives of Early Carolina, 1650–1708* (*Narratives of Early American History* series, J. Franklin Jameson [ed.]) (New York, 1911), 82–108; Francis Yeardley to John Ferrar, May 8, 1654, ibid., 21–29.

miles. Accompaning this increase in total population and the change in its composition was concentration of land into comparatively few hands. One contemporary estimate placed the number of farms and plantations at 11,200 in 1645, but by 1667 only 745 plantations were in operation. Great amounts of capital to buy expensive land and slaves were a necessity. The small planter was rapidly being forced off the land with no place to go. At the same time, sugar prices were falling, which discouraged many large planters.[9] The Barbadians were also experiencing other pressures. Enforcement of the Navigation Acts curtailed the island's trade, much of which had been carried on with the Dutch. This raised the cost of manufactured goods. Taxes were high because the island, due to its exposed position, had to be in a constant defensive posture. Political crises were endemic. The climax came in 1662 when unpopular proprietary rule was ended and the island became a Royal Colony. Even nature seemed to conspire against the settlers. Records of the 1660's are dotted with reports of excessive rains and floodings, crops attacked by pests, and other catastrophes.[10]

It is hardly surprising that some Barbadians would be attracted to any place of reasonable promise. Carolina, Jamaica, and other West Indian islands were some of the places considered. As early as 1650, Lord Willoughby, one-

[9] Much of the material in this paragraph came from Richard S. Dunn, "The Barbados Census of 1680: Profile of the Richest Colony in English America," William and Mary Quarterly, 3rd Series, XXVI (1969), 3–30. In revising earlier views of Barbados in this period, Dunn cites considerable evidence which indicates that there were doubtless many more than 745 agricultural units in 1667. He does not, however, dispute the basic pattern of a falling white population, a rising slave population, and a continuing consolidation of landholding. Also see Vincent T. Harlow, A History of Barbados, 1625–1685 (Oxford, 1926), 151–175, 292–330; Adelaide B. Helwig, "The Early History of Barbados and Her Influence Upon the Development of South Carolina" (unpublished Ph.D. dissertation, University of California, Berkeley, 1931), 88–104.

[10] Helwig, "Early History of Barbados," 41–61, 144–146.

time governor of Barbados, had proposed migration to the Carolina coast. A few years later, various island entrepreneurs banded together into loose organizations to prospect for places to settle.[11] These Barbadians had reasons for moving, they had money, they had colonial know-how; they only lacked legal authority to plant a colony in Carolina.

By the early 1660's Carolina had whetted the appetites of many English colonials. While the charter was legally entangled in England, the King and his court system had the power to straighten out these matters at the appropriate moment. If a settlement were attempted, other problems would have to be faced. Would Spain resist? The odds were against serious interference, inasmuch as Spain had not attacked other mainland colonies. Nevertheless, her attitude might be different toward a new colony much nearer to the Florida peninsula. Though much was known about the natural environment, that, too, would have some surprises for new settlers. None of these seemed to be an insurmountable barrier.

If settlers in America were always on the lookout for valuable lands, it took money, and sometimes influence, to obtain charter rights from the crown. Before 1640 most who obtained overseas lands were English merchants who pooled their resources in joint stock company ventures. After the Restoration those in favor at court, often titled individuals, had the privilege of dabbling in such business affairs. Courtiers used their friendship with Charles II, who had more obligations, monetary and moral, than he had means to pay. They sought and took payment in the form of proprietary grants or other rights disposable by the crown. Those who sought such emoluments were conscious of their selfish objectives, but, as patriotic Englishmen imbued with mercantilis-

[11] Ibid., 172–175.

tic concepts, they rationalized that individual and national profits were complementary, not exclusive. Charles II was not giving away much, since vast overseas tracts or trading rights were of little value to him until they returned something. While several groups in America were exploring the possibilities of settling in Carolina, eight titled Englishmen banded together to obtain rights to the area. They were typical men of affairs in this era. Several of the group, the Earl of Craven, the Earl of Clarendon, the Duke of Albemarle, and Lord Ashley [12] were among the most distinguished peers of the realm. The other four, Lord John Berkeley, Sir William Berkeley, Sir George Carteret, and Sir John Colleton, were not as famous, but they were far from being nonentities. Since most of these men do not figure in the history of Carolina, it is sufficient to note that each had been and was involved in colonial affairs and colonial ventures.[13] Exactly why these eight came together is not known, but the initial impulse must have been supplied by either Sir John Colleton, long a resident of Barbados, or Sir William Berkeley, former and future governor of Virginia, both of whom were in London around the time the charter was granted.[14] Who selected or organized the group is not as important as the obvious fact that these were men of ability, knowledgeable about colonial affairs, with personal re-

[12] Though better known in English history as the Earl of Shaftesbury, a title he received in 1672, to avoid confusion he is referred to as Lord Ashley throughout this work.

[13] Sketches of the public careers of all except Sir John Colleton are included in Leslie Stephen and Sidney Lee (eds.) , *Dictionary of National Biography*, reprint edition (Oxford, 1921–1922) , II, 361–364; II, 368–369; III, 1117–1119; IV, 1036–1055; V, 45–49; X, 370–389; XIII, 594–610, and hereafter cited as *DNB*. Also see William S. Powell, *The Carolina Charter of 1663,* . . . , *With Biographical Sketches of the Proprietors* (Raleigh, 1954) .

[14] Louise Fargo Brown, *The First Earl of Shaftesbury* (New York, 1933) , 151–152.

sources to put into colonization. They could have their way with Charles II because he owed each something.

In the words of the Charter, the eight "humbly besought" the right to transport settlers to a vacant area between 31° and 36° north latitude, the same land given Heath in 1629. A number of articles extolled the religious zeal of the proprietors and their desire to spread the benefit of Christianity among the Indians, but most of the document spelled out the king's terms and conditions. It is rather typical of all such proprietary charters. The proprietors were assured of almost complete governmental powers under the Bishop of Durham clause which was included. The most powerful hold on the economy was the right to "assign, alien, grant, demise and enfoef" the land. To encourage rapid settlement and to benefit the empire, silks, wines, currants, raisins, capers, wax, almonds, oil, and olives produced would be allowed into England duty-free for seven years after production began.[15] Certainly the Lords Proprietors had sufficient powers to insure a handsome return if their managerial skills could translate these rights into inducements and opportunities for settlers.

After they received a charter in 1663, the proprietors' enthusiasm waned. They did little to develop their domains until after 1667. During these four years several groups of established American colonists did initiate negotiations which might have proved an inexpensive way to start to colonize Carolina. In every instance, the proprietors' attitude was less than encouraging. Though these attempts at settlement eventually failed, negotiations revealed the proprietors' consensus about policies to develop their province. The terms offered each group were similar and based upon principles to which the proprietary would adhere as long as

[15] Reprinted in numerous collections of documents including Powell, *Carolina Charter of 1663*, 21–37.

it existed. Settlers in Carolina would have a representative lower house of the legislature, but the governor and council would be appointed by the proprietors. Land would be allocated under a headright system and would bear an annual quitrent.[16]

The proprietors made it clear from the start that they had no intention of surrendering any of the vast political and economic power granted to them under their charter. While there is no doubt of their right to insist upon these principles, such a posture was bound to repel American colonists, such as New Englanders, who had lived under less rigid systems. The first organization to petition for terms of settlement had been "The Adventurers about Cape Fayre," a group of Massachusetts Bay colonists, plus some English merchants brought in for financial support and to use their influence in England to obtain a charter. In late 1662, six months before the proprietors themselves had a charter, these Massachusetts promoters sent out William Hilton to explore the area. He returned from the Cape Fear region with a favorable report. They sent a vanguard to the Cape Fear area, but the group quickly gave up and left. Despite this setback, negotiations continued until the proprietors' stringent terms were learned. Given the inflexible land and governmental policies adopted, it was unlikely that Carolina's future growth could be based on recruiting in America. Certainly the sole possibility of enticing settlers from the thinly settled mainland colonies would be liberal terms.

The proprietors were also approached by the Barbadian Adventurers who wished to obtain a county or colony of 1,000 square miles which they would rule as an autonomous enclave. In August 1663 they sent the available and experi-

---

16 The account of these early attempts at settlement in Carolina owes much to Lawrence Lee, *The Lower Cape Fear in Colonial Days* (Chapel Hill, 1965), 28–53.

enced William Hilton on a second voyage to Carolina. Hilton and his crew explored near Port Royal and then worked their way up the coast as far as Cape Fear before returning to Barbados in early 1664. Hilton's report, the most extensive narrative about Carolina yet written by an Englishman, judged that the land had every attribute necessary for prosperity.[17] Four months after Hilton returned to Barbados, in May 1664, a splinter group of the Barbadian Adventurers led by John and Henry Vassell and Robert Sandford sent a small group of settlers to Cape Fear. Though efforts to gain proprietary sanction failed, the colony, called Clarendon County, existed tenuously for three more years.

Rejecting their original proposal, the proprietors offered to the main body of Barbadian Adventurers terms which contained one important proviso not put to the New Englanders. They wished the Barbadians to settle in the southern part of the province near Port Royal. Thereafter the proprietors always focused on the southern part of their grant. Attempts to settle the northern areas were never hindered, but more generous land grants and other concessions awaited those who would go to future South Carolina. It is possible that the proprietors concluded from mounting evidence that the southern area was more promising for the staples they anticipated. It was also known that the broken coastline in the southern part of Carolina would allow easier access.

After long delays, in January 1665, the main group of Barbadian Adventurers and the proprietary reached an agreement generally known as the Barbados Concessions.[18] Barbadian planters would put up money to transport settlers who could not pay their own passage. Each man who paid in

---

[17] William Hilton, *A Relation of Discovery* (London, 1664). This is reprinted in Salley (ed.), *Narratives of Early Carolina*, 37–61.

[18] "Barbadoes Concessions," Cheves (ed.), *Shaftesbury Papers*, 29–49.

1,000 pounds of sugar was entitled to receive 500 acres of land in Carolina. Settlers were obligated to carry six months' food supply, and a firearm with 10 pounds of powder and 20 pounds of bullets. The proprietors would supply military stores for a fort to be built near Port Royal. Governmental arrangements resembled those offered the New Englanders earlier. The generous scale of land allotments was the strongest inducement to potential settlers. Those who went first and took greater risks would receive larger headrights than those who came later. Settlers at Port Royal, named Craven County, would have larger grants than those of Clarendon County. Those going with the first fleet to Craven County were to have a headright of 150 acres. The headright was then to be reduced in steps until 1667, when it would be pegged at 60 acres. Settlers already in Clarendon County were to be allowed 100 acres and those in Albermarle County (the designation for the irregular settlements near Albemarle Sound), only 8o acres. Future settlers in these two counties would receive sharply reduced headrights.

After months of organizational activity, a small expedition led by Governor John Yeamans set out from Barbados bound for Port Royal in October, 1665. Driven ashore at Cape Fear by bad sailing luck, they joined the miserable remnant of the unauthorized settlement started by the Vassells and Sandford. With the announcement of a larger headright for settling at Port Royal, there was scant hope of further migration to Clarendon County. The settlers tried unsuccessfully to have proprietary land policies revised, but the proprietors would not compromise. Emigration steadily depleted their population. Indian troubles added to their woes, and in the early autumn of 1667 the moribund settlement was completely abandoned.

The venture did have one consequence significant for the future of Carolina. Governor Yeamans had arranged for

Robert Sandford to go on a voyage of exploration south along the coast. Sandford decided to allow one of his party, young Henry Woodward, to remain in the vicinity of Port Royal and live among the Indians. Woodward's knowledge of the tribes and countryside proved of incalculable value when settlement of the region was undertaken by the proprietary. Though Sandford mostly confirmed what others had already discovered, his information resulted in still another account to stir the imagination of interested persons. Such narratives moved the proprietors to subsidize the publication in 1666 of a publicity pamphlet credited to Robert Horne.[19]

Four years after Charles II had awarded the first Carolina Charter, no settlers had been transported to the province as a direct result of proprietary initiative. The only existing settlements were those in the Albemarle Sound area started in the 1650's, hardly the result of proprietary efforts. It was an inauspicious beginning for eight men with vast experience in public and colonial affairs. The difficulty lay with the proprietary itself. Although few causes can be pinpointed with sureness, a number of circumstances suggest reasons for this slow start. While all eight must have originally thought it worthwhile, the project may have been a passing fancy for some. Samuel Pepys knew all with the possible exception of Sir William Berkeley, and he recorded remarks about the other seven and their conversations but failed to mention Carolina.[20] The middle 1660's were noted for disasters—the Great Fire of London, the plague epidemics, and the disas-

[19] Robert Sandford, "A Relation of a Voyage on the Coast of the Province of Carolina, 1666." Apparently this was prepared as a letter to the proprietors. Included in Salley (ed.), *Narratives of Early Carolina*, 75–108; Robert Horne, *A Brief Description of the Province of Carolina* (London, 1666), in *ibid.*, 66–73.

[20] A. V. Goodpasture, "Pepys and the Proprietors of Carolina," *Tennessee Historical Magazine*, VI (1920), 166–176.

trous second Dutch war. These catastrophes disrupted the normal flow of affairs and consumed the energies of leading Englishmen, like the proprietors.[21]

Old age and death figure in the story. Sir John Colleton, the most zealous worker for the proprietary during the early years, died in 1666.[22] The Duke of Albemarle—also quite interested at first—grew infirm; he retired in 1668 and died in 1670.[23] National politics consumed some and destroyed others. It is well known that Ashley and Clarendon became bitter political rivals. Clarendon fell from power and went into judicious exile in 1667. Sir George Carteret was blamed for his failures in the second Dutch war, and he left active affairs.[24] Personal animosity marred relations between Clarendon and Lord John Berkeley.[25] Men who dislike and distrust one another are capable of cooperation, but collaboration for business ends generally leads to better results when relationships among equals are cordial.

The major activity of the proprietary from 1663 to 1667 was to clear up certain legal technicalities about their grant. The proprietors had no more than received the charter when they went to court to void the Heath Patent; the ruling in their favor was handed down on August 12, 1663. To assure that the Albemarle settlements were in their domain, they obtained a second Charter from Charles II in 1665. Though basically similar to the first, it extended the northern boundary from 36° to 36°30′. The southern boundary was pushed from 31° to 29°, making a pretentious claim to some of Spanish Florida.[26]

During these four years, the proprietors exhibited only limited comprehension of the settlement process and little

[21] For example, the Earl of Craven supervised relief for victims of the fire and the plague. *DNB*, V, 45–49.   [22] Brown, *Shaftesbury*, 153.
[23] *DNB*, XIII, 607.   [24] Ibid., III, 1118.   [25] Ibid., II, 362.
[26] In numerous documentary collections including Saunders (ed.), *Colonial Records of North Carolina*, I, 102–114.

concern for their own best interest. They negotiated with various promoters who might have placed numbers of people in Carolina at a minimal expense and bother to themselves, but their responses failed to encourage all potential underwriters and migrants equally. When they did stipulate terms, they spent an inordinate amount of detail on political and judicial relationships rather than concentrating on economic concessions which would people their domains and give the province value. They did not seem to understand how to use the millions of acres they possessed in order to entice immigrants. They tended to offer promoters too much land and common settlers too little. Mostly they appeared to be trying to keep power over all phases of government and economy in their own hands. Their vacillations and their inability to find direction caused the first barren years. It can be argued that the proprietary never completely overcame its lack of leadership.

After four years of drift, the fate of the organization hung in the balance. Lack of progress probably influenced Lord Ashley to assume the role of leadership in the enterprise. It has been difficult for those who have studied his life to account for his sudden emergence, but Carolina became a passion with him. One biographer says that the upswing of his interest in Carolina did not come until 1669.[27] Another authority believes that his assumption of a greater role in the colonial affairs of England after the fall of Clarendon in 1667 was the dividing line.[28] This coincidence of Ashley's interest in Carolina with his peak years as an English politician, 1667–1676, does form a rather intriguing parallel which, nevertheless, may have little significance.

Ashley was uniquely fitted for the role. His biographer

[27] Brown, *Shaftesbury*, 152.
[28] Edwin Ernest Rich, "The First Earl of Shaftesbury's Colonial Policy," *Royal Historical Society Transactions*, 5th Series, VII (1957), 51.

summed up this phase of his varied career by saying that in the 1660's he "was as well informed about the affairs of the colonies in general as was any individual in England." [29] His experience went back at least to the early 1640's when he became part owner of a small Barbados plantation, the type bought out by larger planters. He sold his share in the mid-1650's. He had invested in the slave trade. Besides Carolina, at various times he put funds in the Iron and Steel Corporation, the Africa Company, the Whalebone Company, the Mines Royal, Hudson's Bay Company, Bahamas and New Providence Proprietary, and Bermuda Proprietary. He could afford such risk ventures; his income from lands in England and other sources reached as high as £23,000 annually.[30]

Regardless of the master he was serving, Ashley's public career had one thread of consistency running through it. He was always involved with questions of trade, colonies, and empire. Other issues might be partisan matters, but these were of continuing national importance. All through the 1650's he served on various committees which considered such questions. After 1660 he was on both the Council of Trade and the Council for Plantations. He was, of course, not unusual in serving both Cromwell and Charles II. Men like him were responsible for the continuity of trade and colonial policies from the Interregnum into the Restoration.[31]

Lord Ashley's ideas about colonies had long since matured. His experiences as a governmental official, many contacts with merchants, and personal investments had rounded his comprehensive view. He envisaged a colonial empire

[29] Brown, *Shaftesbury*, 131.
[30] Ibid., 64, 151; Rich, "Shaftesbury's Colonial Policy," *Royal Hist. Soc. Trans.*, 5th Series, VII (1957), 56.
[31] Rich, "Shaftesbury's Colonial Policy," *Royal Hist. Soc. Trans.*, 5th Series, VII (1957), 49–52.

based on commerce, loosely supervised as long as loose controls did not jeopardize the interests of crown and merchants. An orthodox mercantilist, he supported the Navigation Acts. His feeling that trade determined the well-being of the nation brought continuing concern about England's relationship to Ireland and Scotland, but the real key to this trading empire, he maintained, was the overseas domains, particularly the West Indies. In all questions pertaining to colonies and trade, he strove to resolve equitably the conflicting objectives and interests of crown, merchants, and settlers. Though opinionated, Ashley was never doctrinaire about anything. Given a practical bent of mind, he cut corners on his colonial theories when his own interests were at stake. He defended Charles II's policy of granting no more proprietary charters, but he was perfectly willing to become a proprietor in Carolina and in other organizations. Despite his concern for empire, he sometimes advocated freer trade for his Carolina planters when trade with the Spaniards might have aided the growth of the colony. Though he thought in terms of silk, wine, or other tropical produce not then produced in the empire, when plans went awry he wanted Carolina to grow anything which would give him a return on his investment.[32]

In his drive to breathe new life into the Carolina project, Ashley soon enlisted his new friend and confidant, John Locke.[33] Ashley's initial contacts with Locke had been that of a patient seeking help from a medical expert, but friendship became dominant over the patient-doctor relationship. In 1667 Locke became his household physician and secretary,

[32] Ibid., 47–70. For a somewhat different view of Ashley's philosophy about trade, colonies, and empire, see Brown, Shaftesbury, particularly 128–180.

[33] For the relationship between Locke and Ashley, see Maurice Cranston, *John Locke: A Biography* (New York, 1957) , 105–120; Peter Laslett (ed.) , *John Locke's Two Treatises of Government* (Cambridge, England, 1960) , 25–30.

but he was Ashley's protégé and intellectual companion as well. Locke's biographer believes that Ashley was instrumental in Locke's development from a minor scholar and dilettante into a systematic philosopher.[34] Nor was their relationship marred by a social and economic gulf. Although Locke was hardly in the same category with his great lord, he was a member of the landowning class. Some of his inheritance, which allowed him to live the comfortable, independent life of a scholar, had been invested in colonial ventures and other financial opportunities long before he met Ashley.[35] Locke keenly felt his ties to the "investing class" and, his biographer concludes, "was easily infected with Ashley's zeal for commercial imperialism," which both viewed as a source of "personal and national enrichment." [36] Using his position, Ashley obtained for Locke government positions concerned with trade and colonies. In 1668 Locke was appointed as secretary of the Lords Proprietors of Carolina.

Lord Ashley's plans for Carolina were ready by April 26, 1669. On that day the proprietors agreed to certain articles which bound themselves to action. Included was one stipulation of funds to support a group of settlers who were supposed to depart in the near future from England for Port Royal. Every proprietor was to put up £500 at once. To sustain the original colonists and send more, each proprietor would place £200 annually into the hands of an agent for the following four years. This step committed £10,400 as a minimum, and for the first time the proprietors seemed to show some initiative.[37]

Before any settlers left England, it was necessary to translate the proprietary's general powers under its charter into a

---

[34] Cranston, *Locke*, 113.   [35] Ibid., 114–115.   [36] Ibid., 119.
[37] "Articles of Agreement" concluded by the proprietors, April 26, 1669, Cheves (ed.) , *Shaftesbury Papers*, 91–93.

constitutional arrangement defining the relationships between proprietors and settlers.[38] This task was performed by Lord Ashley and John Locke, though the proportional amount of credit, or blame, which should be assigned each will probably never be determined.[39] The document they wrote, the Fundamental Constitutions for the Government of Carolina, generally referred to simply as the Fundamental Constitutions, turned out to be much more than a mere frame of government. It was a complete blueprint of the society they envisioned emerging in Carolina. Into its many articles and clauses, these two men incorporated their vast knowledge of colonies, their own ideas about commerce and empire, their theories on governmental systems and a well-balanced social structure, their advocacy of religious toleration, and a host of other notions which they believed would make the province politically and socially stable and economically prosperous.

Since the Fundamental Constitutions never received the necessary assent from the settlers in Carolina, it never went into effect. This has made it very easy for historians to dismiss the document as unimportant or worth only passing attention. Failure to look behind obscuring details of prolix articles describing the projected society has led to misunderstanding of the proprietors' intentions, and, therefore, to a lack of understanding of some of the reasons for the failure of the proprietary. Though the Fundamental Constitutions was rejected several times by the settlers, the proprietors continued to administer their province with this long-term plan in mind.

The government proposed by Ashley and Locke was an

---

[38] "Fundamental Constitutions," ibid., 93–117.
[39] M. Eugene Sirmans, *Colonial South Carolina: A Political History, 1663–1673* (Chapel Hill, 1966), 8–10; Laslett (ed.), *John Locke's Two Treatises of Government*, 29–30.

adaptation of systems used in other proprietary colonies with some of their own ideas incorporated.[40] The eldest proprietor would be head of the organization, the Palatine of Carolina. The other seven would hold positions roughly analogous to positions held by the king's ministers or councilors. The eight meeting together really acted as a board of directors. The Palatine was to be represented by the governor in Carolina, who would be a liaison between people and proprietors. Each other proprietor would also have a deputy in Carolina who would sit on the council, which was given certain administrative, judicial, and legislative functions. Until the 1690's, apparently these deputies and the settlers' elected representatives sat as one body to act as an assembly or legislature, though the elected members had no power to initiate legislation. A complex court system was provided. At the apex were the proprietors, who could pass down administrative instructions, veto legislation passed in the colony, and hear court case appeals. Needlessly complicated, its feudal forms anachronistic, this basic system never worked much better elsewhere than it did in Carolina.

The Fundamental Constitutions also aimed at coordinating economy and government. This central theme becomes clear when it is remembered that Ashley and Locke wanted Carolina to be a "little England." They had great faith in the English Constitution; the traditional ordering of English society was the best possible arrangement. As men who had spent much of their own lives within a nation in a state of flux, they sought to guarantee stability by insisting that individuals enjoy rights, responsibilities, and titles in proportion to their stake in society. As in England, this class

[40] The legal position of proprietaries generally is explained in a series of articles by Herbert L. Osgood, "The Proprietary Province as a Form of Colonial Government," *American Historical Review*, II (1897), 644–664; III (1897), 31–55; III (1898), 244–265.

structure would be tied to the quantity of land held and the form of land tenure. The problem they had was to try to wed this model of English society to a staple crop colony in a vast wilderness.

Ashley and Locke tried to effect this amalgamation through use of the proprietors' rights to bestow titles and to dispose of land. The holding of a title would signify landholdings commensurate with that rank. A title would also give its holder political privileges and rights. The county would be the basic unit of local administration. Since no one knew how large Carolina was, the total number of counties could not be determined, but each county was to contain 480,000 acres (750 square miles). In every county each proprietor was to have a tract of 12,000 acres (96,000 acres total for the proprietors) or 20 per cent of the whole. The Carolina nobility (landgraves and caciques by title) were to have another 20 per cent. The remaining 60 per cent was reserved for commoners. Commoners would initially get land on terms offered by the proprietors. Large holdings could be subinfeudated, affording another source of land for commoners. There was even a provision for "leetmen" or serfs, though there is no record that anyone ever took this status.[41]

The glaring weakness of this feudalistic conception of society was that it could never be operative unless the proprietors and the Carolina nobility peopled their lands. Even if large holdings were taken up, in labor-short America few would be willing to accept lands under a feudal grant when they could receive acreage elsewhere under more favorable terms. Recognizing this problem and the realities of the American situation, Ashley and Locke made a place for Negro slaves who may have been visualized as replacements

[41] On the land allocation provisions of the Fundamental Constitutions, see Robert K. Ackerman, "South Carolina Colonial Land Policies" (unpublished Ph.D. dissertation, University of South Carolina, 1965) , 7–27.

for the serfs and other forms of subservient white labor which would not be available in America. Though both men are considered advanced thinkers for their era, they apparently had no compunctions about slavery. They knew of its necessity and profitableness in Barbados, Virginia, and elsewhere, though there were not many slaves in the mainland colonies in 1669.

Many other articles of the Fundamental Constitutions showed a keen awareness of the need to work out details before any settlers arrived in Carolina. Ashley and Locke guarded the proprietary economic prerogatives as jealously as they shepherded the political rights. Half the minerals, gold, gems, and so forth, found was to go to the proprietors. Sole power to regulate foreign and domestic trade, manufacturing, public buildings, and highways was reserved to the proprietary. The proprietors could determine the location of towns and designate port towns. The deeper the examination of the document, the firmer the conclusion that this plan was carefully worked out on paper. Whether it would work in practice was to be tested.

Some articles not directly concerned with the economy had economic implications. Both Ashley and Locke accepted religious toleration as a theoretical concept; it also had practical advantages in peopling a colony. They insisted that discrimination against dissenters drove many with tender consciences into exile, to the damage of the nation. Along with others, they advocated that nonconformists to the Church of England be allowed in the colonies. In the Fundamental Constitutions they went a step further and allowed to go to Carolina any person who would acknowledge that God existed and that He should be worshiped. This brand of toleration did not apply to atheists but might let Quakers, Catholics, even Jews, and certainly foreign protestants enter the province.

The first settlers leaving England carried a copy of the

Fundamental Constitutions. They understood that it would not be put into effect until there were more settlers, but assumed that it would be instituted at the proper moment. It became easy for the settlers to blame their troubles on the Fundamental Constitutions which the proprietors refused to abandon. Many of their problems, however, were neither caused by this document nor unique to Carolina. The outlined system was not a theoretical departure from the governmental structure used among Englishmen and was not as radical as its exterior appears. Besides, the Fundamental Constitutions guaranteed personal justice and some liberties not generally granted in other colonies. Theoretically, justice even extended to the native peoples who were generally treated badly everywhere. In Carolina they were given a permanent niche in the projected structure of society.

Nevertheless, Ashley and Locke wittingly or unwittingly laced up the settlers into a closely controlled economic system which was bound to run counter to the free rein capitalism that seemed to work best in America and appealed most to the settlers and potential settlers. The thoroughness of their planning defeated the entire purpose of the blueprint. Instead of preventing antagonisms between settlers and proprietors, it assured that antagonisms would come. Internal turbulence, in turn, would stifle economic growth and deny the profits which the proprietors could never forget for long. It is ironical that two men who thought in terms of a loosely controlled, decentralized empire thought that Carolina would develop most rapidly under a centralized proprietary, controlling government and economy from 3,000 miles away. In the future, when less imaginative proprietors clung to these obviously inapt policies, the inherent weaknesses in Ashley's and Locke's system became ruinous.

CHAPTER II

The Environmental Challenge

IN MID-AUGUST 1669 THE PROPRIETORS' EXPEDITION, DES-tined for Port Royal in the southern part of Carolina, set sail from England under the command of Joseph West. The three vessels of this little flotilla were scheduled to make intermediate stops at Kinsale, Ireland, and Bridgetown, Barbados. Arriving at Barbados, West relinquished command to Sir John Yeamans before the settlers proceeded to Carolina. Departing from Barbados, the vessels headed for Nevis in hopes of picking up recruits. There they did find Henry Woodward who had been left in Carolina three years before by Sandford, subsequently captured by Spaniards, released by an English pirate, and shipwrecked at Nevis. Continuing the voyage, one vessel was wrecked in the Bahamas, another separated and ended up in Virginia, and Governor Yeamans and his party landed in Bermuda. Yeamans then forsook the venture and returned to Barbados after appointing William Sayle as his replacement. A man of vast experience in the colonies, Governor Sayle was able to put the expedition in order despite his advanced age of about 80 years. It was March 17, 1670, before the company went ashore at Port Royal.

The little band quickly became apprehensive about the site designated for settlement. Its swampy lowlands appeared most unhealthy and unpromising for agriculture. From Indians they learned that they were quite near Spanish missions and the lands of Indians allied to the Spaniards. The proximity of the warlike Westo tribe on the Savannah River had to be considered also. Governor Sayle's agents looked to the north along the Ashley River and in early April a nine-acre site was chosen on the western bank several miles upstream from the mouth of the river. Here not more than 150 settlers from England, Barbados, and Bermuda started to carve homes in the wilderness.[1]

All new settlements faced problems of known and unknown dimensions; the unknown was the more haunting. On the Ashley River the unknown had many guises. Destruction could be sudden and violent at the hands of Spaniards, Indians, or a combination of the two. Disintegration could be slow and grinding, stemming from the inability to supply everyday needs or from a long-term failure to find a staple. Weakness of will, a loss of the power of persistence, was the greatest danger of all. Though having some assurance of continuing support from England, these first settlers must have recognized in that spring of 1670 that they would have to rely mostly on their own wills and wits to survive and flourish.

Ultimate success or failure for the colony turned on the settlers' abilities to cope with the environment. Scientific data gathered more recently help provide insights into some aspects of the struggle and into why colonial South Carolina developed as it did. Historical hindsight also aids perspective. Reliance on these approaches, however, might be more misleading than enlightening. The most meaningful frame

---

[1] All secondary accounts of this voyage are based on letters and other documents found in Cheves (ed.), *Shaftesbury Papers*, 117–178.

of reference from which to view this confrontation is the limited knowledge available to settlers and proprietors as they started the task of building their new society. It was necessary for settlers everywhere to adjust their own preconceptions and misconceptions to the realities of the new homeland. Unfortunately, revising faulty notions about the country became a continuous process in colonial South Carolina. Original errors were gradually eliminated, but new errors were constantly being fed into the fund of common knowledge. The proprietors shaped their first plans from a mixture of fact and fiction, and they always found it difficult to obtain dependable information. Bad decisions based on inaccurate knowledge or faulty assumptions are an integral part of the story of this province. Such misjudgments netted a cost in human suffering and money which would reach a staggering sum if there were a way to allocate such values.

Some of the earliest and most persistent misconceptions had to do with the geography of Carolina. Many of these fallacies had been introduced to other Europeans by the Spaniards and French long before the English came to Ashley River. Maps of the Spaniards were rudimentary, sketchy, and full of mistakes. Narratives of their explorers abounded in fallacious detail about the nature of the land. Particularly important in spreading false impressions was LeMoyne, the French cartographer who had been in the region in 1564. He filled his maps with lakes and other features which could not be located on the landscape.[2] From such tracts and maps, the Lords Proprietors and settlers derived their initial impressions about the country and its possibilities. Because they were concerned mostly with the coast and coastline, Hilton

[2] W. P. Cumming, "Geographical Misconceptions of the Southeast in the Cartography of the Seventeenth and Eighteenth Centuries," *Journal of Southern History,* IV (1938), 476–492.

and Sandford did little to correct these earlier assessments in their expansive and optimistic appraisals.

Before the first English South Carolinians could set themselves and others straight, John Lederer added some valid geographical information and many new misconceptions when the results of his explorations into the Carolina backcountry were published in 1672.[3] A German, trained as a physician and scholar, Lederer had been sponsored by Governor Berkeley of Virginia in what was perhaps his only important act as a proprietor.[4] Lederer's maps and narratives added to knowledge of inland areas, including the first clear recognition of the tripartite division of coastal plain, which he called "the flats," the piedmont, and the mountains. Yet Lederer added some unreal features to his maps as well. In the piedmont he placed a 200-mile-long swampy savanna which often appeared on later maps as the Great Lake of the Piedmont. East of this, he showed a large barren stretch, the Arenosa Desert. The proprietors made use of Lederer's information almost immediately. They had already commissioned John Ogilby, the royal cartographer, to design a map. It appeared in 1673, and most of Lederer's valid and specious material was incorporated.[5] Since map makers, like writers, were not bothered by plagiarism in this era, Lederer's distinctive features were copied over and over again. Some maps published as late as the 1720's and 1730's show his influence.[6]

In this way, misleading information about the province was always plentiful. Such mistakes could be erased only by

[3] Sir William Talbot, collector and translator from the Latin, *The Discoveries of John Lederer* . . . (London, 1672) . A recent edition with a valuable introduction has been prepared by W. P. Cumming (ed.), *The Discoveries of John Lederer* . . . (Charlottesville, 1958) .
[4] Cumming (ed.), *The Discoveries of John Lederer*, viii.
[5] Cumming, "Geographical Misconceptions," *Jour. So. Hist.*, IV (1938), 484.   [6] Ibid., 485–487.

future trailblazers. The second map of the Lords Proprietors, published in 1682, reflected the findings of Henry Woodward and others who penetrated the backcountry.[7] When inland travel became more commonplace after 1680, wanderers and Indian traders sometimes contributed new myths or helped to perpetuate old ones. Elimination of geographical errors was more difficult because of the very human failing of trying to substantiate what men had reported earlier as being there. It would be normal not to dispute any notion long held to be true. Most of these aberrations did not start as deliberate hoaxes. Considering the difficulties of travel, no explorer could hope to see such a vast forested area personally and depended, of necessity, on reports from Indians and others.[8]

Being practical men with practical goals, the settlers were more interested immediately in the soil they would work rather than the general topography of the region. Food crops had to be started at once and, after that, commercial crops had to be found. Settlers were hindered by lack of accurate information about soil and factors influencing the productivity of the soil, such as climate. The insights of early explorers proved baneful since their narratives had convinced both proprietors and settlers that South Carolina was in the tropics. Initial calculations about commercially important crops were made upon this erroneous assumption, which died a slow death only after settlers tried unsuccessfully to grow tropical plants.[9]

South Carolina had a coastline unlike any which the settlers could have known previously. First views of the land revealed both promise and challenge. The lush growth of

[7] Ibid., 486.   [8] Ibid., 477.

[9] Some English officials thought of the area as being tropical until almost the American Revolutionary era. See W. A. Foran, "Southern Legend: Climate or Climate of Opinion?," *Proceedings of the South Carolina Historical Association, 1956,* 9–10.

unbroken stands of timber was reported by all early observers as their dominant impression. Such a sight must have been especially overwhelming in that era of hand tools, for these trees meant days and months of hard work to prepare ground for the most easily grown crops. Yet this challenge was found everywhere on the Atlantic coast. It would soon be apparent, however, that South Carolina was peculiarly different from coastal areas farther north. Besides the more obvious indentations from north to south of Long Bay, Winyah Bay, Bull Bay, Charles Town Harbor, St. Helena Sound, and Port Royal Sound, there were almost countless lesser inlets. Into these bays flowed an intricate and extensive system of sluggish streams with ill-defined banks which allowed their waters to spread out into vast swampy areas, estimated to be 1,750,000 acres.[10] Since much of the terrain drained by these rivers and their many tributaries had little elevation, the tides pushed far up into the land. Many areas near the ocean were periodically swept by salt or brackish water.

These lands from the edge of the ocean to the fall line were soon called the low country. This South Carolina coastal plain is the widest found on the Atlantic side of North America. It extends inland as far as 120 miles in places. The land is not over 130 to 135 feet above sea level at the fall line and has few hills. Near the mouths of its rivers, much of the land is only a few feet above sea level at high tide. Most colonial South Carolinians lived and died on this strip of coastal land. While early settlers recognized that the piedmont might be more healthy for Europeans and have better soil over-all, it was almost a century after the first settlement before the cutting edge of the frontier had moved 100 miles inland.[11]

---

[10] David D. Wallace, *The History of South Carolina* (New York, 1934), I, 6.
[11] Ibid., I, 3–10. Wallace anatomizes the geographical base of the entire state.

Since those who obtained the most easily worked lands with the most fertile soil had the best chance of eventual success, settlers were always concerned with the edaphic qualities of lands. It was soon discovered that bottom lands along the banks of streams and the sea islands, divided from the mainland by meandering streams and large swampy areas, had the best soils. These were alluvial in origin and had been built up over the centuries. Though quite fertile, this black, loamy soil was difficult to till because it was wet, heavy, and subject to frequent flooding. The acreage of such soils was obviously limited, so few settlers obtained the best. The rest had to work soils most characteristic of the coastal plain. While these varied widely in quality, even in a given locality, usually they were of comparatively low fertility, made up of mixtures of sand and clay in various proportions over a clay subsoil.[12] These lighter soils offered some advantages to early settlers working with rudimentary tools and few draft animals. There were few rocks to interfere with cultivation of crops. Also, the sandy quality of the land provided such a good cushion that, as often noted, it was not necessary to shoe horses to protect their feet.[13] Nonetheless, settlers who were forced to work these soils of limited fertility and potential labored with an automatic economic handicap.

The drive to acquire land along rivers and lesser streams was one of the chief formative influences upon South Carolina's economic development, indeed upon the life of the province as a whole. Not only did the best lands lie along their banks, but also the rivers provided the easiest means of travel. Since most of the major, and many minor, streams

[12] *Soils and Men: Yearbook of Agriculture, 1938* (Washington, 1938), 1110–1112.

[13] Ralph H. Brown, "The Land and the Sea: Their Larger Traits," *Annals of the Association of American Geographers,* XLI (1951), 204.

were navigable by shallow boats, local and distant travel could best be carried on by water. These waterways made Charles Town the natural center for all trade, government, and social life throughout the colonial era. Attempting to obtain the most fertile lands, settlers dispersed themselves along coastal streams and rivers, interfering with the plans of the proprietors that the province be developed contiguously for safety and orderly settlement.

Here, as elsewhere along the North Atlantic coast, settlers had little difficulty identifying most of the vegetation. They soon paid special attention to trees and other cover on the land as the surest clue to soil quality. Low, swampy fertile soils grew many varieties of hardwoods, including the valuable live oak and cypress. The better, higher sandy soils were dominated by longleaf pines; poorer sandy soils had scrubbier growth. Pines were not common in western Europe and must have seemed strange to those who came directly from England. Eventually nature's gift of extensive hardwood and softwood forests would prove important to the economy of the province. In opening lands, however, forests were an accursed obstacle. In examining the low cover, settlers were most mindful of grasses because of their great importance in feeding domesticated animals. Though grass covered the open areas, these native species were easily overgrazed and worn out. They were inferior in quality to English grasses which were soon introduced, as everywhere in colonial America, to provide fodder for animals.[14]

The woods abounded with game animals, the streams and the ocean with fish. At first, hunting and fishing were necessary to supplement the food supply. Later the skins and furs

---

[14] On this point, see *Climate and Man: Yearbook of Agriculture, 1941* (Washington, 1941), 164; Lewis C. Gray, *History of Agriculture in the Southern United States to 1860* (Washington, 1933), I, 177–178.

of some animals, particularly the hundreds of thousands of deer, would have a major impact on the economy of the developing province. Rivalry over the deerskin trade would figure largely in relations with Indians, the Spanish, and the French. Most of the animals found inland and along the coast were common throughout North America. While fearful tales did circulate, most early accounts tried to play down the danger from alligators and poisonous "serpents"; the latter were greatly feared in that era of rudimentary medical knowledge.[15]

If the terrain appeared promising though challenging, a settler only had to be in residence for a full year, perhaps a summer, to know that the climate exacted its own price. The climate of coastal South Carolina falls into the modern classification, humid mesothermal, which means neither the heat of the tropics nor the cold of the polar caps. The implication of this term is somewhat misleading. This region of South Carolina is usually included in a subgroup, humid subtropical, which connotes much more accurately the characteristic climate. The heat and humidity of summer were overpowering features of day-to-day existence. The newly arrived European, wearing heavy woolen clothes, suffered extremely from high temperatures and high humidity. Yet even those who were acclimated could hardly ignore such weather as they attempted to work.[16]

Summer's heat lulled those with experience in the West Indies into believing that this was truly the tropics. During the summer months, mean temperatures on the South Carolina coast are, in fact, equal to those in Barbados during the

---

[15] Joseph Ioor Waring, *A History of Medicine in South Carolina, 1670–1825* (Charleston, 1964), 32.

[16] *Climate and Man: Yearbook of Agriculture, 1941*, 1099–1108; Glenn T. Trewartha, *An Introduction to Climate*, 3rd edition (New York, 1954), 289, 302–310.

same period.[17] The great warmth of summer was offset, nevertheless, by the sobering cold of winter which, though mild in comparison to that of more northerly latitudes, has frosts and freezes regularly. Early writers often mentioned with amazement that the cold was sometimes extreme enough to form ice an inch or two thick and that snow fell occasionally. Data compiled in recent times show that, after parts of China with a similar climate, this region has the lowest average winter temperatures of any humid subtropical area in the world.[18] Adjustment to the unexpected climate was a slow process. The delusion of the tropics persisted though it was quickly recognized, for example, that some perennial crops of the tropics could only be cultivated as annuals in South Carolina. Despite the wide annual temperature range, settlers did have the advantage of a basically kindly climate with a long growing season of seven or more frost-free months.

Having rainfall spread over the entire year distinguishes the humid subtropical from other subtropical climates which have a dry season. Modern measurements show that approximately 50 inches of rain fall annually in the coastal regions of South Carolina. Receiving rain throughout the year proved a distinct advantage in this area of predominately light soils which percolate rapidly. It helps offset their basically low fertility. Despite a pattern of considerable rainfall with much cloudiness, coastal South Carolina receives much sunshine. Though the sun is another factor in drying out light soils, it too promotes rapid growth of vegetation. Early records also mentioned the violence of the province's weather. Much of the rain came during electrical storms. Sometimes favorable conditions spawned a tornado. Hurri-

[17] W. G. Kendrew, *The Climate of the Continents*, 5th edition (Oxford, 1961), 459, 516–517.
[18] Trewartha, *Introduction to Climate*, 3rd edition, 306.

canes became even more feared, and it was soon recognized that tropical storms would strike at irregular intervals.[19] On more than one occasion, natural phenomena set back the settlement.

South Carolina's social history and political history were permanently influenced by its climate. The demands of the climate were thought to make slavery unavoidable, and the institution was started when settlement began. As the province developed staple crops, the demand for labor grew. During the colonial era, nearly all South Carolinians were convinced that the hot, humid climate and low coastal lands were too oppressive for European laborers. Only an ever-increasing number of African slaves could fill this need. The attrition rate among slaves was high, but blacks were believed better able than whites to stand the debilitating effects of hard labor in the open fields. Slave labor would have been used anyway, because the Barbadians had long depended on it, and Virginia and Maryland provided examples on the mainland. Climate, however, supplied the concrete reason for considering the institution essential to economic development.

Disease was closely associated in the colonial mind with climate.[20] "Seasoning" was reckoned to be one of the first personal crises met by all who arrived in America during this era. It was a particularly dangerous process in South Carolina. Although the exact causal connections would be established over two centuries later, colonial South Carolinians soon recognized that the combination of swampy lowlands

[19] For tropical storms which struck during the colonial era, consult David M. Ludlum, *Early American Hurricanes, 1492–1870* (Boston, 1963). For more detailed analyses of all climate factors see *Atlas of American Agriculture* (Washington, 1936).

[20] Lionel Chalmers, *An Account of the Weather and Diseases of South Carolina* (London, 1776), stresses the connection between climate and disease.

and hot weather contributed to the prevalence of serious, if not always fatal, diseases in their province. No one was exempt from these diseases, but they struck hard at newcomers who had not been exposed previously. The only route to survival was to contract the disease in a mild form which might allow rapid recovery and provide future immunity from that particular one of the many scourges. The victim of illness stood a better chance of survival if he avoided the doctors of the day and their standard prescriptions for all ailments, "blistering, bleeding, sweating, purging, and vomiting." [21] Recovery could be credited to a strong constitution with or without treatment.[22]

There was a fearful variety of maladies. Malaria, known in England and all the American colonies during the seventeenth century, was observed by contemporaries to be particularly virulent in the warm colonies. It was probably the "seasoning fever" which most immigrants reportedly caught soon after arriving and suffered recurrences of for years after. An authority who has traced the early history of malaria in South Carolina concluded that malaria persisted as a problem because the "oak lands," the best lands along river and creek banks, were also the areas heavily infested with the mosquitoes which carried the disease.[23] Dysentery hit nearly everyone at some time. Commonly called the flux or bloody flux, it was sometimes fatal, but more often it caused disability for months, years, and sometimes permanently. Those who eventually recovered were drained of vitality, and became an easier prey for some other malady. Most fatalities from dysentery were among young children and

[21] John Duffy, "Eighteenth-Century Carolina Health Conditions," *Journal of Southern History*, XVIII (1952), 289.

[22] Waring, *History of Medicine in S.C., 1670–1825*, 1–8. Significantly, Dr. Waring entitled this chapter, "Colonists Without Cures."

[23] St. Julien Ravenel Childs, *Malaria and Colonization in the Carolina Low Country, 1526–1696* (Baltimore, 1940), 32–33.

new arrivals, both groups lacking resistance to this attacker. Most other diseases which swept through colonial America were also unwelcome visitors in the low country. Though modern medical experts have difficulty classifying some of these diseases based on the symptoms described by contemporaries, scarlet fever, diphtheria, smallpox, measles, typhoid, tuberculosis, and perhaps typhus would be included in most listings.[24]

Although they could strike anytime, fevers occurred most often from June to October. Hence, slaves and new settlers were commonly brought in during late fall to avoid "seasoning." Few escaped, however. Being incapacitated much of the time, many newcomers were of little value during their first year in the province. The value of a slave who had been a resident for a year was automatically greater for his having survived that period. Indeed, a reason for importing Negro slaves was the immunity they had built up in Africa to smallpox, yellow fever, malaria, and other tropical diseases which wreaked havoc with newly arrived European settlers. This advantage was offset to some extent by the fact that the Negro proved more vulnerable to respiratory ailments, such as pneumonia, to which he had not been exposed.[25]

Although acceptance of disease with its resulting deaths and disabilities was part of being alive in this era, the fact that South Carolina was reputed to be an unhealthy place undoubtedly affected its development. There is now no way for the historian to determine just how much disease and fear of disease retarded recruitment of settlers or curbed productivity in the province. One may note, nonetheless, that the proprietors were always concerned that the prob-

[24] For the most complete general treatment of this subject, see John Duffy, *Epidemics in Colonial America* (Baton Rouge, 1953); for South Carolina epidemics, Waring, *History of Medicine in S.C., 1670–1825.*

[25] Duffy, "Eighteenth-Century Carolina Health Conditions," *Jour. So. Hist.,* XVIII (1952), 300–301.

lems of climate and disease were affecting potential migrants. Their directives to authorities often dwelled on measures which supposedly would make the province a safer place to live. Every prospectus had to deal with this thorny subject. One approach was to be positive: to stress the healthful and invigorating aspects of a climate beneficial to agriculture while downplaying disease as an inevitable part of life in the province. Some publicity tracts ignored the subject altogether, although it must have been of great interest to prospective settlers.[26]

If the settler was able to survive and come to grips with nature, the native peoples remained as contestants for the land. These local Indians were particularly feared in the early years before much was known about them. If nothing else, their presence meant that settlers had to remain on guard against surprise attacks, an expenditure of time and effort which could have been used profitably in other ways. It is easy to say in retrospect that the Indians could no more have stopped this settlement than they stopped others. That the Indians did have sufficient power and knowledge of their native haunts to make settlers pay dearly was proven, however, during the counterattack, known as the Yamasee War, when the colony was in its forty-sixth year. Fortunately for the infant settlement, the savage mind did not think in terms of the relative balance of power between the two peoples. If so, the Indians would have thrown the English back into the sea before they developed unconquerable strength.

By 1670 South Carolina Indians had already undergone major changes as a result of casual contacts with the Spaniards and other Europeans for a century and a half. White man's diseases and artifacts had irreversibly changed their

---

[26] The general problems of promotion have been covered by Hope Frances Kane, "Colonial Promotion and Promotion Literature of Carolina, 1660–1700" (unpublished Ph.D. dissertation, Brown University, 1930).

existence. No one has been able to determine with certainty what these people were like before this process of corruption began. Historians have been handicapped by a lack of documents. The English were in the province for years before preparing detailed accounts of the native people's way of life. In the meantime, Indian tribal structure and culture had undergone further debasement.

Experts vary widely in their estimates of the Indian population at any given time in the New World. Some recent investigators assert that there were more Indians living between Canada and Florida in precolonial North America than previously thought, possibly 125,000 at the beginning of the seventeenth century. Perhaps a third of this total lived on the coastal plain between Maryland and Georgia.[27] Using this estimate, if the Indians were distributed throughout the coastal plain somewhat equally, the maximum Indian population of South Carolina could have been 30,000 to 40,000 in the seventeenth century. Lacking trustworthy figures, authorities assume that the Indian population was always sparse and widely dispersed. The coastal tribes, and some of the inland ones, had already been depleted in numbers by European diseases, perhaps to the extent of decimation, by 1670.[28]

The foremost authority on the Carolina Indians in the colonial era listed 28 tribes which lived within the present limits of the state in 1670. Along the coast and streams from the Charles Town area south to the Savannah River lived the Cusabo, a loose grouping of tribes which included: the St. Helena, the Wimbee, the Combahee, the Ashepoo, the Edisto, the Bohicket, the Stono, the Kiawah, the Etiwan, the Wando, and the Coosa. The Cusabo had been more exposed

[27] Ralph H. Brown, *Historical Geography of the United States* (New York, 1948), 11.
[28] George F. Carter, *Man and the Land* (New York, 1964), 243–244.

than any other coastal Indians to Spaniards who occupied parts of their domains at times and made continuing forays into their territory from missions in Guale and the fort at St. Augustine. Also the Cusabo were permanently weakened just before 1670 by a disastrous war with the Westo, an aggressive inland tribe.

Noted for their prowess as warriors, the Westo were called "man-eaters" by the coastal aborigines who feared them greatly. The fact that they do not fit into any wider tribal grouping has led to the belief that they drifted, or perhaps were driven, into the area from the north. When the English arrived, the Westo made their headquarters on the Savannah River some distance from the coast.

The tribes along the coast north of Charles Town were of Siouan stock. They were primitive peoples, perhaps more so than the Cusabo. Though associated collectively, they were not a powerful grouping being fragmented into many tribes including the Sewee, the Santee, the Congaree, the Wateree, the Sampa, the Winyah, the Waccamaw, the Pedee, the Sara or Cheraw, the Waxhaw, the Sugaree, and possibly others. These tribes had also suffered considerably from early and periodic exposure to the white man.

The inland tribes were larger in population and far better organized. More capable, morally and physically, of maintaining their own cultures, they had not been changed as much owing to their fewer contacts with whites. These tribes would be far more influential in the colonial history of South Carolina. Least powerful among these were the Yamasee who were located on or near the lower Savannah River. Almost due west from Charles Town and far beyond the Savannah, the Creeks, made up of many subdivisions, maintained dominion. These people were one of the two most important tribal groupings on this southern frontier of English America. The other was the Cherokee who lived north-

west from Charles Town. Their lands were from the piedmont back into the mountains and beyond. Farther north
were tribes, such as the Tuscaroras, who did not claim lands
in South Carolina but sometimes roamed into the coastal
area.[29]

All the tribes had some common characteristics which
aided the invaders' purposes. All except the Westo were
basically unwarlike and unaggressive. The Spaniards and
the English were equally impressed with the openness of
these tribes, their friendliness and generosity.[30] While the
proprietors benefited from sad experiences of earlier colonies
and strove to insure adequate food for the first critical years,
the Indians' contribution helped South Carolina avoid a
true "starving time." According to early chroniclers, the
Indians cultivated in extensive fields maize (corn), beans,
pumpkins, squash, melons, native peas or pulse, peaches, figs,
and some native tobacco. As elsewhere in America, corn
proved to be the most sustaining foodstuff for Europeans.

Whites also learned from the natives how to preserve
harvests for winter use and to look to nature's untended
fruits for food. Berries and nuts brought welcome variety
anytime to the settlers' monotonous fare, but, at the beginning, these wild crops were important supplements to the
diet of immigrants relying on half-rotten dried or salted
foods. Grapes, strawberries, blackberries, hickory nuts, and
walnuts were all enjoyed. In an era when guns had limited
range and effectiveness, the English must also have adopted
Indian hunting and fishing techniques.[31]

[29] This material on the Indians has been drawn from Chapman J. Milling,
Red Carolinians (Chapel Hill, 1940) , particularly the following pages: 4, 35–
50, 73–112, 203–230, 266–285; but for the most complete examination of the
Indians and their culture see John R. Swanton, *The Indians of the South-
eastern United States,* Bulletin 137 of the United States Bureau of American
Ethnology (Washington, 1946) .

[30] Milling, *Red Carolinians,* 4–33; Quattlebaum, *Land Called Chicora,* 107–
112. [31] Milling, *Red Carolinians,* 12–19.

To some extent, the Indians had even prepared the land for occupation by Europeans. To facilitate their hunting, the natives had made clearings in the almost complete forest cover by burning the vegetation and trees. Unless prepared for cultivation, burned over areas rapidly filled with browse, a natural place for game, easily stalked by the hunter. Letters of early settlers indicated that some of these cleared "Indian Olde Fields" (or similar designation) were tilled by the whites. While years of cultivation had depleted fertility in some of these fields, they were available for immediate use when there was no time to clear forested areas.

Trade with the Indians, though mutually beneficial in theory, worked mainly to the white man's advantage. Swapping small amounts of European goods for valuable skins and furs was hardly equal exchange. Barter with the Indians constituted the first commerce in the province and was its single most important business enterprise for many years. It was from traders that most Indians gained their predominant impression of Europeans, whether English, Spanish, or French. In this meeting of two peoples, the Indian did gain some items which improved his physical comfort and his way of living, but he also received a lasting impression of the white man's duplicity, as well as his vices and diseases. About a century after settlement started, the destruction of the native culture was complete and most of the Indians native to South Carolina were exterminated.[32] Disease and vice were more important in this process than wars.

The Indian trade was complicated by the role these tribes played as pawns in the chess game of empire. The nation having the strongest Indian allies could best monopolize the trade, destroy the trade of other nations, and militarily control the backcountry. Therefore, England, France, and Spain all sought and maintained alliances with the major tribes.

[32] Ibid., 4.

Although the Treaty of Madrid signed by England and Spain in 1670 declared Charles Town to be safely within English territory, the two nations remained rivals and their colonies fought one another as often as the limited strength of each would allow. South Carolina was organized militarily almost from the start to meet the continual threat posed by Spaniards and their Indian allies. The proprietary era passed away before these potential enemies could be taken lightly.[33]

Indian land claims created additional conflicts between colonists and native peoples. Having no knowledge of European concepts of land ownership, the various tribes occupied some areas and divided the rest into spheres of control. Whenever South Carolinians needed more acreage, agents negotiated treaties with the appropriate tribal chieftains, though it is doubtful that the Indians understood the full implication of such treaties. Payments for land represented only a fraction of the value of the soil. Since the settlers' land hunger could only be satiated temporarily, friction between Indians and whites over this matter was continual. Whether the exchange was for land or other things, South Carolinians and Europeans generally received far more from the Indians than they gave in return.

Viewed several centuries later, the colonists' struggle with the total environment of South Carolina ended predictably. To the first settlers and those who followed them, prospects were not so reassuring. The land presented many difficulties; the Spaniards were too close for comfort; the Indians were an unknown factor. In great measure, South Carolina's economic history is the story of how the settlers adapted to these challenging surroundings.

---

[33] Military plans of the province have been summarized by David Cole, "A Brief Outline of the South Carolina Colonial Militia System," *Proceedings of the South Carolina Historical Association, 1954,* 14–23.

CHAPTER III

Off to a Slow Start
1670–1675

To make the settlement at Ashley River a success, the venture would have to continue to be a cooperative one between colonists and proprietors. The settlers on their own could not hope to overcome the great obstacles they faced. During the initial phase of the settlement process, they would have to spend their labor to clear land, plant food crops, build shelters, and take defensive measures. Only a limited amount of experimentation to find a staple could be conducted at this stage with little likelihood of any production for export. The proprietors recognized, to some degree, the magnitude of the undertaking, and they intended to provide the support necessary for the original settlers and others who might arrive before the colony was firmly established. Yet the advantage for settlers and proprietors of making common cause until the settlement was a success was not sufficient to inhibit dissension.

The proprietors' expenditures to keep the colony going during the early years heightened their interest in the way political and economic developments were proceeding. As investors, they were concerned about the prospects for profits, their basic reason for obtaining the charter in the first

place. As political theorists, they supervised carefully to insure that their directives or the actions of South Carolinians
did not jeopardize their long-term plans as set forth in the
Fundamental Constitutions. They expected that their policies would provide a proper order which would lead to
political stability. Financial returns for everyone would follow naturally and quickly. Not that the proprietors were
insensitive to the views or even the basic rights of the colonists. They reckoned themselves to be just and fair in all
dealings, whether the issue was economic or political; however, they never forgot that their primary motivation in
founding the settlement was not altruism or trial of a political system, but profits.

From the very beginning, the settlers did not take kindly
to proprietary leadership. If the proprietors expected defer-
ence and unquestioning obedience to their policies in appreciation of their subsidies, they did not understand human
nature. The settlers felt that they had come to a strange land
assuming great risks which entitled them to considerable say
about their own destinies. Despite their weak, vulnerable,
and dependent position, they were amazingly frank in their
commentaries and often quite open in their defiance of
directives they thought unsuited to local conditions. Though
some settlers would doubtless have shown an unwillingness
to accept any authority no matter how benevolent and well-
intentioned, most of the opposition to proprietary leadership
was more than mere negativism. Their protests reflected
opinions based on a growing understanding of the realities
of existence in South Carolina. This opposition seldom
spoke with one voice. In fact, some settlers always accepted
proprietary direction, perhaps out of conviction, but also
because the proprietors offered to their favorites such financial plums as offices and land grants. Probably most settlers,
and all the correspondents, at some time recognized their

debts to the proprietors and appreciated the appropriate actions taken in their behalf. Nevertheless, the majority of the settlers and the proprietors rapidly began to see that their interests did not always coincide. The rift steadily widened, and this polarization became a great shaping force of the proprietary era.

Despite growing theoretical and practical difficulties, Lord Ashley tried diligently to go forward with the grand design. Once he had seized the initiative in Carolina affairs, he dominated until his involvement in English politics precluded further attention to Carolina. Because Ashley's papers are a major source for South Carolina history for this 1670–1675 period,[1] it has been far too easy to blame or to credit him for everything which happened to the settlement. This judgment is too sharp. Under the Fundamental Constitutions, as acting Palatine he had considerable power, but there were limits on that power. He might send wordy letters of advice, but on substantive matters he had to have the concurrence of the majority of proprietors. He could scarcely have managed to influence self-seeking men to lay money out of their own pockets time and time again if they had been unwilling to do so. On more than one occasion, Ashley's letters indicated that finding support for his policies was not easy.[2] Though respected in South Carolina, Ashley could not force the settlers to follow proprietary orders or accept the Fundamental Constitutions even in spirit. Perhaps the settlement fared so poorly precisely because the colonists did not pay attention to Ashley's advice. Nor was Ashley to blame for every action taken by proprietary appointees. But it is impossible to camouflage the many ill-advised instructions sent by the proprietary in these early years. If Ashley was not solely responsible for these policies, he agreed with them in

[1] The latest letter in Cheves (ed.), *Shaftesbury Papers,* is dated in June 1675.   [2] Lord Ashley to Joseph West, May 23, 1674, ibid., 446–447.

principle—or at least he defended them with cogent arguments. He genuinely wanted the enterprise to succeed; he tried to be a mediator between the interests of the settlers and those of the proprietors. His stewardship should have been fruitful, but for a variety of reasons, it was not. Yet without his constant attention for five years, the beginnings of the province might have been more grim than they were.

One of the most important, and earliest, issues arising between proprietors and settlers concerned land policies. This was fundamental, for land was the key to wealth and success for everyone. Since the proprietors had all rights to the soil, they could determine these policies without reference to the settlers. Before the first settlers left England, they had done so. Allotment of lands to the common people was to be on the basis of headrights, a proprietary policy which antedated the Fundamental Constitutions. Those who went first were to receive larger grants than those who migrated later. Every free person over 16 years of age who arrived in the colony before March 25, 1670, was entitled to 150 acres. Anyone who brought in his family, servants, or slaves was to receive 150 acres for each adult and 100 acres for each such person under 16. In subsequent instructions, the proprietors pegged the basic headright for arrivals after March 25, 1670, at 100 acres for each adult male. Anyone transporting his family, servants, or slaves could claim 100 acres for each adult and 70 acres for those under 16. These allotments were left in effect until 1679.[3]

[3] Instructions for the Governor and Council, July 27, 1669, ibid., 119–123; Proprietors to Governor and Council, May 1, 1671, as printed in William J. Rivers, *A Sketch of the History of South Carolina to the Close of the Proprietary Government* (Charleston, 1856), 366–369; Proprietors to Governor and Council, May 19, 1679, *Records in the British Public Record Office Relating to South Carolina, 1663–1710* (Atlanta and Columbia, 1928–1947), I, 82–84. Hereafter cited as *BPRO-SC* for those volumes (I–V) which have been published and as BPRO-SC for unpublished volumes which are on deposit in the South Carolina Archives, Columbia, S.C.

The proprietors intended that their land system fill up the province rapidly with both free persons and servants. Basic grants were larger than most offered in America. Those bringing servants, slaves, or having many dependents would, of course, have even greater holdings. Freed indentured servants qualified for 100 acres,[4] more than the reward given in some colonies. The system encouraged the importation of slaves and the creation of an aristocracy obtaining land from headrights on imported slaves, but conditions were not favorable in the first decade for such a development. While the headright was the way most land was obtained, it was not the only way. The proprietors granted many thousands of acres to persons they chose to reward for any reason. Henry Woodward, for example, was at one time given 2,000 acres for his services as explorer and negotiator with the Indians.[5] For all their great eagerness to reap profits, the proprietors never tried to sell quantities of their land, and apparently none was sold in the 1670's.[6]

They thought in terms of perpetual profits from quitrents, and most of the lands granted bore a quitrent.[7] In the feudal past, the quitrent freed the tenant from paying all other annual dues owed his overlord, but by 1670 in South Carolina and the rest of English America, it was viewed as an annual land rent to be paid forever. Settlers who owed these small sums (often a penny or less an acre) felt the obligation noxious and paid grudgingly. To the Carolina proprietors, however, quitrents represented a permanent endowment of considerable proportions if and when rents were paid on the uncounted millions of acres they held. Although a major

---

[4] Ibid.

[5] Lord Ashley to Governor and Council, April 10, 1677, *BPRO-SC*, I, 50.

[6] Ackerman, "S.C. Colonial Land Policies," 17.

[7] For an explanation of the significance of the quitrent, see Beverley W. Bond, Jr., *The Quit-Rent System in the American Colonies* (New Haven, 1919), 25–34.

conflict between settlers and proprietors ultimately developed around quitrents, the dispute was postponed by the proprietors' decision to waive all payments until 1689 (a stipulation of the Fundamental Constitutions) to encourage immigration. This provision of the initial land policy showed considerable foresight and indicated that they could be realistic colonizers, concerned more with the future than with obtaining a quick return for themselves.

Early controversies over land policies centered on the mechanics of land granting.[8] Under proprietary policy, the governor and council in South Carolina were empowered to process each application for land. The handling of claims left considerable discretion to local officials, and their decisions sometimes made both proprietors and individual settlers angry. The proprietors thought that these officials took liberties in their interpretations of precise proprietary directions; some settlers thought that the officials were not lenient enough. Whatever frauds or irregularities were perpetuated, and there appear to have been some, were no major factor for a small band of settlers just getting started. In the first years, both proprietors and provincial officials were most concerned over their failure to find a trustworthy surveyor.[9] Perhaps as a result, there are few land grants dating before 1675, making it impossible to estimate how much land was conveyed.[10] Yet nothing indicates a lack of opportunity to make legitimate land claims. Nor are there signs that settlers were stopped from having lands duly granted eventually. The headright of 100 or 150 acres was, of course, far more land than one man could hope to work.

A source of greater irritation to governor, council, and

[8] Details of granting procedure are described in: Instructions for the Governor and Council, July 27, 1669, Cheves (ed.), *Shaftesbury Papers*, 119–123.
[9] Early letters are full of references to the shortcomings of the first surveyor, Florence O'Sullivan. For example, Stephen Bull to Lord Ashley, September 12, 1670, ibid., 192–196.   [10] Table II, Appendix.

people was the proprietary insistence upon compact, contiguous settlements with people living in towns to advance commerce and facilitate defenses. Ashley admired the town settlements of New England and thought them superior to the scattered plantations of Virginia.[11] Accordingly, the proprietors' instructions were that each man was to have a town lot, no more than one-twentieth of his total land grant. The balance of his holdings would be away from town.[12] There is ample evidence that South Carolina officials tried at first to conform to proprietary wishes. Projects to establish towns in South Carolina during the colonial era must have numbered in the hundreds, but few of the later projects had greater success than the first ones. Proprietary zeal in this matter extended to city planning. They sent several descriptions of what a model town should look like. Each should have a wharf, a common, main streets 100 feet wide, and so forth.[13] These grandiose specifications have often been cited as proof of a visionary approach, but to men who had recently seen the destruction by fire of much of irregularly patterned and cluttered London, planned growth made a great deal of sense. While these plans were impractical for a frontier community and were never instituted, the directives may have had some effect. The fairly regular streets of Charles Town contrast rather favorably with the crooked cow paths of the original part of Boston founded 50 years earlier.

The proprietors' dictum that lands away from towns be laid out contiguously was thwarted as well. Each new grant was supposed to be made for the land adjacent to the last grant made. The proprietors insisted, additionally, that no one usurp frontage on navigable streams. Usually this front-

---

[11] Lord Ashley to Governor Sayle, April 10, 1671, Cheves (ed.), *Shaftesbury Papers*, 310–312.
[12] Proprietors to the Governor and Council, May 1, 1671, as printed in Rivers, *Sketch of History of S.C.*, 366–369.   [13] Ibid.

age was limited to one-fifth of the depth of a plot.[14] The proprietors reasoned that this scheme would insure compact settlements and rectangular plots of land, and would give more people access to the larger streams. Defense measures would also be easier. The colonists were quick to point out that the plan was not feasible. They complained that the proprietors were working from the faulty assumption that South Carolina had an even landscape. In fact, natural obstructions such as creeks and marshes made it impracticable to survey land on a grid system.[15] The proprietors themselves worked against their own orders in this matter. From the first, they insisted that their personal lands and those for the Carolina nobility be laid off and reserved. Since the titled holders of these tracts never appeared in most instances, these large empty reservations interfered with the projected regular and orderly settlement.[16]

Perhaps most important, the elaborate land allocation plan failed when settlers answered the sounder calling of economic self-interest, "the scent of better land." [17] Considering the great variation in land quality within the coastal plain, settlers sought out and local officials granted them good available bottom lands, even though a stretch of pine barrens might be the next logical acreage to be taken up. Ultimately, this pressure from settlers prevailed over instructions which were considered to be based upon false premises anyway. When governors and councils became willing to disregard the spirit of policy or to disobey altogether, proprietary plans for orderly survey and granting of lands broke

[14] By the 1680's instructions for laying out land were quite detailed. For example, Proprietors to Governor Morton, May 10, 1682, *BPRO-SC*, I, 138–157.

[15] Council to Proprietors, about February 14, 1672, Cheves (ed.), *Shaftesbury Papers*, 388.

[16] Ackerman, "S.C. Colonial Land Policies," 41–42, 85–93.

[17] Joseph Dalton to Lord Ashley, January 20, 1672, Cheves (ed.), *Shaftesbury Papers*, 376–383.

down. Land along the Ashley River, obviously not very fertile, was granted at random, for example. Two decades later, when the river front had assumed greater importance for its access to Charles Town, opportunists filled in gaps and claimed land which had been ignored by the first settlers.[18] Influenced by geography, South Carolina developed quite naturally into agricultural units dispersed according to the best available lands, with owners living on "home places" located on the streams which offered easy transit to Charles Town.

If South Carolina were to prosper, many more settlers had to be encouraged to migrate there as soon as possible. In the late 1660's the proprietors had published a number of tracts to attract potential migrants. Why they abandoned this means of publicity is not certain. During the 1670's they depended instead upon letters to governors of colonies which were supposed to be overpopulated. They also appointed agents in England and in some of the colonies. While records name an occasional would-be promoter who was offered a concession, usually a land grant, if he would underwrite a specified number of emigrants, little came of these negotiations. Most, if not all, of those arriving in Carolina during the first decade came as individuals rather than as part of any organized group.[19]

The results of this ineffective advertising are reflected in a slow rate of growth for the first few years. In March 1671 William Owen wrote that they numbered "about 200 and od

[18] A series of articles by Henry A. M. Smith about original land grants in and around Charles Town support this view. Some of these articles are as follows: "Charleston and Charleston Neck; the Original Grantees and the Settlements Along the Ashley and Cooper Rivers," *South Carolina Historical Magazine*, XIX (1918), 3–76; "The Ashley River: Its Seats and Settlements," ibid., XX (1919), 3–51, 75–122; "The Upper Ashley and the Mutations of Families," ibid., XX (1919), 151–198; "Goose Creek," ibid., XXIX (1928), 1–25, 71–96, 167–192, 265–279, 339–340.

[19] Kane, "Colonial Promotion and Promotion Literature," 86.

soules." [20] Some losses by "seasoning" doubtless had occurred. Vessels continued to come throughout 1671, and in
January 1672 Dalton reported that a total of 470 persons had
arrived.[21] John Locke interpreted Dalton's count to mean
that 268 men, 69 women, and 59 children, totaling 396, were
alive in January 1672.[22] Although Ashley wrote in 1671 that
the proprietors intended to send people until the province
was "a thousand strong," this goal was not reached for almost a decade.[23] Since he mentioned in 1675 that 500 or 600
settlers lived in the province, one must conclude that from
1671 onward, growth was very modest.[24] Failure to enlarge
the population may be blamed upon the proprietors alone
who never did what was necessary to attract more people.

If South Carolina's early settlers are difficult to number,
the character of the population is even more obscure. Nothing in the early records of the province contradicts, indeed
much supports, the view that the great majority of settlers
coming to the southern colonies arrived as indentured servants.[25] A few, possibly among the Barbadians, may have been
men of substance, but they were exceptions. The proprietors
were forced to extend so much credit because most of those
who came to South Carolina at the beginning were financially unable to pay passage and support themselves until a
money crop could be grown. In September 1670 West complained that it was difficult to carry on provincial business
because there were not 20 freemen in the company.[26] An-

[20] William Owen to Robert Blayney, March 22, 1671, Cheves (ed.), *Shaftesbury Papers*, 300–307.
[21] Joseph Dalton to Lord Ashley, January 20, 1672, ibid., 376–383.
[22] John Locke's summary of Dalton's letter cited in footnote 21 above, ibid.,
387.   [23] Lord Ashley to Stephen Bull, April 10, 1671, ibid., 312–313.
[24] Lord Ashley to the Governor and Council, June 10, 1675, ibid., 466–468.
[25] Abbot E. Smith, *Colonists in Bondage: White Servitude and Convict
Labor in America, 1607–1776* (Chapel Hill, 1947), 285–286.
[26] Joseph West to Lord Ashley, September 1670, Cheves (ed.), *Shaftesbury
Papers*, 202–204.

other correspondent mentioned in the spring of 1671 that freemen numbered only 40 or 50.[27] By December 1671 a law to regulate the activities of servants was under consideration.[28]

In writing about South Carolina's colonial era, some historians have minimized the number of servants in the early groups.[29] They have emphasized that the servant designation may have been a technique for obtaining land grants for both the master and the servant when his time ended. Such efforts to erase what appears to be a social stigma betray a misconception regarding English society at that time. Though poor, these servants were industrious and ambitious. They were, in fact, the best possible recruits for the colony since they were used to hard work, adjusted better to harsh and rudimentary conditions, and welcomed the opportunity to improve their lot. Had money been a prerequisite to settlement, few Englishmen would have come to America to live permanently.

Agreements between masters and servants were similar to those executed throughout British America. Most of the earlier servants apparently were signed in England on the account of a specific person in South Carolina, although masters of vessels sold the time of some indentured servants upon reaching Carolina. The period of servitude was usually from three to seven years. Servants sometimes signed on for only two years, but the shorter periods of service may have been useful recruiting devices while the province was being established. A servant received passage, maintenance during service, and a land grant at the end of his term. After being freed, through his own ability he could rise to importance in the province.[30]

[27] William Owen to Robert Blayney, March 22, 1671, ibid., 300–307.
[28] Grand Council Journal, December 9, 1671, ibid., 357–359.
[29] For example, Wallace, *History of S.C.*, I, 70.
[30] For more details about the lives of some individual servants, see Warren B. Smith, *White Servitude in Colonial South Carolina* (Columbia, 1961).

Many servants, of course, were not very valuable. Complaining that one group of servants had been "bad," West asked the proprietors in the future to send tradesmen or husbandmen who could contribute more to the settlement.[31] In 1672, 21 stripes were ordered for a recalcitrant servant.[32] The following year two runaway servants were sentenced to execution but the sentence was suspended when the two men begged for clemency and insisted they had repented.[33] These instances typify the sort of indentured servant who had been unsuccessful in England and became a liability in America.

In addition to many servants, some Negro slaves lived among the first settlers. Those who compiled population statistics at the outset did not include slaves. Early records in general contain very few references to Negroes. Nothing among initial laws, for example, pertains to the regulation of slaves. Since the total population was small and striving toward the subsistence level, one may safely assume there were only a few slaves, most of whom had been brought from Barbados by their masters. Most settlers neither had the means nor generated enough capital in the opening years to afford or support many slaves.

Most of the white population came from two sources: England and Barbados. Though hopes remained high that New England, New York, and other West Indian islands would provide settlers, only one shipload, a band from New York, came during the first five years.[34] The Barbadians were comparatively homogeneous and soon formed an important bloc. Political historians have referred to them as "the Goose Creek men" because many settled on that tributary of the

[31] Joseph West to Lord Ashley, about February 14, 1672, Cheves (ed.), *Shaftesbury Papers*, 387–388.

[32] Grand Council Journal, June 4, 1672, ibid., 394.

[33] Grand Council Journal, March 10, 1673, ibid., 421.

[34] For a list of early settlers, their places of origin, the number of slaves and servants they brought, and other biographical information, see Agnes Leland Baldwin, *First Settlers of South Carolina, 1670–1680* (Tricentennial Booklet, Number 1, Columbia, 1969).

Cooper River. They have been considered the dominating political force in the province from 1670 to 1712.[35] Most were experienced planters, belonged to the Anglican Church, and held similar economic views. Similarity of interests and background caused them to ally politically. They became increasingly arrayed against the proprietors and looked down upon other settlers whom they considered poor novices from England.[36] The others, in turn, thought them overbearing, arrogant, and not nearly as valuable to the settlement as they themselves believed. Writing to Ashley on March 21, 1671, Governor West observed that "wee find that one of our Servants wee brought out of England is worth 2 of ye Barbadians, for they are soe much addicted to Rum, that they will doe little whilst the bottle is at their nose. . . ."[37] Yet Ashley probably shared the proprietary view that the self-supporting Barbadians, who could provide colonial experience, money, and leadership during these first hard years, were valuable. The poorer sort, he recognized, "serve only to fill up Numbers and live upon us."[38]

From 1670 to 1675 the most serious friction between proprietors and settlers was caused by the financial backing extended by the proprietors to individuals and to the province as a whole. The proprietors felt that these expenditures, which were considerable, entitled them to dictate in the economic sphere, an assumption soon disputed by settlers. From their vantage point, the proprietors thought they were always subscribing more money. Since much of the money went to support the people and the colony's government, it could not be directly recovered. The eight shareholders assessed themselves equally and then determined at their meet-

[35] Sirmans, *Colonial South Carolina*, 17–100.
[36] Ibid., 17–18.
[37] Joseph West to Lord Ashley, March 21, 1671, Cheves (ed.), *Shaftesbury Papers*, 296–300.
[38] Lord Ashley to Sir John Yeamans, December 15, 1671, ibid., 360–362.

ings how funds were to be disbursed. At their first meeting
on May 23, 1663, each agreed to pay £25 into the hands of
Sir John Colleton.[39] By 1669 their goals had so expanded
under Ashley's leadership that they voted to pay out thousands of pounds at once. The cost of underwriting the initial
venture alone ran to over £3,200, and it is difficult to imagine from accounting details that the proprietors could reasonably have expected to recover more than £500 to £1,000
of this sum.[40] The rest would have to be charged as overhead
and could be regained only after the province prospered
with trade, quitrents were paid, and their own lands produced salable crops.

Failure of individuals to repay personal debts became
particularly galling to the proprietors. Since the majority of
the settlers were poor, the proprietors had to advance more
and more funds to maintain men who had no means to buy
necessities from outside the province. Goods to be advanced
at pegged prices were shipped to the province in the care of
the storekeeper. Joseph West, the first man to hold this job,
was cautioned to keep an account of all transactions and
render a statement to the debtor every three months. The
Register of the Province was also to record details of every
transaction, including an oath by the settler that he would
pay the proprietors. Unpaid debts were to accrue interest at
the rate of 10 per cent per annum, a reasonable charge in that
era. Since money would be short, repayments could be in
kind, at pegged rates.[41]

The proprietors, who had held high hopes for immediate
retirement of the debts, first showed patient though petulant
forbearance, then irritation, and finally anger toward the

[39] "First Meeting of the Proprietors," May 23, 1663, ibid., 5.

[40] Documents pertaining to the first expedition, ibid., 117–152.

[41] "Copy of Instructions to Mr. Joseph West, Storekeeper," August 1669,
ibid., 127–129.

ungrateful wretches living on their bounty. Most of the original debts remained unpaid. Settlers not only asked to delay the start of repayments, they demanded more support in the meantime. As early as the summer of 1670 the council was urging the proprietors to spend more.[42] In the spring of 1671 the council again requested more food, clothing, cattle, hogs, and aid until food crops could be grown.[43] By 1674 these seemingly endless requests had worn proprietary tolerance so thin that they balked at spending any more and sent a letter which was an outburst of disillusionment to officials in South Carolina.[44] Yet they had just voted to spend £700 annually on the enterprise for seven more years, having realized that their only other choice was to see the settlement abandoned and their previous investments lost.[45] Antagonisms over debts persisted for years.

Credit difficulties were related to the much broader question of how quickly the settlers could become self-supporting. How soon would the economy produce enough exportable items to pay for imports and permit profits to be applied to debts? The eventual solution to this web of business lay in the settlers' ability to find a staple that could be grown in commercially significant amounts. During the planning stages and early years of settlement, hopes were high on both sides of the Atlantic that such a staple would be found quickly. Then year after year passed without a suitable commodity emerging from the welter of experiments conducted. Had such a commerical crop been found readily, the province would have grown rapidly and the proprietors soon would have recouped their sizable outlays.

Not only were expectations and projections about a staple

[42] Council to Proprietors, Summer of 1670, ibid., 175–176.
[43] Council to Proprietors, March 21, 1671, ibid., 282–287.
[44] Proprietors to the Governor and Council, May 18, 1674, ibid., 435–438.
[45] "Articles Between the Lords Proprietors," May 6, 1674, ibid., 431–435.

unrealistic, but the food problem persisted for at least four or five growing seasons, limiting all other work. An adequate, locally grown food supply became the primary objective of both proprietors and settlers. All productive capabilities were channeled toward this end; all other economic goals were made secondary. Though the problem was not as desperate as it was elsewhere, the process of attaining self-sufficiency was painful. The proprietors had sent enough food with the first three vessels to support the settlers for 18 months.[46] West estimated, however, that after depletion and losses en route only three months' supply remained when they landed in Carolina.[47] By June of 1670, rations had been reduced to one pint of peas per day.[48] Shortages in provisions, if not actual want, persisted throughout 1670, despite food shipments by the proprietors and purchases from the Indians. Letters from South Carolina in the spring of 1671 described a band of settlers weak from a lack of provisions, but with hope that the 30 acres which they had cleared would grow sufficient quantities for the next winter.[49] An influx of newcomers rendered these plans inadequate, however.[50] Shortages continued. Because the situation remained uncertain during 1672 and 1673, most correspondents told Ashley that each new settler should bring an eight months' supply of food for himself.[51] As late as 1674, corn was reported to be the chief item of diet.[52] Sir Peter Colleton, proprietary agent in Barbados, informed John Locke in July 1674, that the

[46] Samuel Wilson, "An Account of the Province of Carolina . . ." (London, 1682). Reprinted in Salley (ed.), *Narratives of Early Carolina*, 166.

[47] Joseph West to Lord Ashley, November 8, 1669, Cheves (ed.), *Shaftesbury Papers*, 156–157.

[48] Joseph West to Lord Ashley, June 27, 1670, ibid., 173–174.

[49] Joseph West to Lord Ashley, March 2, 1671, ibid., 266–268; Joseph West to Sir Peter Colleton, March 2, 1671, ibid., 271–275.

[50] Joseph West to Lord Ashley, about July 1671, ibid., 349–350.

[51] Captain Halsted to Lord Ashley, about March 1672, ibid., 389.

[52] Jose Miguel Gallardo, "The Spaniards and the English Settlement in Charles Town," *South Carolina Historical Magazine*, XXXVII (1936), 94–99.

food problem had finally been overcome.[53] Though the proprietors may have been increasingly grudging in their support, their supplies saved the settlers from a hungrier beginning.

The settlers should not be blamed overmuch for this slow start. While building homes and clearing land, they remained in constant fear of Spaniards and Indians. The council justified results of the first year by reminding the proprietors that much time was lost standing guard and building a fort.[54] Shortage of food curtailed the amount of work done; men who are underfed lack vitality and stamina. As people became weak and undernourished, they were more vulnerable to the "seasoning" process. During the first ten months of settlement, Dalton calculated, 470 arrived and 48 died.[55] An attrition rate of 10 per cent was high enough to affect productivity, and many others doubtless experienced long periods of illness and disability. A harsh environment clearly took its toll on the first settlers.

Growing their own food was only a first step; the colonists still did not have a commercial crop. Without a staple, the people had nothing to barter for their needs and no means of generating capital to apply against their personal debts or to buy imports. The proprietors encouraged and aided experimentation, though they constantly cautioned that this activity should be limited until the food supply was insured. In 1669 they directed Joseph West, as first storekeeper, to try out a number of potential staples. He was instructed to obtain cotton seed, indigo seed, ginger roots, canes, vines,

[53] Sir Peter Colleton to John Locke, July 22, 1674, John Locke Manuscripts, "Papers Relating to the Colonies," Shelf Mark c. 6, Bodleian Library, Oxford (Microfilm M-3691, Southern Historical Collection, University of North Carolina Library, Chapel Hill).

[54] Council to Proprietors, March 16, 1671, Cheves (ed.), *Shaftesbury Papers*, 287–290.

[55] Joseph Dalton to Lord Ashley, January 20, 1672, ibid., 376–383.

and olive sets in Barbados, then plant them at intervals throughout the start of the growing season—April, May, and June. They were to be planted in as many different places as possible, including sandy soil, light black mold, low land, and higher land.[56] It was a logical way to determine those varieties most suitable for the climate and soil as well as the best planting time. Probably nothing came of this first agricultural testing, but trials never ceased. The early records of the province and letters of settlers are strewn with references to ginger, silk, grape vines, olives, indigo, tobacco, rice, and other plants. A commercially significant crop did not immediately emerge, though the isolation of some which grew well may have occurred. The process of elimination in itself was important. If the colonists had struck upon a staple by 1675, the need to spend time and effort on food production would have prevented developing an unfamiliar or exotic species rapidly. The basic idea of cultivating a crop which would have a ready market in the empire proved sound in the long run, but the task of trial and error in finding such a commodity took years, even decades, longer than either proprietors or settlers had originally anticipated.

Despite the lack of successes in South Carolina, Ashley's interest in agricultural experimentation never flagged. An amateur scientific farmer, he constantly prodded officials about results of their experiments in the province and forwarded advice. Joseph Dalton reported to him in 1672 that while winters were too cold for sugar canes and cotton, he believed that grapes, silk, indigo, tobacco, hemp, flax, and perhaps ginger could be grown. Dalton proposed that plans be made to try dates and almonds.[57] In 1674 Ashley ordered Andrew Percivall to set up his personal plantation at "Locke

[56] "Copy of Instructions for Mr. West . . . ," probably written by Lord Ashley, about July, 1669, ibid., 125–127.
[57] Joseph Dalton to Lord Ashley, January 20, 1672, ibid., 376–383.

Island" where he was to grow Irish potatoes, English grains, and other European crops.[58] Ashley continued to speculate about the commercial potential of his beloved Carolina for the remainder of his life. Although he was in exile at the time of his death, he had trials in progress on his English estate and intended that the plants should be tested further in Carolina.[59] Had his attention not been taken from the proprietary after 1675, his efforts in this area might have brought results much sooner than they did come.

Not surprisingly, tobacco was a successful crop from the beginning. It had been cultivated for so long in colonial America that some of the settlers probably had grown it elsewhere. Stephen Bull judged that Carolina tobacco was better than the best Virginia leaf. To prove his point, he sent a roll grown in 1671 to the proprietors.[60] Four defectors to St. Augustine in 1674 deposed that tobacco was one of the items traded to Barbados for necessities.[61] By 1675 the amount of tobacco being grown for export necessitated the appointment of viewers to guarantee quality of the leaf, and tobacco was made one of the commodities receivable for debts owed the proprietors.[62] Although the proprietors were willing to allow tobacco as a money crop, they did not think it possible to obtain an abatement of customs duties from the crown.[63] Maryland and Virginia had monopolized the tobacco market long before Carolina was opened up. Tobacco continued to be grown and sold, but it stood little chance of becoming important to South Carolina's economy.

As the search for salable tropical and semitropical crops

[58] Lord Ashley to Andrew Percivall, May 23, 1674, ibid., 440–445.

[59] Brown, *Shaftesbury*, 179–180.

[60] Stephen Bull to Proprietors, January 20, 1672, Cheves (ed.), *Shaftesbury Papers*, 386–387.

[61] Gallardo, "Spaniards and Charles Town," *S.C. Hist. Mag.*, 94–99.

[62] Grand Council Journal, November 2, 1675, Cheves (ed.), *Shaftesbury Papers*, 473.

[63] Lords Proprietors to Lord Ashley, November 20, 1674, ibid., 454–455.

became prolonged, settlers drifted into economic activities suited to the local frontier environment. They kept herds of cattle and hogs which ranged on the natural forage of a thinly populated country. The animals thrived, but it took several years to build up herds. Settlers had to import foundation animals and then wait until the natural increase allowed the slaughter of animals not needed for breeding purposes. Irked by the herding, the proprietors exhorted settlers to concentrate on trade and planting.[64] South Carolinians, however, responded to their economic self-interest rather than proprietary goals. Beef and pork salted in barrels had a market in the West Indies. Hides of the butchered animals met the needs for leather within the province and could be exported as well. Furthermore, the herds were a food reserve on the hoof. Given conditions in the colony, it is difficult to believe that many barrels of beef and pork were shipped between 1670 and 1675. Stock raising built up too slowly. As late as 1674 settlers were requesting the proprietors to buy more cattle.[65] Nonetheless, a provisions trade was begun. Each of the four runaways to Florida mentioned such items of trade.[66] The provisions trade, like that in tobacco, had limited potential since every mainland colony could, as many did, send excess food to the West Indies.

The forests provided another natural economic resource to exploit. In the first year, 12 cedar planks were sent to the proprietors as a symbol of the bounty and promise of Carolina.[67] Timbers and lumber were bulky, taking up much shipping space, and the province was too far from the English market to export forest products at a profit. The West Indies, therefore, was the most feasible market for timber,

[64] Proprietors to the Governor and Council, May 18, 1674, ibid., 435–438.
[65] Ibid.
[66] Gallardo, "Spaniards and Charles Town," *S.C. Hist. Mag.*, 94–99.
[67] Sir John Yeamans to Proprietors, November 15, 1670, Cheves (ed.), *Shaftesbury Papers*, 220–221.

and it was shipped to Barbados from the first year onward.[68] If nothing else was available, vessels bound for the islands could always fill cargo space with lumber and timber. Of all lumber products, staves were in greatest demand. As early as 1671 Captain Halsted, an employee of the proprietors, recognized the potential of this trade for South Carolina. He urged the proprietors to buy a "flye-boat" which could carry passengers from Barbados to Carolina and then take a return cargo of 100,000 pipe staves.[69] Staves were always carried to England as fillers in odd nooks and crannies of vessels. As early as 1671 pipe stave viewers were appointed.[70]

The potential for trading lumber was obvious and brought the proprietary into a minor conflict with both settlers and provincial officials. The proprietors complained that settlers were disregarding their orders to load timber bound for Barbados for their account.[71] In the spring of 1671 West requested that the proprietors send horses to draw timber, though the council insisted that loading timber for the proprietors' account was hindering efforts to plant crops.[72] Settlers surely resented their work on the proprietors' behalf, but the preparation and the loading of lumber were one way to repay their debts to the proprietary.

With many possibilities yet to be realized, the early trade in timber and wooden goods shared the limitations of the provisions trade. Profits were small. Every mainland colony had plenty of trees, and every vessel bound for the islands carried some lumber or staves. Perhaps as a result of these limitations, interest shifted to some naval stores, since South

[68] Joseph West to Sir Peter Colleton, March 2, 1671, ibid., 271–273.
[69] Captain Halsted to Proprietors, about September 1671, ibid., 351–352.
[70] Grand Council Journal, December 9, 1671, ibid., 357–359.
[71] T. Colleton to the Governor and Council, December 26, 1670, ibid., 255–256.
[72] Council to Proprietors, March 21, 1671, ibid., 282–287; Joseph West to Lord Ashley, March 21, 1671, ibid., 296–300.

Carolina's potential was known. Some historians have maintained that a naval stores trade to the West Indies actually began during these early years.[73] This is possible but not probable. The processes for manufacturing tar, pitch, turpentine, and rosin were rudimentary. But considering the scope of their other tasks, early settlers likely had little time to do more than experiment. There is little evidence that any of the above naval stores were produced and exported in sizable amounts during the first years. Masts, spars, and ship timbers could have been processed also, but the Royal Navy had concluded prior to 1670 that most American woods were inferior for shipbuilding and it was generally uninterested in the colonies as a source of timber and lumber.[74] Though the navy had sent a vessel in 1667 to obtain a load of cypress masts, during the first years nothing came from hopes to sell the province's forest products in England.[75]

For the first 20 years, the Indian trade was the most significant commerce.[76] It consisted, essentially, of settlers exchanging European manufactured goods with the Indians for deerskins and furs. As this commerce developed, furs became incidental, making up less than 1 per cent of the total value of furs and deerskins which Charles Town exported annually.[77] South Carolina was too far south for animals to have high-quality pelts, and the number of furs obtained from tribes who ranged to the north was always small. Though the Indian trade eventually became formalized, reg-

[73] For example, Sirmans, *Colonial South Carolina*, 23.

[74] Robert G. Albion, *Forests and Sea Power: The Timber Problem of the Royal Navy, 1652–1862* (Cambridge, Massachusetts, 1926), 23.

[75] W. L. Grant and James Munro (eds.), *Acts of the Privy Council of England, Colonial Series, 1613–1783* (Hereford and London, 1908–1912), I, 440, Item 723 (15).

[76] This very brief account of the Indian trade is based on the comprehensive treatment of the subject by Verner W. Crane, *The Southern Frontier, 1670–1732* (Durham, 1928), 3–21.

[77] Murray G. Lawson, *Fur: A Study in English Mercantilism, 1700–1755* (Toronto, 1943), 71, note 12.

ulated, and conducted almost exclusively by professional traders who went into the backcountry as representatives of Charles Town merchants, it began quite naturally and informally. In the first years, any settler could barter casually with any Indian. Many times the Indians came directly into Charles Town, although such direct trading in town ended early. Great numbers of Indians in and around the settlement were regarded as a danger; this was one reason the traders started going to the tribes.

Since they knew that trade with the Indians was lucrative in other colonies, the proprietors were interested in the possibilities of this business activity from the start. They sent a supply of "Indian goods" with the first vessels.[78] These were, of course, used mostly to obtain food and cement friendly relations. Soon, however, the proprietors shifted their attention to the commercial aspects of the trade. Since the weak local tribes neither controlled large land areas, had many hunters, nor had contacts with the inland tribes which proved in time to be the best sources of deerskins, trading in the first few years was limited. An alliance with the aggressive Westo tribe in 1674 to fight the nearby tribes over land rights offered the first opportunity for an important source of skins. The treaty between the province and the Westo was made permanent; from 1674 until 1680 it was the cornerstone of South Carolina Indian policy and the major trading link between settlers and the Indians. Ashley was soon working through Henry Woodward to engross this commerce as the exclusive preserve of the proprietors. In 1677 the proprietors declared that they had the sole right to the trade.[79] Such a policy was utterly unenforceable and brought stiff resistance and noncompliance from the settlers. While the tie to

[78] Documents pertaining to the first expedition, Cheves (ed.), *Shaftesbury Papers,* 117–152.   [79] Crane, *Southern Frontier,* 19.

the Westo doubtless increased this business activity, there is little evidence that much money was made from it before the 1680's.

The major accomplishment of Indian policy up to 1675 was to avoid a major war. A conflict of any proportion with either the Spaniards or Indians or both would have been a disaster. Much of the credit goes to Ashley and Woodward. Ashley clearly recognized the vulnerability of the settlement, and he constantly urged prudence in dealing with the tribes to avoid abrasive actions. Woodward was Ashley's agent. In his role as go-between for proprietors and provincial officials on one side and various tribes on the other Woodward, until his death around 1685, saved the settlement from many troubles during very critical years. Yet the settlers were suspicious that these proprietary attempts to control the frontier were motivated by economic considerations.[80]

Because all attempts to find and develop rapidly a staple trade failed, some settlers engaged in the Indian slave trade as a substitute. Constant skirmishes with Indians over land rights, destruction of crops, slaying of cattle and other animals provided perfect excuses to capture the supposedly offending parties and to send them into exile as slaves. The business started early, perhaps as soon as the first whites arrived, and it continued into the eighteenth century. Some of the unfortunate victims were kept in the province, but most were shipped to the West Indies. The profits involved also encouraged Indians who were allied to South Carolina to waylay, capture, and sell Indians who were allied to the Spaniards. The business jibed perfectly with the Indian way of life and allowed the tribes to make a profit from endemic warfare carried on against traditional rivals. Undoubtedly

[80] Ibid., 18–19.

many traders seeking deerskins also bought and sold Indian slaves.[81]

The proprietors viewed this traffic as illegal from the start, and they constantly railed at the provincial authorities to take steps to prohibit it.[82] The proprietors shared none of the settlers' prejudices and intended, as Englishmen, that the Indians be treated with justice, be allowed lands, and be incorporated into Carolina as set forth in the Fundamental Constitutions. Typical of most frontiersmen, South Carolinians distrusted Indians and probably hated them actively. Because of popular sentiment among settlers and provincial officials, the trade continued despite proprietary attempts to curb it. In fact, some have concluded that Barbadians and governmental officials were the major early slave dealers.[83] South Carolina had the most extensive Indian slave trade of any of the English colonies.[84] It may have been the most important generator of profits during the first five years. Since the trade was illicit, the extent of traffic at any time is not known. However, the presence of numerous slaves in the province after 1700 attests to widespread engagement in this clandestine business.

Contact with the Indians and penetration of the back-country in search of skins and slaves added constantly to knowledge about the interior of the province. Ashley and the other proprietors saw this as a mixed blessing. They did not want the settlers distracted from their primary objective of securing the base on the Ashley River nor did they want

[81] For a fuller treatment of this trade in Indian slaves, see Almon Wheeler Lauber, *Indian Slavery in Colonial Times Within the Present United States* (*Columbia University Studies in History, Economics and Public Law*, LIV, No. 3), (New York, 1913), 118–210.

[82] For example, Instructions from Proprietors to the Governor and Council (this set of instructions is sometimes designated the "Temporary Agrarian Laws"), June 21, 1672, printed in Rivers, *Sketch of History of S.C.*, 355–359.

[83] Sirmans, *Colonial South Carolina*, 40–43.

[84] Lauber, *Indian Slavery in Colonial Times*, 105–117.

dispersal of people to thwart their pattern of orderly settlement. Ashley had the fear of all organizers of colonies that
some rumor of wealth to be found in the interior would
spread gold fever and subsequently disrupt the province.[85]
Systematic exploration of the backcountry to assess its possibilities was not undertaken during the first decade. It was
not until 1682 that Woodward was given an official commission to go beyond the Appalachians.[86]

The proprietors also exercised their right to regulate commerce. In 1669 they charged Joseph West, as storekeeper, to
keep track of goods brought into or taken out of the province.[87] In September 1671 Lord Ashley directed Sir John Yeamans to designate one town on every navigable river as a
port.[88] He himself so designated Charles Town.[89] In December 1671 the council ordered that all vessels arriving should
make entry with the Register's office, listing day of arrival,
point of origin, names of passengers being brought to settle,
and taking out bond not to carry away any present inhabit-
ant without a license.[90] No complete records of entrances and
clearances of vessels survive to indicate if this early and
feeble attempt to comply with the English navigation system
came to anything. The absence of such records before 1717
hinders those wishing to compile meaningful statistics meas-
uring the economic growth of the province.

At the conclusion of five years, South Carolina was only a
partial success. It was a fairly compact settlement of 500 or
600 people living along the Ashley River a few miles from
the ocean. South Carolinians had a foothold, but progress

[85] Lord Ashley to Henry Woodward, April 10, 1671, Cheves (ed.), *Shaftesbury Papers*, 315–317.   [86] Crane, *Southern Frontiers*, 16.

[87] "Copy of Instructions to Mr. Joseph West, Storekeeper," August 1669,
Cheves (ed.), *Shaftesbury Papers*, 127–129.

[88] Lord Ashley to Sir John Yeamans, September 18, 1671, ibid., 342–344.

[89] Lord Ashley to Sir John Yeamans, December 15, 1671, ibid., 360–362.

[90] Grand Council Minutes, December 23, 1671, ibid., 369–370.

had been much slower than either they or the proprietors had anticipated. These dampened, if not dashed, expectations contributed to the growing alienation between proprietors and settlers and aggravated more specific frictions. The most serious economic problems concerned the proprietors' land policy, the individual debts owed the proprietors, and the proprietors' desire to control the Indian trade in skins and halt the Indian slave trade. Proprietary ardor for the project had undergone a serious deterioration after they realized that their large investment was not likely to bring in a return soon, but they had continued to support the settlers during the trial period. By staying five years, the settlers had already committed themselves, though it was not inconceivable in 1675 that the province might yet become a complete failure and be abandoned. No economic foundation had been built. An export which would serve as the basis for future prosperity had to be found before the promise of South Carolina could be realized for both settlers and proprietors.

CHAPTER IV

More Lean Years
1675–1690

THE PATTERN OF SOUTH CAROLINA DEVELOPMENT FROM 1675 to 1690 shows much continuity with the first five years. Having reached the plateau of self-sufficiency in food by 1675, settlers were free to expand their previously limited efforts to isolate one or more commodities which could be produced in quantity for export. No staple had been found, however, by 1690. Since the economy had not become more sophisticated, the great majority of settlers remained poor or in modest circumstances. Only a small minority found ways to accrue wealth from the few commercial activities, some of which were illegal. Most of these trades neither benefited most people nor offered promise for the future.

Because the province remained weak and vulnerable, the proprietors had to continue to supply monetary support. To protect their investment, they were eager to shape economic and political relationships in the colony consistent with their rights and privileges and the spirit of the Fundamental Constitutions. Their policy revisions in the late 1670's and 1680's were intended to foster prosperity and improve the political atmosphere. Under pressure from the crown, the proprietors about 1685 became more concerned about enforcement of imperial regulations within the province. While the proprietors were hardly responsible for the latter, settlers blamed them for trying to enforce imperial regulations as well as their own instructions and, wherever possible, evaded or ignored both. Relations deteriorated, and by 1690 a crisis between settlers and proprietors was approaching.

A major cause of difficulties both in Charles Town and London was the change from strong leaders to weak ones. Governor Joseph West prevented an open break during his term from 1674 to 1682.[1] The settlers exhibited independence of spirit, but he acted as a buffer between the people and their overlords. After West was removed, the proprietors did not have a strong governor in South Carolina for at least another dozen years. West's forceful leadership had concealed temporarily the decline in the proprietary. After 1675 Ashley was fighting first for his political career in England, then for his life; finally, he fled into exile in Holland in 1682. He remained Palatine until 1678, and he signed letters going to Charles Town until near the end of his life, but he could not have had time to supervise the proprietary very carefully. Some have insisted that he was largely responsible for a number of innovations of the late 1670's and early 1680's, but the evidence is scanty.[2]

With Ashley forced into inactivity, the old Earl of Craven became Palatine, a position he held from 1678 until shortly before his death at the age of 91 in 1697.[3] He was the last link within the proprietary to the original underwriters of the project. Though a man of great honor and fidelity, he was also judged to have limited abilities.[4] Upon this aged

[1] Sirmans, *Colonial South Carolina*, 29–30.

[2] Brown, *Shaftesbury*, 176–180.

[3] Though the 1678 date is commonly cited, the earliest letter in the *BPRO-SC* series signed by Craven as Palatine is dated in 1680: Proprietors to Governor West and Council, May 17, 1680, *BPRO-SC*, I, 97–102.

[4] *DNB*, V, 45–49.

and weakening reed, the proprietary's administration depended. Moreover, he did not get much help from the other seven holders of proprietary shares, with the exception of John Archdale, who had purchased a share for his minor son in 1678. But much of Archdale's best work for the proprietary came in the 1690's, not in the 1680's. Most of the rest were inactive, undistinguished, or mediocre in ability. Several shares were held by minors and represented by agents or trustees. Some shares were in litigation for years.[5] The steady decline in proprietary leadership allowed the local government and the settlers generally to assume control of their own destinies much more rapidly than they might have under stronger overlords.

Private debts which individuals owed the proprietors remained a problem and source of friction. By 1675 the proprietors claimed to have spent £9,000 or £10,000 on the venture, and much of this total had been advanced to individuals.[6] In 1679 the proprietors reported to the crown that expenses for the Carolina project had reached £17,000 or £18,000. These figures indicate that they spent almost as much from 1676 to 1679 as they had from 1663 to 1675.[7] There was no way to coerce poor settlers into paying when the province had little to offer in trade. Nonetheless, from time to time, the governor and council were urged to dun the settlers. The proprietors would take either money or commodities, but they must have written off most of these early debts. The records are not very clear, but since complaints declined, the proprietors evidently ceased to advance funds to individuals in the early 1680's.

[5] See William S. Powell, *The Proprietors of Carolina* (Raleigh, 1963), for the identities of all who held proprietary shares.
[6] Lord Ashley to the Governor and Council, June 10, 1675, Cheves (ed.), *Shaftesbury Papers*, 466–468.
[7] Lords Propietors to unspecified addressee (probably the Privy Council), March 6, 1679, *BPRO-SC*, I, 71–72.

The proprietors also sought to reduce the total they were spending by having the province assume the obligation for its own governmental expenses as rapidly as possible. As early as 1675 Ashley had directed that the governor's salary be paid locally.[8] This was not done, but the settlers did concur with some of the many requests that they assume financial responsibility. Perhaps they had to vote taxes or not have many necessary governmental services. For whatever reason, in the 1680's the government of South Carolina did appropriate ever greater sums for general and specific purposes.[9] Possibly the effect of paying their own expenses contributed to their growing independence of spirit. Misunderstandings about the division of financial obligations between proprietors and provincial government endured, however, and ultimately were a cause of the demise of the proprietary.

By 1675 the proprietors must have recognized that promotional activities had to be stepped up. The colony could never produce much with a small population. In all fairness, attracting settlers was difficult and competitive, but Ashley's methods had not proved very successful. In the early 1680's a spate of publicity tracts appeared, representing a return to the approach first used by the proprietary in the late 1660's. The two most detailed were by Thomas Ashe, who came to Charles Town in 1680, and Samuel Wilson, a secretary to Lord Ashley.[10] Nevertheless, it is difficult to connect these

[8] Lord Ashley to the Governor and Council, June 10, 1675, Cheves (ed.), *Shaftesbury Papers,* 466–468.
[9] Thomas Cooper and David J. McCord (eds.), *The Statutes at Large of South Carolina, 1682–1838* (Columbia, 1838–41), I, 3–50. These pages cover most of the surviving laws passed from 1682 through 1690. Since only the titles of some laws remain, it is difficult to analyze the outlays by the provincial government.
[10] Thomas Ashe, *Carolina, or a Description of the Present State of That Country* (London, 1682); Wilson, *An Account of the Province of Carolina. . . .* Both are in Salley (ed.), *Narratives of Early Carolina,* 138–159, 164–176.

pamphlets with any movement of people to South Carolina. To experience rapid population growth, a colony had to offer immediate possibilities; South Carolina did not. The slow development of the economy was a drawback. Moreover, South Carolina's colonizers never found a source of large numbers of immigrants. Even by 1690 the chief lure remained future promise rather than current boom.

Natural increase plus individual immigrants dribbling into the province had only raised the population from 500 or 600 in 1675[11] to 1,000 or 1,200 by 1680.[12] Rather suddenly, between 1680 and 1682, three different group migrations which promised many people for Carolina were begun. There were a small band of French Huguenots, a considerable body of English dissenters, and the purported vanguard of 10,000 Scottish Covenanters. Each of these projected mass migrations owed something to Ashley and his private negotiations.[13] Each could be connected to his insistence that economic potential and religious toleration would be attractive to persons who could no longer live comfortably in European societies. Like so many of Ashley's earlier efforts, however, these fell far short of anticipated results.

Comparatively few Huguenots became settlers in the province. While the terms offered them were generous since their particular talents might be useful to the province, the meager results of these negotiations were quite disappointing.[14] Eighty families were expected in 1680, but only 45 persons

[11] Lord Ashley to the Governor and Council, June 10, 1675, Cheves (ed.), *Shaftesbury Papers*, 466–468.   [12] Ashe, *Carolina*.

[13] For more details on these promotional efforts see Herbert R. Paschal, Jr., "Proprietary North Carolina: A Study in Colonial Govenment" (unpublished Ph.D. dissertation, University of North Carolina, 1961), 163–165; Kane, "Colonial Promotion and Promotion Literature of Carolina, 1660–1700," 73–82.

[14] Documents relating to the proprietors' negotiations with the Huguenots are in *BPRO-SC*, I, 62–81; Arthur H. Hirsch, *The Huguenots of Colonial South Carolina* (Durham, 1928), 11–13; Henry A. De Saussure, "Huguenot Immigration in South Carolina," *Huguenot Society of South Carolina Transactions*, No. 12 (1905), 16–29.

landed.[15] The majority of colonial South Carolina's Huguenot families did not come until after the Revocation of the Edict of Nantes in 1685.[16] While many individuals bearing Huguenot names became prominent, the total number of immigrants was small. An official count in 1699 enumerated only 438 in the province.[17]

To English dissenters, fearful for their future in an England torn by political and religious questions, the promise of religious liberty in Carolina was as important as immediate economic possibilities. A proprietary letter dated in 1690 declared that 500 of these people migrated to South Carolina in a single month, though the month and year were not specified.[18] Most of the dissenters apparently arrived between 1680 and 1682, and they formed the bulk of the increase of the province's population to 2,000 or 2,500, if Ashe is to be believed.[19] The fact that political factionalism was aggravated by religious partisanship in the 1680's bespeaks the admixture of a considerable body of dissenters to challenge the Anglicans. Among their leaders were men like Joseph Blake and Joseph Morton (sometimes spelled Moreton), who would later become governors.

Though a debacle, the story of the Scots' migration is noteworthy because it delineates proprietary shortsightedness and the painful process of establishing a colony.[20] The possibility of obtaining thousands of Scottish settlers influenced the proprietors to make special concessions, the

[15] Henry A. M. Smith, "The Orange Quarter and the First French Settlers in South Carolina," *South Carolina Historical Magazine*, XVIII (1917), 107.

[16] Hirsch, *Huguenots*, 13.

[17] Unsigned memorandum from Charles Town to unnamed official in London, March 14, 1699, *BPRO-SC*, IV, 75.

[18] Proprietors to Andrew Percivall, October 18, 1690, printed in Rivers, *Sketch of History of South Carolina*, 412–414.   [19] Ashe, *Carolina*.

[20] The most complete consideration of this project is by George P. Insh, *Scottish Colonial Schemes, 1620–1686* (Glasgow, 1922), 186–211.

most important of which was the right of the Scots to have their own government, separate and unrelated to the governor and government based at Charles Town.[21] Earlier, the proprietors had foreseen the possibility of a province fragmented into many independent settlements. Moreover, Port Royal, the intended site of the Scottish settlement, was much nearer the source of the lucrative Indian trade than Charles Town. These plans led settlers already in South Carolina to feel that they had been sold out by the proprietors. When 148 Covenanters landed at Charles Town in October 1684, authorities there were negative and unwilling to help the newcomers erect a settlement which would be independent and an economic rival. Their company reduced by malaria, the Scotsmen soon sealed their own doom. Their foolishly aggressive postures toward everyone (including Charles Town settlers) eventually brought retaliation. In August 1686 Spaniards and their Indian allies destroyed the Scottish settlement and several plantations owned by regular settlers as well.[22] At the precise time the invaders were poised to go on to attack Charles Town, a hurricane struck.[23] While the storm itself was destructive, it may have saved the colony by dispersing its enemies. The costly invasion and the hurricane ended the attempts of the Scots. The venture netted only a handful of people for the province.

From a population of 2,000 to 2,500 in 1682, South Carolina must have added enough people to reach the 3,500 to 4,000 level in 1690. One must interpolate between figures, for few meaningful estimates exist for years between 1682

[21] Articles of Agreement between Lords Proprietors and Sir John Cockram [Cochran] and Sir George Campbell, July 30, 1682, *BPRO-SC*, I, 212–219.

[22] J. G. Dunlop, "Spanish Depredations, 1686," *South Carolina Historical Magazine*, XXX (1929) , 81–89; Paul Grimball, "Paul Grimball's Losses by the Spanish Invasion in 1686," ibid., XXIX (1928) , 231–237.

[23] Ludlum, *Early American Hurricanes*, 41–42.

and 1700. Most estimates for 1700 place the total at 5,000 or 6,000.[24] Although the increase in the 15 years from 1675 to 1690 was seven- or eightfold, the province still had comparatively limited human resources. This growth pattern was rather typical of new plantations, however. South Carolina seemed to be filling at a rate only slightly faster than that of Virginia during its first 20 years.[25] Little is known about the demography of this population. It would be valuable to know, for example, how many Negro slaves were in the province. Although trading between servants and slaves and other persons was regulated by law in 1687,[26] absence of a slave code and lack of any accounting of the number of Negro slaves indicate that there were few. Slow progress in producing a staple inhibited the growth of the slave population.

For an individual considering migration to Carolina, the strongest economic inducement remained the ease with which he could obtain a quantity of land. In 1679 the proprietors reduced the headright from 100 acres to 70, and in 1682 it was reduced further to 50 acres for each free person sixteen or older who arrived in the province. Fifty more acres could be obtained for each adult member of the family or for an adult slave or servant imported. Each male servant under sixteen and each woman servant "not marageable" brought an allowance of 40 acres. Freed servants were granted 50 acres.[27] This basic allotment of 50 acres of land for an adult either upon arrival or upon completion of indenture remained the rule until the end of the proprietary era. Land allotments continued to be generous enough to insure that

[24] Evarts B. Greene and Virginia D. Harrington, *American Population Before the Federal Census of 1790* (New York, 1932), 172–173.

[25] Ibid., 135–136, 172–173.

[26] Cooper and McCord (eds.), *Statutes of S.C.*, I, 22–23.

[27] Proprietors to Governor and Council, May 19, 1679, *BPRO-SC*, I, 82–84; Proprietors to Governor Morton, May 10, 1682, ibid., I, 138–157.

any individual could obtain more than he could possibly work alone.

Reduction of the headright value was one of a number of changes in land policy aimed at controlling the sprawl of the settlement. In 1682 Maurice Mathews, the Surveyor General, was instructed to make no grants for lands more than 30 miles south of the Stono River, more than 50 miles north of the mouths of the Ashley and Cooper Rivers, or over 60 miles inland. He was also directed to lay out three counties: Berkeley County centering on Charles Town, Colleton County to the south, and Craven County to the north.[28] In 1685 inland penetration was theoretically restricted further when the governor was informed that no grants were to be allowed if lands were more than 35 miles in from the sea.[29] Such changes were clearly within the spirit of earlier proprietary policies.

Still, neither reduced offerings of land nor restrictions on location of grants adversely affected provincial growth. Immigration is known to have been considerable after 1682, and grants to those promising to transport settlers or rendering service to the province were much more generous than they had been in the 1670's.[30] Also, in the 1680's the proprietors first offered to sell land for hard cash. Persons in England could buy at the rate of £50 per thousand acres (a shilling per acre). Persons in South Carolina paid 12d. per acre or the produce of peas and corn grown on three acres in

[28] Instructions for Maurice Mathews, Surveyor General, May 10, 1682, ibid., I, 130–137. These orders describe the projected boundary lines of the counties in specific terms. Exactly when these counties were actually formed is an open question, though perhaps an unimportant one since they never did become significant administrative or legal districts during the colonial era. Governmental business continued to be carried on from Charles Town. See map in the front of the book for the approximate boundaries of these counties as they were actually laid out.

[29] Instructions for Governor Joseph West, March 12, 1685, ibid., II, 11–24.

[30] For example, Proprietors to Governor Joseph West, July 30, 1685, ibid., II, 81.

a year.[31] Either way of purchase left the grantee with only a nominal quitrent to pay, generally an ear of Indian corn if requested. The proprietors did sell some land to Englishmen, and the proceeds of several hundred pounds may well have been the first clear income the proprietary received. It is difficult to pinpoint how much land was conveyed in this way, but it was a small proportion of the total granted.

Above all, the proprietors looked forward to steady income from quitrents which were supposed to be paid starting September 29, 1689, even sooner on some grants made after 1682.[32] To be sure of collecting, the proprietors changed the form of grants from a deed to an indenture, extracting legal promise that the owner would pay quitrents within six months of the due date or face loss of his land.[33] By 1687 they had taken steps to set up a permanent collection agency for quitrents and appointed Paul Grimball as the first Receiver General of Carolina, but there is little evidence that any were paid before 1690.[34] Confirming the difficulties of collection, in 1690 the proprietors wrote that they were willing to be paid in Spanish money, cotton, silk, or indigo at exchange rates equal to what these items would "clear" in England.[35] Quitrents had become a divisive issue, as the proprietors continued to push for payments while the people dodged these obligations.

The proprietors had no more success in efforts to impose town settlements. The only result of many orders from 1669 onward was the relocation of Charles Town. It was shifted from a short way up the Ashley River to Oyster Point, a peninsula located at the point where the Ashley and Cooper

[31] Proprietors to James Colleton, August 31, 1686, ibid., II, 143–164; Proprietors to Governor Joseph West, March 13, 1685, ibid., II, 27–30.

[32] Proprietors to Governor Morton, May 10, 1682, ibid., I, 138–157.

[33] Form of Indenture for Land, November 20, 1682, ibid., I, 228–231.

[34] Proprietors to Paul Grimball, October 10, 1687, ibid., II, 234–235; Ackerman, "S.C. Colonial Land Policies," 39–40.

[35] Proprietors to Paul Grimball, October 6, 1690, BPRO-SC, II, 289–290.

Rivers empty into the harbor. Though Governor Sayle had planned this move, provincial authorities were slow to carry it out. Under proprietary instigation, the new town was started about 1678.[36] An old and a new Charles Town existed for a few years, but, as the advantages of the new location became apparent, the original town disappeared. Incomplete land records show that at least 40 town lots were granted in 1680 or shortly thereafter.[37] Though its drainage problems were thought to figure in the outbreak of malaria and other sicknesses in the middle 1680's, new Charles Town remained the sole governmental and business center. The emerging plantation agricultural system had little need for many towns.

Fragmentary land records still available reveal that at least 125,000 acres had been granted by 1690, and the actual total was undoubtedly much higher.[38] The existence of large grants and the willingness of people to spread out in search of fertile land support contemporary observations that the country seemed empty or sparsely settled. Maurice Mathews has left a portrait of the province in 1680 which depicts this pattern: new Charles Town, which already had four large streets, would develop into a regularly laid-out town. Contiguous settlement extended from new Charles Town up the Cooper River to the head of Goose Creek, one of its tributaries. Mathews claimed that this was a distance of 15 miles and along this route 115 men had started plantations. Five miles farther up the Cooper was the Midway River which he described as being settled also. Sixteen miles above the Midway was the eastern branch of the Cooper which allowed

[36] Some accounts place the establishment of new Charles Town as late as 1680, but runaways to St. Augustine mentioned that there were two towns in 1679. Gallardo (ed.), "Spaniards and Charles Town," *S.C. Hist. Mag.,* XXXVII (1936), 133–140.
[37] Listed in the index to surviving land grants found in the Search Room, South Carolina Archives, Columbia, S.C.   [38] Table II, Appendix.

boats for eight miles, and this branch had two settlements. The Ashley River, which Mathews estimated to be 30 miles long, was settled continuously, starting from Charles Town. He also said that land between the Ashley and Stono Rivers was populated fairly thickly.[39] If Mathews's description is at all accurate, population was widely dispersed indeed.

Though theoretical problems of government continually bothered the proprietors, settlers concerned with scratching out a living were more troubled by the harsh realities of everyday life. The fact that food was no longer a problem was only a first step. Day-to-day existence must have been monotonous and the quality of life slow to improve. In 1679 some despondent runaways who reached St. Augustine testified to the Spanish governor that they had fled South Carolina because of the poorness of the soil, the harshness of life, and the suffering caused by lack of food.[40] These malcontents seem to have been disgusted and bored rather than in actual want. From 1675 to 1690 there must have been some gradual improvement in the standard of living. Trade and commerce developed, allowing sugar, wine, rum, and other foods and drinks not produced in the province to be imported. Though Indian corn probably remained the chief source of flour, some European grains must have been grown or flour imported from the northern colonies. Increasing herds of cattle and hogs provided meat to supplement local fish and game.

The key to improving life in the province was commerce, and it depended upon isolating an exportable commodity. The proprietors, who felt they had a great stake in the matter, continually assured settlers that they were trying to help find a staple.[41] They supported schemes to bring Hu-

[39] Maurice Mathews, "A Contemporary View of Carolina in 1680," *South Carolina Historical Magazine*, LV (1954), 153–159.

[40] Gallardo (ed.), "Spaniards and Charles Town," ibid., XXXVII (1936), 133–140.

[41] Proprietors to Governor and Council, April 10, 1677, *BPRO-SC*, I, 53–59.

guenots to South Carolina because they came from a country which produced wine, silk, and olive oil—all commodities not available in the English empire except by purchase abroad. The Huguenots have not been credited with adapting any species to the South Carolina environment for production as a staple, though silk culture, for example, was tried intermittently for years. Individuals persisted in their experimentations, however, since even unsuccessful efforts were generously rewarded with sizable land grants from the proprietors.

Luck, rather than design, was the most important factor in finding the first important staple, rice. Although rice did not become a major part of the economy until after 1700, evidence suggests that between 1680 and 1690 early trials leading to successful cultivation of the crop occurred. In fact, records from the 1670's show several such references.[42] Before a permanent settlement was made, rice was mentioned as commercially feasible for Carolina by the Spaniards, French, and English. After 1670, ironically, it was mentioned fewer times in records than any other important possible staple. The most authoritative reference on the start of rice planting does not contain one document dated between 1677 and 1690.[43] Yet, during this period the first small rice crops must have been successfully planted, cultivated, and harvested. Some of the most detailed publicity tracts of the 1680's do not even include rice in lists of crop possibilities. Ashe and Wilson, two men who would have known about trial rice crops, fail to mention rice. Thomas Newe, a man who went to the province in 1682, commented on trade and the commercial situation in letters but wrote nothing about rice.[44]

[42] A. S. Salley, "Introduction of Rice into South Carolina," *Bulletins of the Historical Commission of South Carolina, No. 6* (Columbia, 1919).

[43] Ibid.; also see Gray, *History of Agriculture,* I, 277–279.

[44] "Letters of Thomas Newe, 1682," in A. S. Salley (ed.), *Narratives of Early Carolina,* 181–187.

Little is known of how South Carolinians learned to grow rice. It is certain that few, if any, of them had had earlier experience in cultivating the crop. A large supply of seed would not have been available until numerous growing seasons had passed. Then techniques of cultivation, particularly harvesting and threshing, had to be developed before it could be processed in large quantities. It has been suggested that the first serious experimentations with rice were made about 1685, perhaps using seed left by a Captain Thurber who had obtained it in Madagascar.[45] Some accounts stress that seed rice from Madagascar may have been introduced into the province in the early 1690's after another variety had shown promise. Proving superior, the Madagascar rice replaced the other species.[46] John Stewart claimed in 1690 that six or seven shiploads of cotton and rice would be exported during the year, though he gave no proportional breakdown for the two commodities.[47] This seems an exorbitant amount for either commodity or both combined when compared with Edward Randolph's reported tonnage of rice exported in 1700.[48] Though it is highly questionable that rice had become very important to the economy by 1690, Stewart's account does help isolate the years when rice was being grown on an experimental basis.

From 1675 to 1690 the raising of livestock remained the major agricultural occupation after food crops. Cattle and hogs had the most commercial value of the herding animals because meat was an important part of the provisions trade

---

[45] Duncan Clinch Heyward, *Seed From Madagascar* (Chapel Hill, 1937), 4–5.   [46] Gray, *History of Agriculture*, I, 278.

[47] Summary of contents of letter by John Stewart, 1690, John Locke Manuscripts, "Papers Relating to the Colonies," Shelf Mark c. 30, Bodleian Library, Oxford (Microfilm M-3691, Southern Historical Collection, Univ. of N.C. Library, Chapel Hill).

[48] Randolph's figures are included in Table III, Appendix.

to the West Indies. Once the local food supply was secure, this business must have increased considerably. Excess food, such as barreled corn, was also sold to the West Indies, though it is impossible to gauge the extent of this trade or how rapidly it was expanding by the 1680's. After studying eighteenth century naval lists, it seems safe to assume that exports never exceeded several thousand barrels annually.[49] Of course, such a trade was relatively more important to the economy in the 1680's than later when other commodities were bringing far greater returns. Contemporaries mentioned that South Carolina tobacco continued to have a market in the West Indies, but this, too, was a limited trade.

Since demand in the West Indies for lumber, timber, and staves remained consistently strong, South Carolinians, who had more time to prepare these, shipped more. In the 1680's various schemes were considered to build saw mills in the province and start commercial operations.[50] Freight charges to England were too great to make such a trade profitable,[51] however, and the West Indies, the only feasible market for products of woods operations, was limited. It is doubtful that any of these plans materialized.

Up to 1690 the major step toward provincial prosperity was an expansion of the Indian trade, especially after 1680. Any settler unaware of the trade when he arrived in South Carolina soon came to know that profits were to be made in this business. The Indian trade had already become a political issue between the proprietors who wanted to monopolize it and enterprising settlers who wanted full freedom to deal with the Indians for their own gain. Moreover, to acquiesce

[49] Table III, Appendix.
[50] A. S. Salley, "Documents Concerning Huguenots, 1686–1692," *Huguenot Society of South Carolina Transactions,* XXVII (1922) , 71–72.
[51] Ashe, *Carolina.*

in proprietary monopoly would have ended or curtailed the lucrative trade in Indian slaves.[52] Some of the most prominent politicians in the province were also leading slave traders and not about to be suppressed by directives from faraway London. In this matter, as in others, some settlers were willing to ignore or defy a proprietary which acknowledged defeat by directing in 1680 that no more slaves should be taken from tribes within 200 miles of Charles Town.[53] Yet the proprietors were reluctant to abandon the objective of stopping this business. In 1683, they deprived Maurice Mathews and James Moore of office because they were Indian slave traders.[54] Two years later, they ordered that Mathews and John Boone be removed from the council for the same reason.[55] Indeed, they may have relieved Governor West because they believed that he was involved in the trade or at least did nothing to stop it.[56] Still the Indian slave trade did not cease, and the South Carolina government continued to ignore the proprietors' commands. A large segment of popular opinion supported the slave traders, and regulation became one of the many unresolved issues irritating relations between settlers and proprietors.

This friction over the Indian slave trade led, in 1680–1681, to the virtual annihilation of the Westo. The few surviving fled south of the Savannah River where they were absorbed by other tribes, and the designation of a Westo nation soon disappeared from maps. It has been alleged that the desire of the traders to enslave the Westo led to the war.[57] Possibly the Westo were destroyed because they symbolized

---

[52] The proprietors always held to the European idea of the noble savage entitled to his rights. Nowhere is this better expressed than in Proprietors to Governor and Council, September 30, 1683, *BPRO-SC*, I, 255–263.

[53] Proprietors to Joseph West and others, May 17, 1680, ibid., I, 97–102.

[54] Proprietors to Seth Sothell, November 6, 1683, ibid., I, 266–267.

[55] Proprietors to Governor Morton, September 10, 1685, ibid., II, 89–92.

[56] Wallace, *History of S.C.*, I, 97.   [57] Crane, *Southern Frontier*, 19–21.

proprietary attempts at dominance.⁵⁸ Correspondence from
South Carolina officials, all of which was after the fact,
justified the war on the grounds of Westo aggressions, but
the proprietors did not accept these rationalizations.⁵⁹

Following the destruction of the Westo, the Indian traders
turned to the Savannah tribe for trade, and the provincial
government made a military alliance with them.⁶⁰ Apparently only recently having wandered into the area, this tribe
had willingly aided the whites in defeating the Westo and
then occupied the lands vacated by the vanquished. They
had a number of liabilities, however, which limited their
usefulness as commercial partners. Nomadic and restless, in
time they migrated from the area just as they had drifted
there. They did not control much more territory than the
Westo had, and they did not have trading ties with the
interior tribes who could provide great numbers of deerskins. They were vigorous warriors who soon developed the
reputation for selling any unsuspecting Indian, friend or foe,
into slavery; they apparently found eager buyers among the
Charles Town slave traders. Nevertheless, the South Carolinians used the Savannah as their chief trading tie during much
of the 1680's.

As the Charles Town Indian traders came to recognize the
advantages of doing business with the major Indian nations
of the interior, they began to woo the tribes which were
collectively called the Lower Creeks. Known to the Spaniards as the Apalachicola, these tribes held sway on the
southside of the Savannah River to its headwaters, and then
westward to the Chattahoochee River. While they lived on
lands nominally claimed by Spain, they were numerous

⁵⁸ Wallace, *History of S.C.*, I, 101.
⁵⁹ Proprietors to Governor and Council, March 7, 1681, *BPRO-SC*, I, 115–120.
⁶⁰ Material in the following three paragraphs has been drawn from Crane, *Southern Frontier*, 22–37; Milling, *Red Carolinians*, 84–97.

enough, strong enough, and independent enough to switch allegiance when the time and price were right. They rapidly became pawns, though by no means powerless ones, in the struggle between the Spaniards, who were trying to maintain control of Guale, and the English, who were trying to take over. During the 1680's the South Carolinians with their English trading goods gradually gained the upper hand over the Spaniards and their weak mission system. Many of the Lower Creeks actually moved north of the Savannah River to be nearer the South Carolina traders. Guale was being emptied of its tribes. The migration guaranteed Charles Town merchants a steadily increasing deerskin trade for many years to come. Even before 1690 and until 1715, this trading arrangement with the Lower Creeks was the single most important link to the tribes in the interior.

The Spaniards were incensed at the English for luring these tribes to the north. Destruction of the Scottish outpost at Port Royal was, in part, a reprisal for the migration. Spain's last attempts to reassert control over the Lower Creeks failed between 1689 and 1691, leaving the Charles Town Indian traders in a position to control the flow of deerskins and Indian slaves from a vast hinterland. But in 1690 this trade was only in the first stages of its development. As a side effect of South Carolina's expansive moves in the backcountry about this time, imperial authorities came to recognize that this colony was pivotal in any fight to control the southern frontier of English America.[61]

By 1690 the province was not close to reaching a favorable balance of trade. Shipping deerskins to England was the only

---

[61] Edward Randolph to Lords of Trade, written from the "Common Jail at Boston," May 29, 1689, in Robert N. Toppan (ed.), *Edward Randolph: Including His Letters and Official Papers . . . 1676–1703*, (*Publications of the Prince Society*, XXIV–XXVIII, XXX–XXXI, [7 vols.]) (Boston, 1898–1907) XXVII, 271–281.

important export trade to European markets. Timber, provisions, and Indian slaves to the West Indies were the other trades worth noting. Both trade patterns advanced in volume and total value from 1675 to 1690, but how much and how rapidly may never be determined.

The Charles Town export trade to other mainland colonies was virtually nonexistent. Although South Carolina never had a sound commercial basis for trading extensively with colonies to the north, eighteenth century trade patterns do include a substantial volume of exports destined for both Boston and Philadelphia. Such a pattern had not developed by the 1680's. To enforce his special instructions regulating trade in Boston, Governor Andros had a record of port activity kept from December 16, 1686, to April 12, 1689. During these two and one-half years, 441 vessels cleared. Of this total, only fourteen sailed for Carolina and only three were bound specifically for South Carolina. The smallest of these fourteen vessels was 4 tons burden and the largest, 50 tons. Most were in the 15 to 30 tons burden range, rather typical of coasting vessels in the seventeenth and eighteenth centuries. Though many were not listed by home port, most headed for Carolina were designated as based in New England.[62] Francis Nicholson noted in 1688 that vessels from Carolina brought very little to New York except logwood. A dye wood that grew in Central America, it was picked up there or in the West Indies, then eventually shipped to England. Nicholson mentioned no commodity of South Carolina production being sold in New York.[63]

Trading with pirates was another significant business

[62] Data summarized from Robert Earle Moody, "Massachusetts Trade with Carolina, 1686–1709," *North Carolina Historical Review*, XX (1943), 43–53.
[63] Francis Nicholson to Edward Randolph, October 21, 1688, in Toppan (ed.), *Edward Randolph (Publications of the Prince Society)*, XXVII, 246–247.

activity conducted at Charles Town in these years.[64] Pirates were active periodically in the seventeenth century, and in the middle 1680's a number of bands preyed on shipping along the Atlantic Coast and in the West Indies. The development of this illegal business is further evidence of the dearth of legitimate trade to and from Charles Town. Since South Carolina as yet produced little to export to England, there was a shortage of European merchandise flowing into the province. The pirates were a source of manufactured goods, selling at prices considerably below open market or intrinsic value. The pirates wanted in return at least one thing South Carolinians had in plentiful quantities—food.

This illegal commerce could only flourish with the open or tacit approval of the local government. When pirates had booty or needed supplies, they put into a convenient port where few questions would be asked. Charles Town fit the needs of pirates because its governmental regulation was lax, and apparently, some officials welcomed the freebooters. Certainly the proprietors acted on the assumption that pirates were being permitted to land at Charles Town with official sanction. In 1686 they removed Robert Quarry from the office of Secretary because of his alleged complicity in allowing a known pirate vessel to do business in the province.[65] Again in 1687 they named Quarry along with Captain Daniell and Colonel Godfrey as having conspired with pirates to circumvent the law.[66] The proprietors did not name more of these men, as one might wish, yet, it is clear that at least some of those dealing with pirates were the same men trading in deerskins and Indian slaves. These were the most aggres-

---

[64] Shirley C. Hughson, *The Carolina Pirates and Colonial Commerce, 1670–1740* (Herbert B. Adams (ed.), *Johns Hopkins University Studies in Historical and Political Science,* Twelfth Series, VII) (Baltimore, 1894), 9–34.

[65] Proprietors to Governor Morton and others, February 15, 1686, *BPRO-SC,* II, 121–124.

[66] Proprietors to Governor Colleton, March 3, 1687, ibid., II, 177–183.

sive entrepreneurial spirits in South Carolina and were not averse to making money in any way possible. Many were also members of the council, or holders of other offices. They have often been characterized as being the backbone of the anti-proprietary faction, the Goose Creek men.

While trying to stop traffic with pirates, the proprietors conducted a stout defense of their stewardship of the province in their correspondence with crown officials. Though Craven denied all knowledge of widespread dealing between pirates and South Carolinians and insisted that only one pirate had ever been caught in South Carolina,[67] letters to provincial authorities reveal great proprietary anxiety about the problem. In 1684 they ordered South Carolinians to pass a law making trade with pirates illegal.[68] The request was honored in 1685 by a statute which delineated the criminal aspects of piracy or of having dealings with pirates.[69] It is doubtful that the law changed anything immediately, however; references in letters of 1686 and 1687 indicate that the problem persisted.[70] Proprietary pressure may have led to enforcement of the laws after 1687, but possibly the problem continued into the 1690's.[71]

Some historians have claimed that since the freebooters of the 1680's often paid for supplies with stolen coin, they supplied South Carolinians with hard money.[72] Undoubtedly the pirates did leave some coins in the province, but this gold and silver (most likely in the form of Spanish money) probably did not remain in South Carolina very long. Any coins which did enter the commerce of the province would have flowed quickly to England or into other legitimate trade centers to pay for the goods that South Carolinians had to

---

[67] Earl of Craven to Lords of Trade, May 27, 1684, ibid., I, 284–285.
[68] Ibid.   [69] Cooper and McCord (eds.), *Statutes of S.C.*, II, 7–9.
[70] *BPRO-SC*, II, 121–124, 177–183, 221–228.
[71] Hughson, *Carolina Pirates*, 27–34.
[72] Sirmans, *Colonial South Carolina*, 39.

purchase elsewhere. In statutes of the 1690's one finds various commodities being used as money for the purpose of paying obligations,[73] concrete evidence that this temporary influx of coins did little to bolster the economy of the province permanently, aid its development, or provide a circulating medium.

Despite the low volume of trade to and from South Carolina, a number of things point toward increasing commercial activity in the 1680's. One such index is shipbuilding and repairing, though conclusions must be based on occasional references in the records. Ship refittings occurred in the province almost from the start of settlement. This is understandable in an era when almost every sailing vessel making port had to undergo some overhauling to remain seaworthy. Such repairs could be made under the most primitive conditions, but shipbuilding, which required proper facilities and skilled craftsmen, was another matter. During the first years, some vessels had been purchased outside the province, but by the late 1670's shipbuilding must have started. Maurice Mathews reported in 1680 that several vessels had been built in South Carolina and that, as he wrote, three or four more were on the stocks.[74] By 1687 a South Carolina statute provided for the giving of bond for vessels built in the province.[75] This law was in accord with the Acts of Trade then in force. It is difficult to assess the extent and importance of shipbuilding at any time in the colony's history and impossible to guess how many vessels were built in the province before 1690. Nevertheless, by 1690 shipbuilding had started in a meaningful way.

Purchases of vessels outside South Carolina further illustrate that the growing mercantile community had money to

[73] For example, Cooper and McCord (eds.), *Statutes of S.C.*, II, 96–102.
[74] Mathews, "Contemporary View of Carolina," *S.C. Hist. Mag.*, LV (1954), 159.   [75] Cooper and McCord (eds.), *Statutes of S.C.*, II, 32–34.

invest in small craft for the coasting or Islands' trades. In October 1681 William Allin of Newport, Rhode Island, sold Henry Simonds, described as a vintner living in Charles Town, the sloop *Endeavor* for £190 sterling. Simonds, in turn, sold three-fourths of the vessel to William Rirad, a Charles Town merchant who formerly lived in Boston. They renamed their 30-ton vessel, *Johanna of Carolina*.[76] While hardly typical, the record of another transaction involving a vessel does reveal leading, sometimes controversial, figures involved in trade. Stephen Bull appeared before the council on August 25, 1682, to testify that he had bought his ship *Success* from men having no right to sell it, a fact he had not known at the time. Bull certified that he had spent £114 sterling to make her seaworthy and that he wanted repayment by the rightful owner or owners should they appear within a year and a day. Apparently Bull became satisfied that no one would put in a claim, for he sold the vessel on November 2, 1682, to Maurice Mathews, James Moore, and George Robinson for £300 sterling money of England.[77] Mathews and Moore were, of course, the alleged Indian slave and deerskin traders who played such a prominent role in defying proprietary authority.

Also during the 1680's the proprietary became acutely concerned with trade regulation. Earlier attempts to enforce the Navigation Acts had not been observed in South Carolina, but in the 1680's increasing imperial surveillance became a threat to the existence of the proprietary. Considerable sentiment existed in England for putting all proprietaries under the crown, and reorganization of English America did begin with the short-lived Dominion of New

[76] Records of the Register of the Secretary of the Province, 1675–1696 and 1703–1709 (bound manuscript volume in South Carolina Archives, Columbia, S.C.) , 150–152.
[77] Records of the Court of Ordinary, 1672–1692 (bound manuscript volume in South Carolina Archives, Columbia, S.C.) , 99–102, 120.

England. Failure to suppress piracy in the province and failure to enforce imperial trade regulations were two of the charges leveled against the proprietors, placing their charter in jeopardy. In 1684 they sent a copy of all appropriate Navigation Acts to the governor and council with instructions that these laws be observed.[78] Several subsequent letters reiterated that all the laws of trade be obeyed in Carolina. Pressure on the proprietary also led in 1685 to the appointment of George Muschamp as first collector of customs in South Carolina.[79] Robert Quarry, Secretary of the Province, was named naval officer and charged to prepare lists of vessels arriving in or departing from the province.[80] In 1687 the proprietors again instructed the governor and council to maintain naval lists. Every three months the Secretary of the Province was to forward them to the proprietors who would send them on to the Commissioners of His Majesty's Customs.[81]

South Carolina officials may have been as lackadaisical and defiant in this matter as in others, for if naval lists or other official records of trade were prepared, they are not known to survive. Instead, the matter of enforcement became part of the greater political fight between proprietors and the anti-proprietary party. One has the suspicion that Quarry never did prepare or submit any naval records, for he was a target for removal because of his dealings with pirates. Some officials were doubtless opposed to observing the trade regulations because of their own illegal activities, but they had support from many who were opposed to any

[78] No addressee but probably Proprietors to Governor, April 10, 1684, *BPRO-SC*, I, 276.

[79] Extract of undirected letter, probably Proprietors to Governor, March 5, 1685, ibid., II, 204.

[80] Proprietors to Robert Quarry, March 13, 1685, ibid., II, 43–46.

[81] No addressee but probably Proprietors to Governor, October 10, 1687, ibid., II, 221–228.

manifestations of acquiescence to proprietary authority. Some South Carolinians claimed that the Navigation Acts did not apply since these acts were passed after the charter for the province had been granted.[82] The proprietors, of course, denied any such exemption from the laws of empire.[83]

Once South Carolina authorities decided to enforce these laws, they began to use the laws as instruments to condemn as prizes vessels which were violators. Informers always received a portion of any condemnation, and certain persons might have recognized the value of this weapon. At least the proprietors thought that specious evidence and trumped-up proceedings were used in such cases. They believed the culprits to be those who opposed proprietary authority at every turn.[84] Mr. Muschamp eventually despaired of enforcing the Navigation Acts in South Carolina and petitioned for a transfer.[85] Enforcement of the Acts of Trade must have been somewhat sporadic and capricious in South Carolina in the 1680's, with some unscrupulous persons benefiting whether the laws were obeyed or ignored. This defiance of the proprietors and sometimes of imperial regulations and the eagerness for any trade, legal or otherwise, seem part of the larger pattern of friction developing throughout the 1680's.

Despite the political controversies of the 1680's and other problems still unsolved at the end of the decade, South Carolina had made progress. Though the pattern of settlement was haphazard and sprawling, the population had reached a level where the province could feel more secure. Promise of a better life for most white settlers awaited the

[82] George Muschamp to Proprietors, April 11, 1687, ibid., II, 194–195.
[83] No addressee but probably Earl of Craven to Lords of Trade, not dated but marked as July 1687, ibid., II, 199–201.
[84] No addressee but probably Proprietors to Governor, October 10, 1687, ibid., II, 221–228.
[85] Thomas C. Barrow, *Trade and Empire: The British Customs Service in Colonial America, 1660–1775* (Cambridge, Massachusetts, 1967), 27.

outcome of experimentations to find a commercial crop, for, despite the few gaining in wealth, the general level of existence remained humble. The proprietors had proven inept and unsuccessful in directing or in coercing the settlers. Most of the province's growth owed nothing or very little to the proprietors. The question looming by 1690 was whether the proprietors could render the political and economic order necessary in South Carolina to save the proprietary from being taken over by the crown.

CHAPTER V

Improving Prospects
1690–1705

BETWEEN 1690 AND 1705 SOUTH CAROLINA MADE GAINS toward the goal of establishing an economic base for future prosperity. Although documentation is lacking in some particulars, all available evidence attests to commercial growth over these 15 years. By 1705 future prospects seemed bright. The political crisis which was deepening by 1690 was resolved by 1696, bringing the stability and tranquillity that stimulate economic growth. Relations between settlers and the proprietors improved also. This euphoric state did not last long, however. South Carolina politics had a feisty quality throughout the proprietary era, and with the interjection of new issues, deterioration began again. Some of these disputes bore directly on economic activities, indeed the entire future of the province.

In 1693 the situation seemed critical. After Governor James Colleton had been overthrown in 1690, the provincial government had degenerated into impotence. The assembly drew up a list of 14 grievances against the proprietors and their officials as a measure of the urgency many settlers felt. Significantly, the unsatisfactory method of conveying lands was placed first on this bill of particulars.[1] Until a fair and reasonable system of land tenure was adopted, no settler could feel secure in his holdings nor could migrants be attracted to the province. In England officials were recommending that proprietary charters be called in. Aware that the crown might use protests from Carolina as a pretext to take this action against them, the proprietors decided to send one among them to South Carolina to put their unruly house in order. John Archdale, who held a share in the name of his son, agreed to go. Reaching Charles Town in the fall of 1695, Archdale bore not only the authority of being a proprietor but the power to use his own judgment in working out compromise agreements to satisfy as many settlers as possible.[2]

Though Archdale's instructions were sweeping, a number of specific problems were slated for solution. For example, he was to stimulate the development of Charles Town by having laws passed which would encourage building there, and he could grant a charter to the city if it would encourage "Sobriety and vertue as well as trade." Other towns were to be built at places which would help commerce. The Fundamental Constitutions was to be examined and, with the help of the council, recommendations made concerning which parts should be imposed. Charles Town was to be fortified by act of the assembly. Marshes were to be drained and other improvements, such as building mills, encouraged to speed development of the country. The Indians were to be protected, with steps taken to civilize them. Sale of lands was to be pushed at £20 sterling per 1,000 acres near the settlements and £10 per 1,000 acres "at 200 miles Distance or nere

[1] Assembly to Governor and Deputies, no specific date but prepared in late 1692 or 1693, as printed in Rivers, *Sketch of History of S.C.*, 433–435.
[2] See *BPRO-SC*, III, 135–142, for documents pertaining to Archdale's appointment and his instructions.

ye Mountains." A quitrent of 12 pence per 100 acres was to be reserved. Lands which had been taken up but not improved within three years were to be foreclosed and recovered by the proprietors.[3] Obviously the Lords Proprietors were unaware that during the 1680's their powers to influence the settlers and local policies had diminished. Archdale's work in the province would dramatically point up that this shift in power was taking place.

Despite his elaborate instructions, Archdale dealt mainly with three controversies during his brief stay in Carolina. These were land policy, regulation of Indian trade, and the status of Huguenot settlers. Archdale regarded resolution of the land question as vital, and this achievement alone made his mission successful. Caught between obdurate proprietors who could veto any law they disliked and settlers who might rebel against any arbitrary proprietary ruling, Archdale's compromise land system is the more remarkable. The agreements, commonly called Archdale's laws,[4] were passed by the assembly, which indicated their acceptance by the people of South Carolina. Though the proprietors never assented to these laws, the statutes were allowed to stand unchallenged to the end of the proprietary.

Under Archdale's Laws the purchase price for 1,000 acres was pegged at £20 current money. In this decade more land was needed as rice production increased rapidly, and this arrangement satisfied established settlers who had the purchasing price. Lands bought at this new price, which superseded earlier proprietary offers to sell land, were to bear an annual quitrent of 12 pence (one shilling current money) per 100 acres. Lands previously granted were to bear a yearly quitrent of one penny per acre. Quitrents could be paid in indigo, cotton, silk, rice, barreled beef or pork, or

[3] Proprietors to Governor Archdale, August 31, 1694, ibid., III, 140–142.
[4] Cooper and McCord (eds.), *Statutes of S.C.*, II, 96–104.

English peas instead of in money. Lands would be forfeited to the proprietors should quitrents remain unpaid or lands remain unworked or undeveloped after being conveyed. Lands taken up by newly arrived settlers or servants whose time had been completed would bear no quitrent for the first five years while such persons were becoming established. This was intended to attract new migrants, but in practice it was interpreted to mean that anyone taking up new lands was entitled to a five-year moratorium on his quitrent payments for the new lands.[5] The form for granting all lands sold in the future was spelled out. One clause specified that the Lords Proprietors could not change the system of granting land for at least six years and then only after a year's notice.

The proprietors compromised in an effort to recover some of the past due quitrents. Archdale agreed to let the assembly pay £1,700 (apparently current money) owed by the proprietors for local governmental expenses. In return, the proprietors remitted a portion of past due quitrents.[6] The law was intended to reduce the outstanding quitrents by about two-thirds for most landholders by requiring payment of quitrents owed for the previous two years but canceling all quitrents for earlier years. All persons in arrears were to pay one half their obligation in money or commodities by December 1, 1696, and the other half December 1, 1697. The proprietors could extract past due payments through action in the Court of Common Pleas. In effect, the changes in the land laws brought on a great rush to validate claims to lands which had never been conveyed by grants.[7]

Even after Archdale's land reforms, the proprietors did not obtain all the quitrents due them. Data are incomplete, but it is safe to conclude that by 1705 several hundred thousand acres of land had been granted. Despite the vary-

[5] Ackerman, "S.C. Colonial Land Policies," 60–61.
[6] Proprietors to Governor Archdale, June 17, 1696, *BPRO-SC*, III, 174–175.
[7] Table II, Appendix, seems to indicate the rush to register lands.

ing kinds of grants, much of this should have been bearing quitrents which should have brought the proprietors hundreds of pounds per year in income. In addition, every land sale was a direct return for the proprietors. Some money did flow into the proprietary. In 1695, Paul Grimball, the Receiver General, reported that he had on hand over £73 current money from quitrents and £277 from land sales.[8] When Archdale left the province, his report to the proprietors disclosed that he had collected £1,838 9s. current money from the sale of lands and from quitrents due through 1696, including £835 2s. 4d. which Grimball had previously collected.[9]

Yet the Archdale settlement did not permanently improve the collection system of quitrents, and the proprietors continued to receive sparse returns from their modest investment in Carolina. Only three years after Archdale left, in 1699, the proprietors claimed that settlers were already £2,000 current money behind in their quitrent payments.[10] In 1702 they directed James Moore, the Receiver General, to sue those who were over a year in arrears of quitrents. Moore, like every other Receiver General, seems to have been instructed to prepare a rent roll listing all lands granted and the rents due.[11] Yet there is no evidence that one was kept until at least 30 years later.[12] No wonder the proprietors continued to be frustrated and irritated over a land system which was supposed to provide a steady income to meet their obligations to the province but remained ineffective because of inadequate collection methods and the willingness of many to evade their lawful obligations.

Archdale's success with the land question was not matched

[8] Proprietors to Paul Grimball, April 12, 1695, *BPRO-SC*, III, 156–157.

[9] John Archdale's Account with the Proprietors, September 21, 1697, ibid., III, 220–228.

[10] Proprietors to John Ely, September 21, 1699, ibid., IV, 109.

[11] Proprietors to James Moore, June 18, 1702, ibid., V, 79–81.

[12] Ackerman, "S.C. Colonial Land Policies," 64.

in his handling of two other serious problems. A law was passed providing for the adjustment of controversies between whites and the Indians and among the Indians themselves.[13] Commissioners were appointed by the assembly to adjudicate such conflicts and injustices. Because its powers to regulate abuses of the Indian trade did not go far enough, the act did not serve its purpose. The most specific prohibition was a general statement stopping the dispensing of liquor to the Indians. Otherwise the act did not define the commissioners' authority. As long as the deerskin and Indian slave trades were valuable, only a strong body with broad powers could hope to regulate relations between whites and Indians effectively.

Archdale was also unable to follow instructions that a statute be passed to define the political and economic rights of Huguenots in South Carolina. When he arrived in the province, anti-Huguenot feeling had reached a new high.[14] This repressive sentiment which had been growing for years had two goals. If Huguenots could be restrained from voting and participating in government, they could not form a political "swing" group which would constitute a majority when joined with one of the regular factions. Furthermore, though most could buy and hold land, the Huguenots were restricted from competing commercially with native-born or naturalized English subjects. Huguenots insisted that they were being denied rights which the proprietors had intended they should have,[15] but Archdale, forced to bargain with the province's factions, sacrificed their cause to obtain the rest of his statutes.

In 1697 South Carolina Huguenots were given a legally

[13] Cooper and McCord (eds.), *Statutes of S.C.*, II, 108–110.

[14] Hirsch, *Huguenots*, 117–118; Sirmans, *Colonial South Carolina*, 61–62.

[15] The proprietors affirmed this point of view several times. For example, Proprietors to Governor Archdale, January 29, 1696, *BPRO-SC*, III, 166–168.

stronger position including unquestioned rights to their lands, but they still lacked economic parity with native-born Englishmen.[16] By a questionable interpretation of the Navigation Acts, Huguenots were barred from owning vessels.[17] In 1708, however, Parliament passed a naturalization law for all Huguenots in English domains, which removed any stigmas still inhibiting them in commercial enterprises.[18] By the decade 1710 to 1720 some South Carolina Huguenots were leading merchants, principal owners of vessels, and important politicians.

The handling of the above controversies clearly illustrates a shifting in the power balance from the proprietary to the South Carolina people and their government. Archdale's use of the local government certainly accentuated the trend which was under way before he reached South Carolina and continued after he left. By the 1690's the proprietors were surrendering their prerogatives willingly in an attempt to bring stability to the province and, hopefully, profits for them. As the initiative for policies moved to South Carolina, the settlers' elected representatives took power and used it to reflect the sentiment of the people. After gaining recognition as a separate body in 1692 and winning the right to initiate legislation, the Commons House of Assembly moved ahead rapidly during the 1690's to define its constitutional position. The proprietary acquiesced; from 1693 to 1718 it did not veto a single South Carolina law.[19]

The political significance of this change has been widely recognized and described in considerable detail, yet there

[16] Cooper and McCord (eds.) , *Statutes of S.C.*, II, 131–133.

[17] Sirmans, *Colonial South Carolina*, 62, 66; Edward Randolph to Board of Trade, June 28, 1699, *BPRO-SC*, IV, 88–95.

[18] Hirsch, *Huguenots*, 106–111.

[19] Sirmans, *Colonial South Carolina*, 67; the long term implications in a wider context have been explored by Jack P. Greene, *The Quest for Power: The Lower Houses of Assembly in the Southern Royal Colonies, 1689–1776* (Chapel Hill, 1963) .

were many economic implications here, too. An assembly making land and Indian policy would soon be making policy affecting economic arrangements within the province. Yet local option was by no means attained. After the 1690's South Carolinians found new limits on economic matters which came, not from proprietary directives, but from the bonds of empire.

Assumption of governing powers by the South Carolina authorities was certain to dash the intentions of the proprietors. While they continued to recommend, sometimes even demand, this action or that, whatever power they had once possessed as well as moral suasion was falling from their grasp. Still they clung to the proprietary dream. In 1698 they urged the acceptance of what proved to be the final version of the Fundamental Constitutions.[20] Even they could not have been too surprised that this revision, much simplified from the original edition of 1669, was rejected. Not easily persuaded, even after 1700, they sometimes acted as though they expected acceptance eventually. Yet their own actions on many substantive matters had undercut their theoretical professions of consistency. In 1669, the proprietors provided for a landed nobility, the elite of Carolina. By 1690 the proprietors offered to sell baronies for £20 per annum.[21] In 1698 they offered to sell the title of landgrave or cacique to anyone who would take up the land.[22] In 1709, they permitted Peter Colleton to break up his barony and sell the land piecemeal though such grants had originally been entailed.[23] Whether they acknowledged it or not, the proprietors had taken cognizance of the erosion of their brand of feudalism by the South Carolina environment.

[20] Fundamental Constitutions, April 11, 1698, *BPRO-SC*, IV, 27–39.

[21] Minutes of meeting of Proprietors, November 17, 1690, ibid., III, 1.

[22] Ackerman, "S.C. Colonial Land Policies," 63.

[23] Proprietors to Governor Edward Tynte, April 14, 1709, *BPRO-SC*, V, 278–279.

In vain, the proprietors tried to keep the pattern of land development under their own control. Spelling out some rules for granting land in 1693, they ordered that a port town be laid out on each river and stipulated that no grants were to be made more than 30 miles south of the Stono River or more than 50 miles north of the Ashley and Cooper Rivers.[24] In 1699 they wrote that no one person was to be granted more than 500 acres and that lands must be settled in four years or be escheated.[25] But the drive to seek out lands favorable for rice or other specific purposes was stronger, if possible, than previously. There is little indication that their rules stopped land-grabbing. In 1697, perhaps bowing to the facts, they rescinded their orders against taking up lands farther than 30 miles south of Charles Town.[26]

The population continued to spread out, and no new towns were added. Although the great majority (perhaps three-fourths) of the people continued to live in Berkeley County,[27] surviving land grants issued between 1690 and 1705, as well as political controversies over the representation of Colleton and Craven counties in the assembly, substantiate this distribution. Alarmed about the province's vulnerability to attack, the proprietors offered on several occasions to give up part of the lands reserved for themselves to help concentrate settlement.[28] Eventually the provincial government became concerned about the open frontier, but a lack of popular support and factional squabbling over the Indian trade prevented the passage of laws which might have limited the areas open for granting or might have set up fortifiable towns.[29] This was a people chiefly intent on taking

[24] Rules for granting land, February 6, 1693, ibid., III, 51–68.
[25] Proprietors to Governor Blake, December 20, 1699, ibid., IV, 128.
[26] Proprietors to Governor Blake, August 30, 1697, ibid., III, 217–219.
[27] Proprietors to Governor Ludwell, April 12, 1693, ibid., III, 84–98.
[28] Proprietors to Governor Blake, August 30, 1697, ibid., III, 217–219.
[29] Crane, *Southern Frontier*, 144–148.

advantage of an economy which had begun to expand.

South Carolinians after 1690 were more concerned about the rapidly changing ratio of whites and slaves in their population than about how it was dispersed. Wishing to augment the flow of whites into the province, they found that in the area of promotion, the decline of the proprietary was a disadvantage. Though never very successful in their haphazard schemes to fill the province with people, the proprietors had, nonetheless, tried from time to time to find settlers. After 1690 they made few attempts to influence people to go, and European migration to South Carolina slowed to a trickle until after 1730.[30] There were probably a number of reasons for this, but proprietary withdrawal must have been a major cause.

To offset this rapidly growing Negro slave population, the provincial government had to assume responsibility for promotion. Their efforts centered on obtaining indentured servants. By a statute passed in 1698, any merchant, master of a vessel, or other person not intending to settle would be paid £13 current money for every male servant between the ages of 16 and 40 who was brought into the province. Every boy under 16 would bear a bounty of £12. A system of allotment required planters owning six or more male slaves to take one servant so imported for every six Negro man slaves owned.[31] The act was repealed on the grounds that its purpose "is already accomplished." [32] If this law did make enough male servants available to correct the population imbalance, it could have succeeded only temporarily. The most authoritative population statistics show 110 white male servants and 1,500 Negro men slaves in 1703; then only 60 white male

[30] This view of the immigration pattern is not new. For example, see Edward McCrady, *The History of South Carolina under the Proprietary Government, 1670–1719* (New York, 1901) , 337–338.

[31] Cooper and McCord (eds.) , *Statutes of S.C.*, II, 153–156.

[32] Ibid., II, 165–166.

servants and 1,800 Negro men slaves in 1708.[33] These hardly seem the proportions envisaged as a safe ratio under the 1698 statute.

The lack of white immigration is reflected in the population figures from 1690 to 1705. Despite the indexes of increasing productivity, the white population remained about the same over the 15 years. If the white population was in the range of 3,500 to 4,000 in 1690, by 1700 it may have reached 5,000 to 6,000, and may actually have declined to about 4,000 by 1705.[34] Governor Nathaniel Johnson computed the total at 4,080 in 1708, according to his calculations an increase of only 280 in five years. He further concluded that there was an actual drop of 140 adults and 80 white servants since 1703. Another way to view this pattern is to point out that the white population in 1708 was only 1,500 greater than it had been in 1682. The most hopeful aspect of Governor Johnson's appraisal was the increase in white children from 1,200 in 1703 to 1,700 in 1708, a trend he attributed to more healthful conditions in the colony after a long period of illnesses.[35] In 1697–1698 smallpox caused 200 to 300 deaths. Both smallpox and yellow fever raged in and about Charles Town in 1699. These were the first great epidemics in the province's history. In 1706 yellow fever broke out again. So severe were these epidemics, immigration may have been inhibited for years to come. Besides disease, Charles Town had a disastrous fire in 1698.[36] A devastating hurricane hit in 1700, the second such storm in the 30-year history of the province.[37] It is little wonder that in 1700 the province was growing slowly in population and

---

[33] Governor Nathaniel Johnson and Council to Proprietors, September 17, 1708, *BPRO-SC*, V, 203–210.   [34] Table I, Appendix.

[35] Governor Nathaniel Johnson and Council to Proprietors, September 17, 1708, *BPRO-SC*, V, 203–210.

[36] Wallace, *History of S.C.*, I, 140.

[37] Ludlum, *Early American Hurricanes*, 42.

those living in South Carolina periodically had real doubts about their future.

While there was slow growth, perhaps even slight loss, in the white population, the number of Negro slaves had begun to increase rapidly. Neither proprietors nor local government had anything to do with stimulating slave importations; they were bought to fill economic need. Since none of the early population estimates list Negro or Indian slaves or offer an impression of their proportion to the whole, one must conclude their numbers were small before 1690. By 1708 Governor Johnson recorded 4,100 Negroes and 4,080 whites, implying that the number of Negroes increased by 1,100 in the five years from 1703 to 1708. Assuming that Johnson's count was approximately correct, the total population advanced from 6,800 in 1703 to 8,180 in 1708.[38] This demographic revolution becomes manifest when it is noted that the total population of the province doubled from 1690 to 1705, and nearly all the increase was in blacks. These slaves allowed the first great upsurge of productivity in this plantation society.

The first laws to regulate slaves, passed in 1690 and 1696, offer further evidence of the increasing attention being paid to the visible alteration to society. The law passed in 1690 under Governor Seth Sothell was disallowed by the proprietors, but the settlers showed that they felt the need for a comprehensive act to define the place of blacks.[39] The delay until 1696 to re-enact the slave code suggests that slavery was not yet the pressing problem it was soon to become.[40] Possibly the disrupted condition of the provincial government forced the postponement. Regardless, the law of 1696 went to

---

[38] Governor Nathaniel Johnson and Council to Proprietors, September 17, 1708, *BPRO-SC*, V, 203–210.

[39] Cooper and McCord (eds.) , *Statutes of S.C.*, VII, 343–347.

[40] Title only in ibid., II, 121.

great lengths to define the legal status of slaves and the regulations which were to govern their behavior. The time-honored interpretation insists that South Carolina modeled its laws and customs relating to slavery after Barbadian practices, particularly the Barbados law of 1688, because a number of leading South Carolinians were Barbadian immigrants. The South Carolina law followed the Barbadian practice of deliberately defining the legal status of the slave vaguely, depending on custom to enforce slave discipline.

A slave was any person who had ever been or would ever be bought and sold. The category included not only Negroes but Indians, mulattoes, and mestizos. Some question has been raised about whether slaves in South Carolina were freehold property, tied to a plot of ground with the master having use of the slave for life, or whether the slave was a chattel, personal property which could be bought and sold as any other personal property. Whatever the legal technicalities were, in practice South Carolina slaves were regarded as personal property by the early eighteenth century. They were bought and sold, mortgaged for debt, and listed as personal property in inventories. Since slaves were a majority of the population after 1708, South Carolina had no difficulty erecting a slave code, even if it were largely customary and unwritten. In a society fearful of slave insurrections, it was tacitly assumed that masters would exert great powers over their slaves. This system of controls worked unchanged until 1740 when, following the slave revolt in 1739, many essentials of the slave laws were altered and more specifically set forth.[41]

Early records reveal very little of how this early Negro

[41] M. Eugene Sirmans, "The Legal Status of the Slave in South Carolina, 1670–1740," *Journal of Southern History*, XXVIII (1962), 462–473; Edward McCrady, "Slavery in the Province of South Carolina, 1670–1770," *American Historical Association Reports, 1895*, 629–673.

slave population was trained for their field tasks in South
Carolina. If many were brought in from the West Indies,
they were at least used to slave discipline. Since a number of
early laws put higher import taxes on slaves who had been
domiciled in the West Indies than on those imported directly
from Africa, one must assume that most Negro slaves came
completely untrained to South Carolina. How rapidly they
became useful, how efficient they were, and a host of similar
questions must go largely unanswered. The tasks were simple, and those who had mastered the work doubtless passed
these routines on to those newly arrived. While training this
first influx of new field hands, the planters were also learning
how best to use labor in growing rice and in producing naval
stores, both processes which were somewhat in the experimental stage. Eventually rice hands worked by the task
method, but whether this was introduced in the first years of
serious rice growing is not clear. The surest conclusion is
that the planters were able to adapt slave labor rapidly to
South Carolina needs so that the total output of major staples increased dramatically within a comparatively short period of time.[42]

As Negro slaves came in, local use of Indian slaves declined.[43] Sometimes Indian slaves were included in population estimates, though such inclusions must be seen in context. The number of Indian slaves varied widely from year
to year. In 1703 Governor Johnson reported 350, but, following Indian campaigns, he counted 1,400 in 1708.[44] But this
increase was temporary. Sooner or later most Indian slaves

[42] The most useful work on this subject is by Ulrich B. Phillips, "The
Slave Labor Problem in the Charleston District," *Political Science Quarterly*,
XXII (1907), 416–439; also see Frank J. Klingberg, *An Appraisal of the
Negro in Colonial South Carolina* (Washington, 1941), particularly 1–26.

[43] Crane concluded that the peak use of Indian slaves was about 1708.
Crane, *Southern Frontier*, 112–113.

[44] Governor Nathaniel Johnson and Council to Proprietors, September 17,
1708, *BPRO-SC*, V, 203–210.

were shipped from the colony either to New England or to the West Indies. Although the women and children proved tractable, Indian men were neither trustworthy nor equal to Negro men as field hands.[45] Moreover, the inland tribes were proud people who did not tolerate the rigors of slave life without objection. An Indian slave who escaped could most likely make it back to his tribe.

While the actual number of indentured servants in the province at any one time was seldom recorded, the trend is obvious. The decline of the employment of white servants parallels the decline in the use of Indian slaves. Governor Johnson recorded a reduction in the number of servants from 200 in 1703 to 120 in 1708.[46] After this time, they were always a small minority in proportion to Negro slaves in South Carolina. Of course, indentured servants were a dwindling source of labor in the eighteenth century. There were simply not enough laborers in Europe who wanted to come to America, despite America's insatiable demand for workers. Besides, the shift to rice cultivation fairly well eliminated the use of white field labor in South Carolina since it was widely believed that they could not stand the conditions of the low country.

With the weakening of the proprietary hold, the South Carolina government was often swayed, particularly after 1696, by bold leaders who got the province into difficulties. Some new questions, such as the fight over the establishment of the Church of England, were strictly internal and might not have upset the economy or inhibited developmental processes other than to give the place a bad reputation for constant political strife. How this fight, for example, affected

[45] This view of the Indians as slaves is widely held among authorities. For example, Crane, *Southern Frontier*, 113.

[46] Governor Nathaniel Johnson and Council to Proprietors, September 17, 1708, *BPRO-SC*, V, 203–210.

attempts to recruit new settlers is almost impossible to fathom. Other situations, however, were much more danger-ous to the political and economic future. Beginning in the 1690's South Carolina's position on the southern frontier became quite precarious, although many South Carolinians never seemed fearful of her enemies or restrained by the niceties of international relations. Eager to move against the Spaniards at St. Augustine and the French on the Gulf of Mexico, the South Carolinians soon became the concern, not only of the proprietors, but the crown as well. Controversy with the proprietors centered on whether they or the South Carolina assembly should pay the bills for defense.[47] The crown, on the other hand, aware of the key position of this province, determined to keep a closer watch over events in that corner of the empire but urged the proprietors to con-trol the settlers' rasher impulses which might lead to interna-tional complications. Despite the aggressive instincts of the colonists, South Carolina played a minimal role in King William's War. Governor James Colleton stopped a South Carolina raiding party from hitting St. Augustine in 1690; however, even this projected expedition was not part of the war effort but was viewed as revenge for the Spanish invasion of 1686. The chief loss for the South Carolinians during the war may have been that of most of its small vessels.[48]

By the time Queen Anne's War started in 1701, South Carolina expansionists had the upper hand and took advan-tage of a legally declared war to strike a blow for South Carolina's economy. Schemes were soon afoot to raid against both the Spanish and French to make the frontier secure and increase trade with the Indians. This time there would be no

[47] Proprietors to "My Lords" (probably Board of Trade), December 6, 1703, ibid., V, 112–113. The proprietors reported that the cost of defense was greater than any profits they would receive.

[48] On South Carolina's role in King William's War, see Edward Randolph to Board of Trade, March 16, 1699, ibid., IV, 88–95.

proprietary governor to hold them back. In fact, Governor James Moore, who assumed office after the death of Governor Joseph Blake in 1700, was a leading exponent of the aggressive spirit. Elected temporarily by the council until the proprietary made a permanent choice, Moore was confirmed in his office by Lord Granville, the Palatine. Moore was leader of the Anglican party, an Indian trader, and, above all, an opportunist. Though the religious question had brought factionalism back into South Carolina politics, the right of the assembly to control the province's administrative machinery and its right to regulate the Indian trade were being contested by Moore. While many settlers wanted reform and regulation of the Indian trade, Governor Moore may not have since he feared restrictions on his own business activities. On the other hand, the assembly would not vote funds for a military expedition. The stalemate delayed Moore in his intentions to take the field against the enemy. In August 1702, with war officially declared, the assembly finally voted to support Moore's project to go against St. Augustine before Spain reinforced it. After more haggling, Moore himself took command.[49]

In October 1702 the South Carolina expeditionary force appeared before St. Augustine.[50] The invaders easily drove the inhabitants into the main fortress, but the South Carolinians had no means to penetrate such fortifications. After trying to starve out the garrison and people for a month and a half, Moore and his small army retreated when Spanish reinforcements arrived. It is doubtful that Moore's precipitate actions accomplished much that was permanent. Some have concluded, however, that he did push the frontier farther to the south.[51]

[49] Sirmans, *Colonial South Carolina*, 81–86.
[50] For the military campaign, see Charles W. Arnade, *The Siege of St. Augustine in 1702* (Gainesville, Florida, 1959).
[51] Sirmans, *Colonial South Carolina*, 85.

Most significantly, South Carolina was left with a debt of £4,000 sterling for the costs of the expedition above and beyond the assembly's original authorization. Governor Moore proposed that £4,000 in bills of credit be issued to pay holders of this debt. To obtain this objective, some of his opponents tried to force Moore to accept measures which would regulate the Indian trade and make naturalization for Huguenots more difficult. Governor Moore won his point. In 1703, an act was passed to pay the debt plus provide some operating funds by issuing £6,000 in bills. It included a rationalization that the province was "following the examples of many great and rich countries who have helpt themselves in their exigencies with funds of credit, which have fully answered the ends of money, and given the people besides a quick circulation of their trade and cash." Commissioners were authorized to make the bills which were to be in denominations no smaller than 50s. and no larger than £20. These bills were to be placed in circulation by the Receiver General to meet the outstanding obligations of the province. To prevent counterfeiting, the bills were to be indented and numbered with the counterpart retained in a book held by the Receiver General. Bills were to bear 12 per cent interest per year until withdrawn from circulation by being paid to the Receiver General, who canceled them as scheduled under law.[52]

The actual sum of £6,000 in bills of credit was probably not excessive, considering the population of the province and its growing economy, but it was a dangerous precedent. Unless this means of financing were handled with discretion, further issuances would tend to devalue this currency below hard money. Anticipating such a debasement, those framing the law included a clause which said that bills were "to be a

---

[52] Cooper and McCord (eds.), *Statutes of S.C.*, II, 206–212.

good payment and tender in law, and if any person or persons shall refuse to take and receive the same in payment, he or they so refuseing shall forfeit double the value of such bills so refused." This was an attempt to forestall strained relations between debtors and creditors, particularly when South Carolinians offered bills as payment to English merchants. From scanty evidence, one concludes that this first issue was handled well and brought few problems to the conduct of business, though the bills of credit were discounted when exchanged for sterling.[53] Nevertheless, a dubious means of financing governmental adventures had been initiated. Neither proprietors nor crown stepped in to veto this act.

As South Carolina loosened proprietary restraints, it came under closer surveillance by the English government, though the two trends were not interconnected. It was at this time that England was tightening its rules of empire and setting up new enforcement procedures. In 1696, the very year that Archdale made an obvious donation of legitimate proprietary powers to the assembly and the people of South Carolina, major reforms were instituted in the English colonial system. Some of these reforms, indeed, were aimed at proprietary colonies which were never known to be zealous generally in enforcing imperial laws. Edward Randolph, a crown functionary who visited South Carolina later, was one of the chief instigators of these reforms.[54]

The Navigation Act of 1696 drew together many stipulations included in several earlier acts. Colonial trade was still confined to Englishmen and English colonials sailing under the English flag in English or colonial-built vessels. Enforcement provisions were strengthened. Colonial-based customs officers were given the same rights as customs officers serving

[53] Ibid., IX, 766.
[54] Michael G. Hall, *Edward Randolph and the American Colonies, 1676–1703* (Chapel Hill, 1960), 154–177.

in England, including the right to go on board any vessel or search on land for goods suspected of having evaded duties. Naval officers, responsible to the governor of the colony, were given greater powers to help with enforcement. All officers directly involved with enforcement procedures, including proprietary colony governors, were required to give bonds to guarantee performance. Vice-admiralty courts, crown courts as opposed to colonial courts, were created to try alleged offenses under the acts of trade.

That same year, the administrative machinery to supervise all phases of the relationship between colonies and mother country, including enforcement of the above act, was overhauled. From 1675 to 1696 a committee of the Privy Council, commonly called the Lords of Trade, had controlled trade and colonial affairs for the crown. Under an Order in Council, dated May 15, 1696, the Lords of Trade were superseded by a new body, Lords Commissioners of Trade and Plantations, which was generally called the Board of Trade. The agency was similar to others functioning under the Privy Council at this time. Some of its members were Privy Councillors, but it had salaried members with specific jobs plus a working bureaucracy. The Board was to promote trade generally, care for the poor, and look after the plantations. In practice, its major task was to find ways to make the colonies profitable for crown and merchants. To fulfill this portion of its mission, the Board was given a long list of specific powers of supervision including the following: correspond with governors; recommend persons to be governors, deputy governors, members of colonial councils, and a host of other positions; review laws passed by colonial assemblies; decide which laws should be recommended for confirmation or disallowance and why; hear complaints from the colonies; and investigate and take testimony under oath on the state of affairs in a given colony, a given trade, or other matter affecting commerce. Legally, the Board of Trade was not the final authority, but its recommendations were generally confirmed by the Privy Council.[55]

The importance of these changes for all the American colonies cannot be overemphasized, yet the proprietary colonies would be especially affected by the new machinery of supervision. As the leading authority on the empire pointed out, "the private colonies, protected by their charters, had hardly felt the weight of England's hand, but now they were to see the long arm of authority reaching out across the intervening waters to curtail their prized independence." [56] In South Carolina the results were mixed. Assumption of supervisory powers by the crown did not produce great changes immediately. South Carolinians did register their vessels,[57] and the proprietors did appoint officers specified in the Parliamentary act. In February 1698, for example, they appointed as Naval Officer, Nicholas Trott, who was to play an important role in the province for years.[58] In addition, the records are dotted with references to admiralty court jurisdiction from about 1697, though proceedings for this court in South Carolina do not survive for these early years.[59]

In the long run, there were perhaps three consequences of these reforms for South Carolina. There was, necessarily, increased correspondence with London, much of it directly to and from the Board of Trade. Accordingly, a fuller pic-

---

[55] For a discussion of these changes in the English government in the 1690's, see Charles M. Andrews, *The Colonial Period of American History* (New Haven, 1938), IV, 178–317.

[56] Ibid., IV, 227.

[57] These are to be found interspersed with other documents and were apparently never collected and put in one volume. "Wills and Miscellaneous Records, 1694–1704" (Manuscript volume in South Carolina Archives, Columbia, S.C.), 105–135.

[58] Proprietors to Nicholas Trott, Commission as Naval Officer, February 5, 1698, *BPRO-SC*, IV, 3–5.

[59] Records of this court are on deposit at the Federal Records Center, East Point, Georgia.

ture of economic development in the province emerges after 1696. Second, Board of Trade recommendations led to the enumeration of some staples exported from South Carolina, and to the offering of bounties on certain commodities which might be produced in South Carolina. Finally, South Carolinians found, in time, that being under the protection of the crown had more advantages than disadvantages, but they also learned that the crown was much more difficult to ignore than the proprietary had been. So the reforms of 1696 in England bear ultimately on the changing relations between settlers and their government on one side and the proprietary on the other, and may have conditioned the settlers to revolt in 1719 when the proprietary was unable to cope with the crisis.

Despite the rise of the mother country as a factor in the existence of South Carolina, the Indian trade for deerskins, the most profitable commercial activity between 1690 and 1705, remained under the control of the province. Though interested in the frontier, England did not try to supervise white-Indian relations until late in the colonial era. The proprietors by 1690 had already attempted to shape the business for their own benefit and failed. So local interests dominated the trade, and, as a result, the provincial government ran into stiff opposition whenever regulation was attempted. To be fair, devising rules for an activity taking place many miles from the edge of civilization was a most difficult task at best. As early as 1691 a law to control the trade by limiting it to certain geographical areas had been tried.[60] The act passed while Archdale was governor was ineffective and unenforceable without some agency empowered to supervise. Partisan politics prevented passage of any comprehensive law before 1712, though most settlers proba-

[60] Cooper and McCord (eds.), *Statutes of S.C.*, II, 55; Crane, *Southern Frontier*, 40, 45.

bly realized that shoddy treatment of the Indians by the traders might bring Indian reprisals.[61]

In casting about for taxable commerce, the assembly early took to placing duties on exported deerskins. This willingness to tax the first prosperous business in the province suggests that the value and volume of the trade were viewed with envy by those who did not participate in it, and also that the Indian traders occupied a special niche in commerce. The 1691 law rationalized the tax on skins and furs on the grounds that Indian traders could not help defend the province when emergencies arose. It was only fair, therefore, that a duty be placed on their trade to help pay for fortifications. While duty acts were revised and re-enacted at frequent intervals, the tax or duty was generally a few pennies current money per skin. The 1691 law, for example, rated untanned deerskins at threepence each. Other skins and furs such as beaver, fox, cat, otter, boar, and raccoon were taxed and must have been exported on occasion.[62] By 1703 taxes were laid on a long list of imports as well, including liquors, biscuit, and herring. This taxation was doubtless necessary as the financial plight of the province grew more desperate.[63] But deerskins seem to have been the only major export consistently taxed. In the 1690's nearly all such taxes were tagged for defense. Later, some taxes on exported skins were reserved for supporting ministers.

The impact of such tax laws and their renewals may not have been borne by local traders at all since such levies are generally passed on to the buyer. When the act of 1700 was passed, an innovation was added which gave local merchants the advantage over English merchants in the deerskin

---

[61] Crane, *Southern Frontier*, 141.

[62] Cooper and McCord (eds.), *Statutes of S.C.*, II, 64–68. Since this was passed under Governor Sothell, it is doubtful that it was long enforced. A similar act was passed in 1696; see ibid., II, 110–112.

[63] Ibid., II, 200–206.

trade.[64] At least Michael Cole, master of a London-based vessel who claimed to have been trading to South Carolina since 1693, lodged a vigorous protest over the recent discriminatory legislation. Though he said he could not obtain a copy of the law, Cole asserted that under its provisions skins or furs shipped by South Carolina residents were taxed "three farthings" per skin while nonresidents paid 1½d. per skin exported. He insisted that this was no small matter since it amounted to £3 per ton on exported furs and skins or an amount equal to half the freight per ton. According to Cole, this law meant that English vessels had to stay in South Carolina "till the Wormes shall rot their bottoms out." Cole interpreted the purpose of the act to be to place English merchants at a disadvantage, since South Carolinians were eager to trade directly to England on their own. He protested that such a law was illegal under imperial laws.[65] This particular enactment probably reflects the rise of the spirit of antagonism between South Carolinians and English merchants, a feeling not uncommon throughout colonial America.

The act of 1703 continued the tax concession for local merchants, though under a different formula.[66] Under this law, skins, furs, and other items taxed upon exportation would bear only half the stated duty if exported on board vessels built and wholly owned in the province. If exported on a vessel owned in the province but not built locally, duties would be two-thirds the stated rate. These concessions to local shipowners may be found in several subsequent acts which placed taxes on the skin trade. It is doubtful, therefore, if Michael Cole obtained the relief he sought. The law failed to give much advantage to Charles Town vessel own-

[64] Title only, ibid., II, 162.
[65] Michael Cole to Board of Trade, February 17, 1702, *BPRO-SC,* V, 25–26.
[66] Cooper and McCord (eds.), *Statutes of S.C.,* II, 200–206.

ers because the natural market for deerskins was England, and they owned few, if any, ships large enough to sail directly to England. Cole's persistent correspondence with the Board of Trade and the subsequent inquiry do illustrate the overseeing by imperial authorities and their potential for interference.[67]

Freed of proprietary restrictions, unhampered by imperial regulations, and unregulated by provincial laws, South Carolina-based Indian traders flourished after 1690. Taking advantage of the trade ties cemented with the Lower Creeks between 1689 and 1691, they steadily expanded their business in slaves and deerskins despite temporary checks during King William's War and Queen Anne's War. These daring men, mostly nameless to history, who pushed deeper and deeper into the continent, reached the Mississippi River, a thousand miles from Charles Town, before 1700.[68] They always attempted to broaden their hold by bringing more and more tribes within their sphere of influence. They were leaders in the push against French and Spanish traders, soldiers, and administrators who were also actively engaged in the same enterprise.

While the international implications of this confrontation in the backcountry have been told in detail, the impact of this trade on the South Carolina economy has never been analyzed as thoroughly.[69] For the first time, the province was in a position to supply something which had considerable value, which had an almost insatiable market in Europe. Though the trade brought some individuals considerable profit, a comparatively small number of settlers shared this income. The capital generated doubtless helped to develop other aspects of the economy, for financial opportunists of

[67] For other documents pertaining to these tax levies, *BPRO-SC,* V, 37–40.
[68] Crane, *Southern Frontier,* 44–46.
[69] Crane made little attempt to explore the business side of the trade.

that day seldom confined themselves to one activity. While it is impossible to be specific about this process, it is obvious that individuals making profits in the deerskin business did not invest in vessels to any great extent, since Charles Town did not claim a very large merchant fleet. Most of them probably expanded into other export trades developing at this time and invested in lands which would produce these exportable commodities.

Aggressive moves into the backcountry resulted in wars which sharply increased the number of Indian slaves available for market. Most of the action took place as tribes trading with the South Carolinians attacked tribes allied to the Spaniards and French. Yet, to obtain slaves, unscrupulous traders fomented raids even in peacetime and, more than once, against friendly tribes. Part of the willingness of South Carolinians to participate in wilderness raids was the possibility of being paid handsomely in booty in the form of marketable captives, though in the long run "of small economic significance." [70] Nevertheless, Indian slaves transported from Charles Town after 1690 numbered in the thousands, since outbreaks of warfare were frequent. Governor Johnson's population statistics reflect the impact of such actions on the supply of Indian slaves.[71] The failure of the provincial government to curb such abuses and control the most unethical traders was one of the more costly errors made between 1690 and 1705.

In the long run, deerskins provided a far more lucrative business than did selling Indian slaves. If the Earl of Craven's evaluation that the total South Carolina trade to England in 1687 was not worth £2,000 in skins and cedar was

[70] Crane, *Southern Frontier*, 112.
[71] Governor Nathaniel Johnson and Council to Proprietors, September 17, 1708, *BPRO-SC*, V, 203–210.

correct,[72] by the middle 1690's the value of exported deer-skins alone was more than several times that sum. Because of the Navigation Act of 1696 and the increasing efficiency of English officials, some meaningful statistics are available to measure the volume of this trade. Prospects for assessing the figures fully are dim, however, for it is difficult to be sure of the worth of skins in any one year or of the profit structure of the trade. Few business papers and little pricing data are to be found for any period before the 1730's.

Considering all the qualifications about figures, one may only be sure that the number of deerskins exported increased dramatically between the 1680's and 1700. Profits probably increased proportionally. According to figures compiled from British customs records, from 1699 through 1705 more than 317,000 deerksins were imported into England from South Carolina. The average for the seven years was over 45,000 annually, with a high of 64,488 in 1699 and a low of 10,289 in 1705 (a war year).[73] Assuming that the average deerskin exported was worth 10s. sterling on the dock in Charles Town, the value of the average annual deerskin exportations in this period could have ranged between £15,000 and £25,000.[74] Even if this trial figure is overesti-mated by a considerable margin (as it may be), the total value of exported skins was much greater than the value of other exports before 1705. It must be reiterated that this trade gave financial gain to a comparative few. How much of

[72] Unaddressed but probably from Earl of Craven to Lords of Trade, un-dated but with 1687 papers, *BPRO-SC*, II, 218–220.

[73] "Custom House Inspec. Genls. Office June 1716," BPRO-SC, VI, 135–136; the same figures were used by Crane, *Southern Frontier*, 328; see Table III, Appendix.

[74] From scanty pricing information, it appears that deerskin prices were increasing in this era, but how rapidly is difficult to determine. Even when a price is found, it is impossible to judge whether the price is typical since most often the weight and quality of the skins being valued are not given.

the total value of the exported skins represented profit and who among merchants, Indian traders, and Indians received the profits remains largely a moot point.

Rice emerged as the second most important export commodity after 1690, and it was of much more importance to the average settler than was the development of the more specialized Indian trade. If, as seems likely, rice was first cultivated in South Carolina between 1685 and 1690, it took several more years before commercially significant crops were grown. The steps in tilling and harvesting to provide a marketable staple had been mastered before 1705, but this was not accomplished rapidly and procedures were not fully perfected. As with all agricultural pursuits, innovations were being introduced constantly. Nevertheless, rice growing had progressed sufficiently so that it headed the list of staples by 1705. It had supplanted provisions as the leading agricultural export.

The increase in the cultivation of rice owed little to the proprietors, local government, or imperial officials. Its development must be credited almost solely to the initiative and persistence of individual settlers, whose names are not recorded. Success, however, did bring the province to the attention of English authorities. Soon after cultivation began, some of the rice was sent directly to Spain and Portugal, a leading market for this grain, and to Holland.[75] Such shipping patterns prevented the English customs service from collecting duties which were normally paid when rice was imported into England. Since 1660, it had been taxed at the rate of £1 6s. 8d. per hundredweight or about 3d. per pound.

---

[75] South Carolinians always claimed that rice was shipped to Europe before 1705, but the trade could not have been extensive since rice cultivation was in its infancy. For confirmation, see Report of Commissioners of Customs to Lord High Treasurer, December 7, 1704, Joseph Redlington (ed.), *Calendar of Treasury Books and Papers, 1557–1728* (London, 1868–1889), III, 306.

Additionally, there was a 5 per cent ad valorem duty.[76] To protect the royal revenues, Parliament, upon the advice of the Board of Trade, enacted a statute which forbade the export of rice from the colonies to other than English ports after September 29, 1705.[77] At the time of passage, the effect of this enactment could not be predicted, but South Carolinians soon recognized that restricting the market cut profits for them. For the first time, South Carolina felt the power the mother country possessed to shape trade relations to the disadvantage of its offspring.

Most of the late eighteenth and nineteenth century accounts barely touch on the early trials and problems before launching into a discussion of tidal culture. Sometimes it is not even noted that it took 75 years of experience before this method of cultivation was put into practice. It was therefore the earlier methods of growing the crop which produced nearly all the rice grown and exported from South Carolina during the colonial era. This early experience is important, for the conclusions drawn from it shaped many aspects of the province's development.

According to most botanical experts, all the cultivated rice belongs to one genus, *Oryza L.* The many species which belong under this genus have two genetic sources, Asia and Africa. First cultivation, however, was probably in Asia, most likely China, and probably several thousand years B.C. From its point of origination, rice was spread as a cultivated crop. The Malays probably carried it to East Africa and Madagascar from whence it was carried to South Carolina. This sequence is logical, feasible, and supported to some degree by South Carolina records and traditional accounts.[78]

Rice was introduced into the Mediterranean basin as a result of the growing trade with the Far East at the dawn of

---

[76] Gray, *History of Agriculture,* I, 284.   [77] 3 & 4 Anne, c. 5.
[78] D. H. Grist, *Rice,* Fourth Edition (London, 1965), 3–9.

the modern era. It came to be grown in Italy, Spain, and Portugal among other countries before European expansion to the New World. Spaniards carried it to Central and South America, and the Portuguese grew it almost from the start of settlement in Brazil.[79] Strangely, the Spanish and Portuguese experience with the crop in the New World does not seem to have influenced methods of culture in South Carolina. The records frequently mention that the English learned about agricultural crops from other nationalities involved in the West Indies. Yet, there seems to be no hint that any Barbadian who migrated to South Carolina had any knowledge of rice based on personal contacts with the crop in Central and South America. So it appears that, despite centuries of rice cultivation in many areas of the globe including the western hemisphere, South Carolinians drew very little upon this experience and mainly learned how to grow rice by trial and error.[80]

Although rice does best and produces the largest crops under certain optimum conditions, it may be cultivated in quite different physical situations. Most rice, but not all, has been grown in tropical and semitropical areas of the world. Abundant water seems to be the most important element for success, but rice will mature in comparatively dry climates. An examination of the criteria specified by modern agriculturists reveals that coastal South Carolina is an area that provides excellent over-all conditions. Most of the high-yield areas of the globe fall between the 30th and 45th parallels north latitude. These areas have high average daily temperatures ranging from 68 to 100°F. during the growing season; a

[79] Ibid.

[80] Some authorities do believe that knowledge of Chinese planting practices were influential, though they offer no documentary proof. Heyward, in *Seed From Madagascar*, 8–10, concluded, however, that information about cultivation in China was brought to South Carolina much later than the period covered in this study.

great deal of sunshine is quite necessary. Furthermore, of the many satisfactory soil classifications, alluvial soils formed by river deposits are among the best.[81] Leaving further description of the ideal rice environment to the agriculturist, one may conclude that South Carolina was naturally suited to the profitable cultivation of this crop if the settlers could master the secrets of tillage.

Since rice cultivation started in South Carolina before much systematic classification of plant species had been undertaken, it is almost impossible to be sure about which varieties were tried when. The records are very contradictory. One rice planter of a later date concluded that the variety called Carolina gold rice (after the color of the outer hull) was introduced from Madagascar in 1685.[82] Another rice planter asserted that the first variety grown was "white rice." He said that gold rice, first tried around the time of the American Revolution, was then developed into the "long grain" rice of the nineteenth century.[83] A more recent writer, after sifting conflicting evidence, decided that soon after the introduction of Madagascar rice, another variety was imported from the East Indies.[84] For the general student, the species grown is of minor importance. Mostly these confusing contradictions offer proof that experimentation was necessary to determine the best variety or varieties for growth in South Carolina and that details about early rice culture are scanty.

The first rice crops were planted in open fields without any attempt to irrigate the land. Possibly Madagascar rice, which grew well under such conditions, was used when rice was cultivated in this way. One author claimed that white rice was always judged the best variety for what South Caro-

---

[81] Grist, *Rice*, 10–31.   [82] Heyward, *Seed From Madagascar*, 4.
[83] Robert F. W. Allston, *Essay on Sea Coast Crops* (Charleston, 1854), 29.
[84] Gray, *History of Agriculture*, I, 277.

linians called "upland culture," rice planted in open fields depending on natural rainfall to supply moisture. Growing rice by this method was supposed to be no more difficult than growing any other grain crop. Only hoeing was required to keep down stifling weed growth. Some rice was grown by the "upland culture" method at least until the late nineteenth century.[85]

The second method of cultivation involved planting inland swamps fed by freshwater streams.[86] When and how the transition from open field culture to swamp culture began is uncertain. The change was made because it was found that rice yielded better if grown in very moist places, but whether the information came to South Carolina from rice-growing areas elsewhere or was discovered locally is not known. Inland swamps were converted to fields (paddies) by a laborious process sometimes taking several years. South Carolina's swamps near the ocean are often brackish, since salt water is pushed some distance inland by the tides. Farther away from the ocean, swamps are fresh, being fed by streams, and normally are beyond the push of the tides. Sometimes in these freshwater swamps are ridges of land standing a few feet above the level of the swamp. Some imaginative planter conceived the idea that the area between two such ridges could be dammed by piling up earth at either end. The dam at the lower end of the artificially created field would keep water on the field and prevent unwanted water from being

---

[85] Amory Austin, *Rice: Its Cultivation, Production and Distribution* (U.S. Dept. of Agriculture, Division of Statistics, Miscellaneous Series, Report No. 6) (Washington, 1893) , 16–24; Allston, *Sea Coast Crops*, 31.

[86] This account of the inland swamp culture and the planting-harvesting cycle is based on the following sources: Heyward, *Seed From Madagascar*, 11–21; Robert F. W. Allston, *Memoir on the Introduction and Planting of Rice* (Charleston, 1843) , 4–17; *American Husbandry*, . . . *Agriculture of the British Colonies in North America* . . . (London, 1775) , I, 391–397; Gray, *History of Agriculture*, I, 279–284; Thomas Nairne, *A Letter From South Carolina* (London, 1710) .

pushed into the field by the tides; the dam at the upper end of the field would control the water flow into the field or would hold out and divert the flow around the field. A gate was placed in the lower dam to allow water on the field to be drained off; the gate in the upper dam allowed water to flow into the field to the desired depth.

Putting in the dams and gates was a comparatively simple part of the process of preparing a field. The land still had to be cleared of trees. Fortunately, not many large trees grew in such areas, according to most accounts. Those which were there presented a real problem, since the land was so soft that draft animals could not be used to drag off the logs and stumps. Roots were often left to rot because they could be taken out much more easily after they had deteriorated. The land also had to be leveled. This, too, was hand labor, but the softness of the ground was an advantage when it came to digging and cultivating.

This was not a foolproof system of cultivation. The most obvious weakness showed up when there was a freshet which would destroy the upper dam or flood over it. The crop in the field would then be washed out or buried under many feet of water. Especially high tides or hurricanes might affect some fields by forcing saltwater far inland and past the lower dam, destroying the crop and fouling the field. Still, this method grew better and larger crops than the upland culture method. It continued in use by some planters long after most rice was grown by the third method, tidal culture, which was widely practiced from about the time of the American Revolution. Most inland swamp fields were abandoned by the middle of the nineteenth century, apparently because of soil exhaustion and the cluttering of fields with grass and weeds.

No large crops of rice could be planted until the supply of seed was built up. This could only be done over a number of growing seasons. If one had a good yield, the return on seed was considerable. Thomas Nairne, Indian agent and pamphleteer, wrote that a peck planted an acre which would return 30 to 60 bushels of cleaned rice. Later reports said that it took up to three bushels of seed per acre planted. These contradictory accounts lend support to a theory that if a small bag of rice were planted in 1685 or thereabouts, it would have taken up to ten years before seed was widely available and cheap in price.[87]

While details of culture are best left to the agriculturist, an outline of the planting-harvesting cycle helps explain why rice growing was such an arduous series of tasks. Seeding time was between April 1 and May 20, with the seeds planted in drills about 18 inches apart. After germination of the seed, the rice had to be hoed and weeded constantly whether grown in open fields or inland swamps. Much of this phase of rice growing was backbreaking labor conducted with hand tools in water or muddy soil, under hot and humid conditions. Harvesting time was from early September to early October. The crop was cut with sickles and stacked in the field to dry.

Two onerous tasks remained before the finished grain was ready for market. Threshing, separating the grains from their stocks, came first. The method followed in the colonial era was to place bundles of cut grain on the ground with the heads outward. Slaves walked down the rows of bundles swinging a flail to beat off the heads of rice. Rice grains with the hulls still on were known as rough rice.

The second task is generally called pounding in most descriptive accounts. This designation gives a wrong impression, since during the colonial era the action was more grinding than pounding. The objective was to remove the outer

---

[87] On this point, see Gray, *History of Agriculture*, I, 280.

coats on the granule of rice to expose the kernel, a process which took several steps. First, the recently threshed grain was winnowed, most likely by sending it down a netting strung from a building. After the grain was separated from the chaff, the rice had to be ground to take off the outer husk and inner cuticle. Each laborer put two or three pecks of rough or unhusked rice in a wooden mortar made of common pitch pine. A pestle of lightwood or the heart of pine was worked in the mortar with a grinding motion. The husk came off rather easily, but removal of the inner cuticle or film required care. A careful workman might produce 95 per cent unbroken rice grains fit for market, but a careless one could easily shatter half his rice, making it unfit or reducing its value. Randolph reported in 1699, "They have now found out the true way of raising and husking Rice," [88] but it is apparent that the South Carolinians had only developed techniques to the point that a crop might be grown and harvested commercially. Threshing and pounding machines by the score were tried, but it was late in the eighteenth century before substantial improvements in these methods became widely adopted.

The tremendous amount of hand labor, the wearing and dangerous nature of the work, and the full yearly cycle of growing and harvesting a rice crop influenced the pattern of life and commerce of the colony. Since much of the repetitive, strenuous labor could only be performed on swampy ground under adverse climatic conditions, it became generally accepted that only Negro slaves could stand it. The slow process of pounding took months and delayed getting the crop to the vessels until late fall or winter. Most of the export trade of the province was conducted in the winter and spring

[88] Edward Randolph to Board of Trade, May 27, 1700, *BPRO-SC*, IV, 189–190.

when this bulky and profitable staple was available to ship to England.[89] Once the pounding was completed, preparations were started to get the fields ready for the next year's crop. Winter apparently was the only time of year when activity on a rice plantation slackened, and some of the hands could be put to other tasks, including clearing more land and making tar and pitch.

Rice was slow to gain acceptance as a staple. At least a decade passed between introduction of the crop and the time the South Carolinians were able to take some advantage of its commercial possibilities. Undoubtedly, a shortage of seed, the slow development of cultivation techniques, and the cumbersome method of preparing the grain for market caused this lag. Despite the delays involved, rice steadily increased in importance after 1695. Even a casual survey of provincial records after that year reveals more and more references to rice. In 1696, it was acceptable as a commodity in payment of quitrents.[90] A sample of Carolina rice was laid before the Board of Trade for their perusal and information by 1699.[91] All evidence points to the period, 1695–1700, as the approximate time when rice began to take its place as the leading commodity produced on the soil of South Carolina.

There are few meaningful figures for exports of rice from Charles Town before 1717, but those available indicate a rapid increase of production after 1700. The most valid estimate was provided by Randolph, who reported that 330 tons of rice were shipped from the harvest of 1699.[92] Proba-

---

[89] Converse D. Clowse, "The Charleston Export Trade, 1717–1737" (unpublished Ph.D. dissertation, Northwestern University, 1963), 203–204; 210–211; 243–257.

[90] Cooper and McCord (eds.), *Statutes of S.C.*, II, 96–102.

[91] Minutes of Board of Trade, July 25, 1699, *BPRO-SC*, IV, 99.

[92] Edward Randolph to Board of Trade, May 27, 1700, ibid., IV, 189–190; Table III, Appendix.

bly this was an export of 2,000 to 2,200 barrels, based on an average barrel holding 350 pounds of cleaned rice.[93] By 1712–1713, five or six times as much rice was shipped.[94] Customs figures of rice imported into England show that rice from Carolina was beginning to make an impact on that market by 1705.[95] The method of compiling these figures, however, raises so many questions that they must be used only to indicate trends.[96] It was this increase, nevertheless, which must have influenced English officials to have rice placed on the enumerated list when they feared that much of the South Carolina rice would be shipped directly to Europe. Even if the export of rice from Charles Town reached the 5,000-barrel level by 1705, the gross value of the rice probably had not exceeded the value of deerskins exported. But rice clearly had vaulted into first place as the major staple of South Carolina.

At least two other related trends correlate to the increase of commercial rice production between 1695 and 1705: the rapidly increasing slave population and the granting of land, with more rapid dispersal of settlers. Since rice was the only crop with an unexploited market and a good profit potential, it is logical to assume that slaves were purchased during these ten years to obtain labor to open up rice fields and to cultivate the crop. At least 200,000 acres of land were granted from 1694 through 1705. It is impossible to estimate how much of this land had been previously opened up and worked without legal claim, but was now being registered

[93] On the question of the size of the rice barrel at any one time, see *Historical Statistics of the United States: Colonial Times to 1957* (Washington, 1960), 750–751; Clowse, "The Charleston Export Trade, 1717–1737," 27–28, 188–190.

[94] Table III, Appendix.

[95] *Historical Statistics of United States,* 768 (Series Z 274–280).

[96] George N. Clark, *Guide to English Commercial Statistics, 1696–1782* (London, 1938), ix–xvi; Elizabeth B. Schumpeter, *English Overseas Trade Statistics, 1697–1808* (Oxford, 1960), 1–14 (introduction by T. S. Ashton).

under Archdale's land reforms. The more than 100,000 acres granted from 1698 through 1705 must be a reflection of headrights obtained for slaves imported. White population in this period was static or actually declining slightly and white immigration was negligible; land purchases were never very great. Moreover, though most of this land granted was in Berkeley County, the area around Charles Town, considerable amounts of it were in Colleton County, to the south of Charles Town, and some in Craven County to the north. This pattern is part of the quest for suitable rice lands.[97] Rice had made substantial impact on the economy and the province's life even before 1705.

With rice emerging as a money crop, England gave the colonists' hopes another boost when Parliament passed an act in 1704 providing for bounties on naval stores shipped to the mother country. This was the positive side of imperial power, a power to give benefits as well as to regulate to the colonies' disadvantage. The movement to impose bounties was not new, but colonials and merchants had been unsuccessful in earlier lobbying efforts. As usual, when the crown made the decision, it was based on the advantages the system would have for England with any profits for colonists being incidental. As early as the 1690's, there were signs that something might be done to give price support to colonial-produced naval stores. Creation of the Board of Trade to oversee commerce was an important step, for this agency became a sounding board for advocates of bounties.[98] The Admiralty had projects of its own afoot in the 1690's. Their survey of New England forest resources showed that conditions there

[97] Table II, Appendix.
[98] Eleanor L. Lord, *Industrial Experiments in the British Colonies of North America* (Herbert B. Adams (ed.), *Johns Hopkins University Studies in Historical and Political Science,* extra volume XVII) (Baltimore, 1898), 5–9.

were generally unfavorable to naval stores production. Transportation from the deep forests to the seaports was impossible in an area where most streams were navigable only a few miles inland.[99] In 1704 Thomas Byfield, representing several groups of traders, tried to contract with the Board of Trade and the Royal Navy to supply them with tar and pitch from Carolina. After many petitions and hearings, the Board of Trade recommended against the scheme on the grounds that such a project would not be in the national interest and was only for private profit.[100] Nothing was done to subsidize the shipment of American naval stores to England.

With the advent of the War of the Spanish Succession, those responsible for England's defense had to protect her supply of naval stores. The normal source in the Baltic could now be cut off rather easily. Moreover, the Swedes began practicing stricter adherence to their own mercantilistic doctrines. In 1703 the Stockholm Tar Company, the Swedish monopoly, commenced a policy of refusing to ship tar to England unless the goods were delivered in Swedish vessels.[101] In 1704, after weighing all the ramifications of the situation, Parliament passed the statute instituting bounties to encourage the manufacture of naval stores in the American colonies, with the following bounties to be paid on goods arriving in England after January 1, 1705/6: [102]

Tar: £4 per ton, with each ton in 8 barrels, each barrel to gauge 31½ gallons

Pitch: £4 per ton, with each ton to be 20 gross hundreds (112 pounds each) in 8 barrels

---

[99] Albion, *Forests and Sea Power*, 238–239; Lord, *Industrial Experiments*, 9–14; Joseph J. Malone, *Pine Trees and Politics: The Naval Stores and Forest Policy in Colonial New England, 1691–1775* (Seattle, 1964), 10–27.

[100] For documents relating to Byfield's petitions, see *BPRO-SC*, V, 120, 121, 129, 130, 131–139.

[101] Lord, *Industrial Experiments*, 56.   [102] 3 & 4 Anne, c. 10.

  Turpentine and rosin: £3 per ton, with each ton to be 20
   gross hundreds (112 pounds each) in 8 barrels
These proved to be the meaningful stipulations for South
Carolina, but bounties were also included for hemp, masts,
yards, and bowsprits.

  When the law was passed, no one could foresee exactly
how it would affect South Carolina. But the development of
a trade in naval stores was natural in a country endowed
with millions of acres of easily accessible pine forests. In 1699
the observant Edward Randolph wrote the Board of Trade
that when he had been in New York he had believed himself
in the best area for the production of naval stores, "But since
my arrival here [South Carolina] I find I am come into the
only place for such Commodities upon the Continent of
America." [103] His judgment, of course, was confirmed by Byfield's interest in Carolina as a source for tar and pitch.
Parliament, however, had not guaranteed a profitable commodity. It had merely given a bounty sufficient to underwrite transportation costs for these bulky products. Techniques for manufacturing tar and pitch commercially were
not unknown in South Carolina, yet these had to be perfected. Still, this was one more hopeful development which
made the future of the province even brighter. No evidence
exists which indicates that naval stores were widely manufactured before 1705, and the few barrels produced earlier had
been shippped to the West Indies. Now naval stores could
possibly become a major product of the province.

  While commerce generally was expanding, the provisions
trade probably held its own, though there are no statistics to
substantiate that conclusion. Various attempts to regulate

  [103] Edward Randolph to Board of Trade, June 28, 1699, *BPRO-SC,* IV,
88–95.

this trade offer the best proof that South Carolinians continued to view it as important. In 1691 a statute was passed to stop "deceits" in the selling of barreled beef and pork and other commodities. Henceforth, South Carolinians were to ship their goods in standard-sized barrels of the same gallon content used by shippers in other colonies. Beef and pork were to be packed in 28-gallon barrels and tar and pitch in barrels of at least that size. All barrels were to be of seasoned wood and branded with the cooper's mark. Beef and pork were to be wholesome with no bull's flesh, boar's flesh, or other corrupt matter.[104] The general provisions of this act were renewed periodically thereafter. Abuses were never fully stopped by such laws. Former Governor Kendall of Barbados once reported to the proprietors that the South Carolinians packed their beef with "so much Carlessness or rather design" that the reputation of the province was damaged.[105]

Lumber and lumber products were also shipped, probably in greater quantities than previously, since this business seems to have been growing all through the colonial period. An interesting court case in 1705 shows the meager profits in this business to have been one reason for its slow development. John White and James Todd sued John Guerard, merchant, for £63 7s. 8¼d. current money allegedly due for 13,960 pipestaves and 2,097 pipe headings. These sold at the rate of £4 5s. per thousand for staves and £2 per thousand for headings, modest sums even for that time.[106] Small wonder that the forest offered little opportunity for business until the passage of the naval stores bounty act.

[104] Cooper and McCord (eds.) , *Statutes of S.C.,* II, 55–57.
[105] Proprietors to Governor Archdale, June 28, 1695, *BPRO-SC,* III, 159–160.
[106] Court of Common Pleas, Judgment Rolls, 1705–1706 (Documents in South Carolina Archives, Columbia, S.C.) , No. 536.

From 1690 to 1705 the usual references to experimental crops were plentiful. Cotton seems to have been widely tried, but nothing suggests that much was grown or shipped. Silk seems to have undergone a similar scrutiny.[107] Possibly the Huguenots were experimenting with it. In 1699 a sample of silk was sent to London,[108] and Randolph confirmed that it was being cultured at this time.[109] Hopes for these commodities did not lead to anything.

Vessel ownership and shipbuilding also reflect the growing strength and diversity of the economy. While South Carolinians never owned or built many vessels, it seems likely that they did own and build more from 1690 to 1705 than previously. Under the Navigation Act of 1696, all vessels had to be registered, and some of those registrations survive. The largest vessel owned locally was 50 tons burden, two others were 40 tons burden each, and several more were 30 tons or less. Since these registrations listed where vessels were built, it is possible to conclude that a small but continually active shipbuilding industry existed in the 1690's. In 1696 the sloop *Joseph of Carolina* was built; in 1697, the 30-ton *Sea Flower of Carolina;* in 1698, the sloop *Dorothy and Ann.*[110] Most of these were coasting vessels, incapable of undertaking the dangerous voyage to England. Yet it was possible to build larger ships in South Carolina by this time. In 1704 John White, shipwright, claimed that he had a contract with John Fenwick and John Severance, planters, to construct a vessel of 80 or 90 tons burden, with the width at the keel no greater

---

[107] For example, Governor Nathaniel Johnson to Board of Trade, September 17, 1708, *BPRO-SC,* V, 203–210.

[108] Proprietors to Sir Nathaniel Johnson, October 19, 1699, ibid., IV, 117.

[109] Edward Randolph to Board of Trade, May 27, 1700, ibid., IV, 189–190.

[110] Registrations were interspersed with other documents in "Wills and Miscellaneous Records, 1694–1704," (manuscript volume in South Carolina Archives, Columbia, S.C.) , 105–135.

than 50 feet nor less than 40 feet.[111] While this vessel was probably never built, the agreement would not have been made unless those entering into the contract thought that the province had, with the exception of a few items such as iron parts, all the necessary materials and the skilled builders. So strong was the pull toward the expanding agricultural endeavors that South Carolinians generally did not seem very interested in the possibilities of ship construction, despite the superior building materials at hand.

With all the signs of economic advancement for South Carolina between 1690 and 1705, such improvement in position must be kept in perspective. The changes seem greater than they really were, for the volume of trade until around 1690 had been so insignificant. The total export trade in 1705 was still confined to deerskins, a limited provisions trade, and a small, but growing, rice trade. While it is difficult to calculate, logically there is no way that this small export trade paid for what the South Carolinians had to import, particularly manufactured goods and costly slaves. The shortage of capital must have continued to be acute. Several questions remained to be answered in 1705. No one was sure how enumeration might affect the rice trade, and it was yet uncertain how rapidly, if at all, the South Carolinians would be able to take advantage of the naval stores bounties.

South Carolina may have been in the process of finding an economic foundation, of building a more sophisticated society, of losing its rougher edges, but much of the process was still to be finished in 1705. The great majority of white people were not a great deal better off than they had been a decade before. The Society for the Preservation of the Gos-

[111] Court of Common Pleas, Judgment Rolls, 1705–1707 (manuscript records in South Carolina Archives, Columbia, S.C.), No. 631.

pel in Foreign Parts sent its first missionaries to the province in 1707, and nearly all put remarks in their letters about the poverty of the great majority.[112] In the years ahead, the greatest opportunities for money-making were in enterprises requiring land and slaves. Nevertheless, with all their nagging doubts, most settlers in 1705 had concrete reasons for the first time to feel optimistic about the future.

[112] For example, Commissary Gideon Johnston to Lord Bishop of Sarum, September 20, 1708, Frank J. Klingberg (ed.), *Carolina Chronicle: The Papers of Commissary Gideon Johnston, 1707–1716* (Berkeley and Los Angeles, 1946), 19–30.

CHAPTER VI

An Expanding Economy
1705–1715

D URING THE DECADE FOLLOWING THE ENUMERATION OF RICE and the allowance of the first bounties on colonial naval stores, the province showed a rapid rate of economic growth. By 1715 South Carolina was booming as never before. While there is a lack of data to measure all configurations of this increased productivity, most of it was concentrated in rice, naval stores, and enlargement of the long-established deerskin trade. Early prophecies foretelling a great future for the province seemed about to be realized.

But thoughtful men in South Carolina were concerned about the bases of the provincial economy. The profitability of each of the three major export trades hinged on circumstances largely beyond the control of the settlers. Much of the rice shipped to England was re-exported to the continent, and one of the best markets was the Iberian Peninsula ports during the early spring months. Once rice was enumerated, merchants were automatically barred from this trade since it was impossible to ship the autumn's harvest to England for re-export to Spain and Portugal by early spring. No one is sure how much the loss of this outlet curtailed the total market for rice, but South Carolinians regarded this trade restriction as a great hardship. A successful naval stores trade depended upon developing techniques of manufacturing tar and pitch which would meet the quality requirements of the Royal Navy. Moreover, the bounty law had been put in for only ten years on an experimental basis, so full dependence on producing naval stores appeared risky in the long run. The deerskin trade was conducted in a volatile atmosphere, subject to quick change. Good relations with interior tribes to the south and west were essential. These good relations depended upon the ability of the South Carolinians to outbid the Spaniards and the French as the three groups vied for the friendship and trade of the tribes.

Fears about the future of rice and naval stores trade proved groundless between 1705 and 1715. Although rice production increased rapidly, markets were not saturated despite the prohibition to trade directly to Spain and Portugal. The experiment to subsidize production of naval stores in America proved successful enough for Parliament to continue the bounty until 1724, though grumblings from England about the poor quality of colonial naval stores never ceased. South Carolina had begun by 1715 to increase its shipments of tar and pitch to take advantage of the bounties. Despite a state of international war during most of the period from 1705 to 1715, South Carolinians were able to maintain their grip on the Indian trade and even to expand it in the face of constant competition.

Although several laws relating to the deerskin trade were passed, partisan politics made effective regulatory legislation impossible from 1705 to 1715.[1] All might agree that some regulation was necessary for the safety of the province, but this was one of several divisive and inflammatory issues in which personal prejudices and vested interests overruled

[1] This account of the political issues closely follows Sirmans, *Colonial South Carolina*, 89–93.

prudence. The proprietors had long since given up any pretense of controlling the trade, and their correspondence to the province after 1705 reflects minimal concern over trading conditions. Laws passed earlier purported to provide supervision for the Indian trade, but agencies created had no powers to stop evils in the trade. One sticking point was the manner in which the Indian trade was to be organized. One faction wanted a trade open to all. Another group desired a system of licensing which would close the trade to all but a few. If regulations were imposed, who would control the regulatory body? The governor, supported by the council, wanted to maintain his grip on the administrative machinery, but the lower house, already widening its authority, was demandng the right to supervise any new agency created. This was the first major confrontation between governor and commons.[2]

The controversy over regulation raged from the spring of 1706, when Governor Nathaniel Johnson requested action, until July 19, 1707, when a law was hammered out. Debate was acrimonious, full of charges and countercharges. Moreover, the central question was clouded by a number of minor but hotly disputed issues. One was the matter of gifts given annually by tribes as symbols of loyalty and friendship and traditionally kept by the governor for his personal use. Governor Johnson had no intention of losing these perquisites which, valued at several hundred pounds, were greater than his official salary. His opponents, led by Thomas Nairne, claimed that the governor was primarily interested in protecting the interests of his son-in-law, Colonel Thomas Broughton, an important and allegedly slippery Indian trader. The commons, pushing for a law which would create commissioners who would be answerable to them in running

---

[2] Crane, *Southern Frontier,* 146.

the trade, threatened to carry their case to the proprietors and, if necessary, the crown. They even advocated, briefly, the creation of a publicly held company to have exclusive right to the trade.

The compromise which was enacted represented a considerable victory for the Commons House which was able to siphon off certain powers previously belonging to governors. Under the 1707 law,[3] nine commissioners, holding office at the pleasure of the commons, were appointed to supervise the trade. They met each August and February to arbitrate disputes concerning conduct of the trade. Most important, an Indian agent was appointed and directed to live among the tribes for at least ten months of the year. He was to dispense justice between Indians and traders and traders and Charles Town merchants. He was given broad powers to insure that fair and amicable trading conditions were maintained. Only the commissioners were the agent's superior. Furthermore, annual licenses would be required for any trader, and these would be granted by the commissioners.

This law, along with a similar one passed in 1712,[4] should have brought order to the Indian trade and have guaranteed safety from Indian uprisings. But the laws failed. Thomas Nairne, bitter foe of Governor Johnson, was appointed Indian agent. Nairne did a good job under the circumstances.[5] Attempting to clean up abuses in the trade, the agent soon brought charges against Colonel Broughton, and the governor came to the defense of his son-in-law by having Nairne thrown in jail on a charge of treason. Though

[3] Cooper and McCord (eds.) , *Statutes of S.C.*, II, 309–316; for an explanation of the provisions of the act and its implications, see Crane, *Southern Frontier*, 148–153.

[4] Cooper and McCord (eds.) , *Statutes of S.C.*, II, 381. The editors could not find the text of the act, but this law appears to have been a continuation of the 1707 act.

[5] Crane, *Southern Frontier*, 152.

later exonerated of the trumped-up charge, Nairne was replaced as agent by John Wright, who has been judged "ineffective." [6] The licensing provision proved difficult to enforce. The trade continued to be unethical and cutthroat since the traders were not restrained.

Protecting the Indian trade from the Spaniards and French led to South Carolina's financial problems during this decade. The province spent proportionally large sums on military affairs. Some money went for defensive purposes. Fortifications were built in and around Charles Town to stop either land or sea invasions. [7] These proved their worth in 1706 when a Spanish invasion was repelled. Much of the money, however, went for aggressive actions taken by the provincial government against the Spaniards, French, and hostile tribes. Doubtless some of these involvements were necessary, and they were often justified as part of a larger struggle during Queen Anne's War in the colonies. Yet, South Carolinians often appeared to be more concerned with control of the deerskin trade than with the interests of the British Empire, though the two objectives were generally compatible. [8] Numerous, filibustering expeditions were undertaken solely to protect South Carolina's position in the backcountry. Some of these episodes cost dearly.

The provincial government bore the brunt of these expenses. The proprietors, who were now content to have the South Carolinians conduct and pay for their own defense, never vetoed their decisions. Given the weak condition of the plantation and its limited resources for fighting, it is amazing that South Carolina so readily took to the field against its

[6] Sirmans, *Colonial South Carolina*, 94.

[7] Several laws were passed between 1700 and 1709 relating to defensive measures for Charles Town and the province. Cooper and McCord (eds.), *Statutes of S.C.*, VII, 17–56.

[8] Crane concluded that interest in trade was the most important motivation. Crane, *Southern Frontier*, 137–161.

enemies. Such policy is indicative of the economic importance of the trade and the political power of the Indian traders. But war is an expensive habit, and the only way South Carolinians could meet the costs was to borrow against the future, to issue bills of credit which were to be retired by future taxes.

But these bills of credit, which were authorized ostensibly to meet military expenses, were vital to the economy for another reason. They provided a local money supply. Although the occasions for issuing paper money between 1703 and 1715 were related to the protection of South Carolina's interests in the backcountry, there was growing sentiment in the province to put bills of credit into circulation and to keep them in circulation as a useful currency to carry on business transactions within the province. This impetus culminated in the Bank Act of 1712, which created a semipermanent currency issued by the government but backed by private assets.

To understand how South Carolinians came to such a decision in 1712, one must remember that their financial problems, like those of most other English settlements in America, arose partly from the shortage of hard money throughout the colonial era.[9] There were several reasons for this shortage. Most persons coming to the colonies did not bring great quantities of sterling with them. Moreover, as in any undeveloped area with few trade items of local production, hard money in America soon flowed back to England to buy manufactured items. Even after a colony produced quantities of salable export items, the need for English goods

---

[9] The explanation of the money situation which follows owes much to Curtis P. Nettels, *The Money Supply of the American Colonies Before 1720* (*University of Wisconsin Studies in The Social Sciences and History,* Number 20) (Madison, 1934), 202–283.

remained great enough to prevent the colonists from tipping the balance of trade in their favor. South Carolina, whose planters invested all they had, or could borrow, in slaves, experienced an additional drain since slave traders sold on a cash basis.

England never made more than halfhearted attempts to provide a circulating medium for her American colonists, yet they remained tied to sterling as an absolute value. The pound sterling was the standard for all monetary exchange in English domains. Goods shipped to America by English merchants were originally priced in terms of sterling. American colonists, who might not see an English pound from one year to the next, had to determine prices or values in terms of sterling. Any local currency which might be devised had to be given some arbitrary value relative to sterling. Despite its pegged legal value, local currency generally had a different open market value which was determined by how much sterling it would buy. Merchants set this open market price when they accepted local currency in a certain ratio to sterling.

Various devices were tried to overcome this shortage of English money and provide a medium for local business. Every colony tried legalized barter quite early. Under this scheme, certain items of local production were given a specific value per unit. Sometimes items so designated were called commodity money or country pay. Wampum was commonly used in New England; tobacco in Maryland and Virginia. Barreled beef and pork, naval stores, staves, and rice were only a few of the goods designated as commodity money in South Carolina at various times. Payments in kind at legally pegged rates were accepted for taxes and other obligations to the colonial government. Objections to the use of commodity money were constant. The legal value of a given commodity could never be kept equal to the open market price. When items were bulky agricultural products, transactions were awkward. The obvious difficulties of this method of settling obligations made it at best a stopgap. Most colonies abandoned the system early. By the end of the proprietary period, South Carolina tax laws generally stated that payments were to be in money, although a law passed as late as 1719 did specify that quitrents due the proprietors could be paid in rice, tar, and pitch.[10]

Colonies also attempted to use foreign silver coins (mostly Spanish) as a local money supply. The worth of the silver in these coins was known, but because of competition to attract as much specie as possible, the coins were overvalued legally by colonial legislatures. These foreign coins, rated in terms of English shillings, were generally called "current money" or "current lawful money." Since the pegged rate was constantly being revised, the legal value of current money to sterling was particularly important to English merchants doing business with colonials. South Carolina consistently maintained one of the highest ratios. In 1701 it was 161:100, that is, it took £161 current money of South Carolina to buy £100 sterling.[11] This may have been one of the attractions Charles Town held for pirates, who were a major source of pieces of eight and other coins. In 1704 the Queen attempted by proclamation to stop competition among colonies for coins by pegging the exchange rate of foreign coins to sterling at 133⅓:100. Naturally enough, foreign coins so valued were known as "proclamation money." The proclamation was defied by the leading trading colonies including South Carolina, and in 1708 Parliament passed a law to enforce the proclamation. Again, the colonies refused to

[10] Cooper and McCord (eds.), *Statutes of S.C.*, III, 44–49.
[11] Ibid., II, 178. The editors list the title only, since the text is lost. However, Nettels, *Money Supply*, 241, sets this as the ratio.

adhere to the legal ratio. South Carolina maintained its 161:100 differential.[12]

With all their manipulations, the colonials still found it difficult to retain this form of hard money just as they could not retain sterling. It was cumbersome to do business in terms of foreign money. Besides, all hard money was drawn to England to pay off unfavorable ledger balances. Even without an unfavorable balance of trade, English monetary policies of the period would probably have prevented the colonists from keeping a supply of English money for commercial purposes. The export of English coins to the colonies was not allowed; the minting of coins in America or for use in America was opposed. Exploring other possibilites for a circulating medium, the colonial governments turned rather naturally to paper issues. From the start of settlement in all colonies, business had been carried on through endorsable personal promissory notes and bills of exchange. Finding themselves short of funds, colonial governments often authorized the issuance of promissory notes to pay the colony's debtors. These were generally short-term notes to be retired when taxes were next collected. South Carolina may have used this expedient in 1702.[13] Such borrowing against future tax collections educated the settlers to accept deficit financing and to recognize the advantages of these bills as commercially negotiable paper.

Starting in 1703 the government issued bills of credit to meet emergencies and provide funds for defense.[14] Each new enactment moved closer toward making bills of credit a permanent circulating medium. As noted earlier, the first issue bore interest of 12 per cent, a good return even in that day. In fact, some authorities think that the bills may have been hoarded for this reason. The issue was limited to

[12] Nettels, *Money Supply*, 248.   [13] Ibid., 251.
[14] Cooper and McCord (eds.), *Statutes of S.C.*, II, 206–212.

£6,000. The smallest notes were 50s.; the largest £20, indicating a degree of control of the paper. Since the first issue had been successful, in July 1707 the assembly authorized the issue of £8,000 of "new" bills of credit. These were to pay for fortifications, costs incurred when repelling the invasion by the Spaniards, as well as to retire the 1703 issue bills of credit still outstanding.[15] Denominations of the bills ranged from £1 to £20. These "new" bills were made legal tender for all future debts under 40s., with a penalty of double the debt for refusal. The wording is rather important: "That all and every the bills of credit made and established by this Act, shall be current for the sum or sums of money therein mentioned. . . ." It made bills of credit lawfully of equal value to current money, legal tender for small debts, and, by issuing bills in smaller denominations, encouraged their increased use in commerce.

After 1707 it became easier to use the fiat money device to meet the immediate needs of the province for funds.[16] Each law had provisions for retiring all bills of credit outstanding, but somehow new emergencies always arose which meant that more paper money had to be issued before the old was removed from circulation. In this way, at irregular intervals, the total amount of paper money in circulation was gradually increased. In the spring of 1708 more bills of credit were authorized to provide funds for defense against Indians.[17] The acts authorizing these bills did not make the issue legal tender. However, all the bills were to be in £1 and £2

[15] Ibid., II, 302–307.

[16] For more details about the confusing issues and reissues of paper currency, see Richard M. Jellison, "Paper Currency in Colonial South Carolina, 1703–1764" (unpublished Ph.D. dissertation, Indiana University, 1953); "An Account of the Rise and Progress of the Paper Bills of Credit in South Carolina, . . ." in Cooper and McCord (eds.), *Statutes of S.C.*, IX, 766–780 (William Bull, Sr., is generally listed as the probable author of this narrative); *An Essay on Currency, Written in August 1732* (Charles Town, 1734).

[17] Cooper and McCord (eds.), *Statutes of S.C.*, II, 324–327.

denominations, probably those most useful in local business transactions involving small amounts. The 1710 act said as much, pointing out in the preamble the "inconveiences which hath happened through the want of smaller bills of credit." [18] This £3,000 issue was to consist of 8,000 five-shilling notes and 2,000 ten-shilling notes. The Act also specified that these small bills would be "tender in law" and "current" for the sum or sums mentioned for debts of 40s. or less. Bills were now, more than ever before, serving a business purpose. Moreover, each new issue increased the total number of bills as well as the total amount in circulation. This made it less and less likely that all the outstanding bills could be retired in the foreseeable future given the province's weak tax base.

There is evidence that before the Bank Act of 1712 bills issued had not depreciated seriously. In fact, a committee of the assembly in 1711 recommended payment of the province's debt by emitting £40,000 in bills of credit.[19] Since the majority of the committee was made up of prominent Charles Town merchants (Benjamin Godin, William Gibbon, Alexander Parris, and Samuel Wragg), it is hardly likely that serious depreciation existed at that time. Before this drastic expedient could be instituted, however, the Tuscarora War broke out in 1711 in North Carolina, requiring South Carolina's military support and, of course, more bills of credit.[20] South Carolina's outlay to aid her sister province added to the province's growing financial crisis. Until 1712 confidence in the South Carolina government to retire the bills out of future tax revenue kept the value of the bills of credit quite high in proportion to the value of hard money.[21] Yet, if the total in circulation were to be increased drasti-

---

[18] Ibid., II, 352–354.   [19] Jellison, "Paper Currency," 55–57.
[20] Cooper and McCord (eds.), *Statutes of S.C.,* II, 366.
[21] Jellison, "Paper Currency," 46.

cally, as it was in 1712, confidence could be impaired, particularly among the merchants.

The Bank Act of 1712,[22] arising out of pressing financial problems, is, nonetheless, the logical culmination of a decade of experience with paper money. Although the law was passed to raise funds to pay off provincial obligations, it was also to create for the first time a semipermanent circulating medium for internal commerce. Of the total of £52,000 authorized for emission, £16,000 would be used to exchange old bills (previous issues) for the new, £4,000 would be held for governmental contingencies, and £32,000 was to be "lent at interest." Of the several earlier issues, only the Tuscarora bills (£4,000 of these) were left in circulation. This enactment would give South Carolina a total of £56,000 currency for circulation.[23]

Anyone wishing some of this paper money could contract to borrow at least £100 but no more than £300 from the government. The borrower secured the bills by bonds or mortgages on his own land or slaves in double the amount borrowed. Bills were to be retired in 12 years by having the borrower pay back annually one-twelfth of the principal, plus 12½ per cent interest on the balance. The scheme not only gave the government means to meet its immediate obligations, but interest payments promised considerable profit to the province over the 12 years. These loans appeared secure, since land and slaves were the best collateral that the country offered. This general method of backing paper issues, sometimes called a "land bank" scheme, was used at various times in many other American colonies, though frowned on by English authorities.[24]

Since the bills were negotiable and were made legal tender

[22] Cooper and McCord (eds.), *Statutes of S.C.*, IX, 759–765.
[23] Bull, Sr., "Account of Bills of Credit," ibid., IX, 769–770.
[24] Andrews, *Colonial Period of American History*, IV, 350–351.

for all debts, the Bank Act was fraught with economic and political implications. Not only did the Act provide a large supply of circulating paper, but for the first time required acceptance of this paper money at face value for all debts, including the larger commercial transactions which had not been touched by previous enactments. If, as before 1712, the issue had been small in total amount, land and slaves might have been sufficient security, but the magnitude of the debt of the provincial government and its ability to retire the paper issue on schedule were soon in question. The open market exchange ratio between South Carolina bills of credit and sterling rapidly widened. In 1710 South Carolina currency was exchanged at 3 for 2; £150 South Carolina bills of credit to £100 sterling. After 1712 the ratio quickly changed to 3 to 1 and perhaps to as much as 4 to 1.[25] By 1715 there does not seem to have been a further decline.

With the weakening of the open market value of South Carolina bills of credit, creditors (generally English merchants) with open accounts saw outstanding debts cut in proportion to the fall in value of the legal tender bills of credit. Debtors could pay off obligations in bills of credit which were worth only a fraction of their face value when converted to sterling. Protests from merchants claiming to have been defrauded of lawful obligations started at once, and their petitions flowed into the Board of Trade for years afterwards. The proprietors who took note of the act and the protests speculated in their correspondence to the province that if paper issues were not controlled, the crown would disallow this law and prevent passage of other currency acts.[26]

It is difficult to know exactly how great the impact of this

[25] Jellison, "Paper Currency," 65–66.
[26] Proprietors to Governor and Council, September 8, 1714, BPRO-SC, VI, 69.

law was on the province and its commerce. Circumstances would suggest that merchants did not lose as much as they tried to make everyone believe, and debtor planters did not gain as much as many hoped they might. No doubt, the act immediately made winners and losers, as currency manipulations always do, but the process was not a continuous one. English merchants had factors in South Carolina who adjusted prices so that transactions kept abreast of fluctuations in the exchange ratio. Merchants also may have tended to price goods higher after 1712 to be sure to have a greater margin as a hedge against future declines in the value of the paper. To benefit local debtors continually, inflation of the South Carolina currency would have had to be more frequent than it was before 1715. The great fear of the merchant community must have been that the Bank Act was the prelude to more drastic monetary legislation.

Despite the furor it caused and the evidence of some real impact, it is almost impossible to show that the Bank Act curtailed South Carolina's economic growth. It would be difficult to prove that any great number of merchants were ruined or that English merchants refused to trade to the colony for fear that they would be losers. The contrary seems true. If some merchants decided to curtail their operations, others would have welcomed the easy entree into the trade of an expanding colony. In fact, it was about this time that South Carolina began to have an important group of resident merchants, many apparently arriving in these trying years. Whatever instability the Bank Act caused, commerce was unchecked as far as can be determined. Perhaps the Bank Act actually encouraged economic growth because it provided not only money for a circulating medium, but funds so "borrowed" fed speculation in land and slaves, the two essentials for participating in the rising agricultural businesses of this province.

Note should be taken that the emergence of this strong,

specialized merchant class between 1705 and 1715 was important politically as well as economically. The natural concern within the merchant community over the issuance of paper money brought the group to the fore as a political force. Until recently, however, historians have assumed that all merchants (supposedly creditors) were opposed to paper currency on principle. Fortunately, this view has been sharply modified of late, and it has been recognized that the merchants did not coalesce into a monolithic bloc.[27] Unfortunately, lack of personal papers and full biographical information about individuals makes it difficult to account for the positions of these men regarding paper money legislation. It is indisputable, nevertheless, that not all merchants were adamantly against bills of credit; some apparently did not object to their issuance.

The reason for these divisions in the merchant community must be related to the diversity of the group, the backgrounds of the individuals, and the various financial and investment interests represented. These considerations influenced positions to various degrees, but we do not know exactly which consideration was topmost in the value system of each man. Andrew Allen and William Gibbon were partners. They are always designated as merchants, but they had wide investments in vessels and they owned a 3,000-acre plantation.[28] They may have been generally favorable to reasonable amounts of paper money, or at least did not join the protesters.[29] Benjamin de la Conseillere and Benjamin Godin were also partners with wide investments, but they

[27] For example, Sirmans, *Colonial South Carolina,* 110–111.
[28] Agreement between Andrew Allen and William Gibbon made May 1, 1722. Recorded: March 18, 1724. Miscellaneous Records, 1722–1726 (Manuscript volume in South Carolina Archives, Columbia, S.C.) , 249–252.
[29] Their names are conspicuously absent from the petitions of merchants dated from 1712 into the 1720's. Governor Nicholson, no staunch opponent of bills of credit, portrayed Allen as his friend. Francis Nicholson to William Hammerton, August 22, 1726, BPRO-SC, XII, 136; Sirmans, *Colonial South Carolina,* 147.

opposed paper money issues with a vehemence.[30] Other merchants signed every petition for years which was sponsored by opponents of South Carolina financial statutes.

Three general groups of merchants emerged with motivations for their positions. There were those who might be designated England-oriented or export-import merchants, men who sometimes came to the province to trade, but were hardly classified as residents. Some were factors for English mercantile houses. Most had no intention of remaining in the province permanently. They had no investments locally and little concern except for their trade interests. These men probably were a large proportion of all men trading from Charles Town, and almost without exception they opposed paper money. Even their petitions imply that they are traders to the province, not residents of it.[31]

Other merchants were South Carolina-oriented, men who had long lived in the province and were permanent residents though engaged in overseas trade. Some may have started out as local planters, then branched out to make trade their major emphasis. All in this category had ties to the soil, for few entrepreneurs of this era specialized to the extent that they would not take advantage of an agricultural boom. They might correctly be called merchant-planters. As local men, they were sensitive, perhaps for diplomatic reasons in part, to the local point of view, and they understood the problems of planters since they, too, had invested extensively in land. This local orientation caused men such as Allen, Gibbon, and others to appear to go against what would be the logical merchant position, but they were certainly not jousting against their own over-all best interests.

[30] They signed most merchant petitions in this period. Sirmans, *Colonial South Carolina*, 110, 138, 147.

[31] "The Memorial of the Merchants . . . in Behalf of Themselves and Several Merchants of Great Britain Who Trade to and have Considerable Effects in This Province" (about 1722), BPRO-SC, IX, 179–190.

But such theorizing has its problems. One must account for the adamant opposition to paper issues by such as Conseillere and Godin. They certainly qualified as local merchants who were very prominent. Conseillere, in particular, was a member of the council and held other posts for years. Their opposition appears to have been rooted in the type of investments they had. They were primarily traders. They were money lenders in a society without banks.[32] In this positon, they were much more vulnerable to being ruined by depreciated currency. One suspects that some other local merchants may also have had their reasons for joining their English friends in petitions and letters protesting the action of the assembly. While any simple anatomization of a complicated situation is dangerous, perhaps someday the evidence now uncovered may be pieced together to give a more sharply focused picture of the merchant community and the reasons why it fragmented as it did in reaction to paper money. Despite recent modifications, the central fact remains that the majority of merchants trading to and from Charles Town, whether Charles Town residents or transients from England, were opposed in varying degrees to the bills of credit. Their opposition was a new force which had vast influence on the economic future of the province.

While the proprietors remained aloof and uninvolved in the paper money controversy and most other local political matters, they continued to reveal their lack of managerial skill and understanding of their own best interests. In the fight over establishment of the Anglican Church culminating in 1706, proprietary assent to an act railroaded through by the Anglicans under Governor Johnson alienated perhaps half the colony's white population.[33] Many dissenters re-

[32] Based on a survey of the Court of Common Pleas, Judgment Rolls. It is doubtful if any individuals initiated more actions to recover loans than Conseillere and Godin from 1705 to 1720.

[33] Wallace, *History of S.C.*, I, 171.

garded this act as a breach of faith between proprietors and settlers, and they threatened a mass exodus if excluded from participation in government.[34] Because of effective lobbying by their agent, Joseph Boone, in London, the original law was disallowed by the House of Lords. The new establishment act passed did not give the Church of England party all that it hoped, but it did give the Church a special relationship to the government, including financial support. The failure to exclude dissenters from political life, however, allowed the dispute to subside into an uneasy armistice between the factions. Only when Governor Craven assumed office in 1712 did the matter recede from political importance as other questions became more pressing. A serious religious crisis which could have disrupted the economy as well as other aspects of the province's life was averted, despite proprietary bungling.[35]

From 1705 to 1715 the proprietors mostly affected the economy through their land policy. Even if they had begun to surrender their once exclusive sway in this area before 1705, they did not bow completely to the will of the people and its assembly. In contrast to the alterations in the land system between 1690 and 1705, basic policies were not changed as drastically after 1705. The two basic avenues to obtaining land remained open. Purchase at the rate of £20 current money per 1,000 acres was one method and the other was by claiming a headright of 50 acres for each adult immigrant, white or black. Since some land purchases were made in England, the proprietors may have made some money in this way. Most lands, however, continued to be obtained by headrights.[36]

[34] Rivers, *Sketch of History of S.C.*, 230.
[35] For more details, see Sirmans, *Colonial South Carolina*, 96–100.
[36] This is the generally accepted conclusion of historians; however, Thomas Nairne, *A Letter From South Carolina*, 43, says that most purchased their lands.

The proprietors were mostly concerned with collecting their elusive quitrents. They needed the funds to pay the salaries of their appointees in South Carolina which amounted to £610 sterling annually by 1708.[37] They requested several times that a rent roll be prepared to list property granted, the owners, and quitrents due. In 1708, they were hoping that the assembly would pass a law to help with the collection process.[38] These pleas were not honored. Even their own appointees, who supposedly represented the proprietors' interests, seldom obeyed directives in this matter. Nathaniel Sale, who became Receiver General in 1709, reported that his predecessor had not collected the hundreds of pounds of quitrents past due and that there was no quitrent roll.[39]

As a result of the evasion of quitrent payments, the proprietors moved to curtail land sales and headright grants. In 1709 they ordered that neither grants nor sales of land exceeding 640 acres should be made without special warrant or license from them.[40] In 1713 a further restriction allowed land sales but at the expensive price of £10 sterling per 500 acres with a 500-acre per warrant limit.[41] Fearing that the proprietors might move to repossess land granted but undeveloped or land upon which the quitrents had not been paid, the assembly passed a statute in 1712 specifying that any land title which was "without lawful interruption" for over seven years could not be legally forfeited.[42] This law, clearly a challenge to proprietary prerogatives, was not vetoed.

[37] "The Charge of the Civill List," marked received April 22, 1706, *BPRO-SC*, V, 151.
[38] Proprietors to William Saunders, undated but probably December 11, 1708, ibid., V, 218–221.
[39] Nathaniel Sale to Proprietors, September 28, 1709, ibid., V, 300–303.
[40] Proprietors to Deputies and Council, April 9, 1709, ibid., V, 271–274.
[41] Proprietors to unspecified addressee, August 21, 1713, ibid., VI, 56.
[42] Cooper and McCord (eds.), *Statutes of S.C.*, II, 583–588.

The land records surviving do suggest that the tightening of rules to limit the size of grants had some effect after 1712. The settlers, however, had been busy for several years polishing up their claims. Available records show that at least 320 grants representing almost 152,000 acres were made from 1710 through 1712. The only comparable earlier period of land granting seems to have been from 1695 to 1697, when activity was brisk after Governor Archdale's reforms. From 1706 through 1715 remaining records include at least 427 grants totaling over 198,000 acres, including some in Granville County (area between the Combahee and Savannah Rivers).[43] Since we can be reasonably sure that at least this much land was granted, proprietary rules did not stand in the way of agricultural, therefore commercial, development of South Carolina in this period. After 1712, however, some individuals may have been unable to obtain large grants.

While the proprietors had been concerned with shaping the economy of their province from the beginning, by 1705 their influence in this area had declined sharply. They did not completely forget this function which had supposedly been reserved for them. From time to time, they commented on economic matters. In 1711 their instructions to newly appointed Governor Charles Craven included orders to establish a fishery, promote trade, enforce the imperial trade

[43] Table II, Appendix. Exactly when Granville County came into being as a legal entity is difficult to determine. The proprietors, as was their right under their charter, had designated the names and boundaries of the first three counties created about 1682; however, the first mention of Granville County in their directives is in 1711, in their instructions to Governor Craven (BPRO-SC, VI, 43–46). Yet, the earliest statute recognition of the county came in 1712, when St. Helena parish was designated as consisting of the area "commonly called by the name of Granville county" (Cooper and McCord (eds.), *Statutes of S.C.*, II, 372). This wording suggests that the title was used, and had been for some time, for a specific area, but the designation had never been made official. This view is substantiated by surviving land grants which show that land was obtained in Granville County as early as 1705.

acts, and found a port at Port Royal where naval stores might be loaded.[44] Beaufort was the town founded, but it is doubtful whether the proprietary actually created the town or determined its site. Granville County had been filling with people for some time, and the town may have already been in existence before 1711. Beaufort did not grow rapidly, never rivaled Charles Town in trade, and was not a factor in the colony's trade until after 1730. The proprietors could not give momentum or direction to the economy; that was being supplied by the settlers as they pursued the opportunities then available.

Nowhere is the waning of proprietary power more obvious than in the matter of recruitment of settlers. In 1709 they wrote that they would encourage German Palatines to migrate to Carolina, and they backed up their promise by offering 100 acres to each immigrant.[45] This was about the extent of their promotional activity during the ten years. Those Palatines who did come ended up in North Carolina, and South Carolina was left with the task of doing its own recruiting.

The provincial government did what it could to seek white immigrants for the province. It was essential to offset the growing slave population which might soon be in such imbalance that the feared slave revolt could become a reality. The South Carolina government continued to experiment with financial inducements to stimulate importation of indentured servants. There was a basic unwillingness to take the second step and limit slave importations, given the local view about slave labor. A 1706 act, repealed soon after passage, had such a low tax rate on slaves that it appears to have been more of a revenue measure than regulation

[44] Instructions for Governor Craven, about April 1711, BPRO-SC, VI, 19–38, 40–42; Instructions for Governor Craven, June 6, 1711, ibid., VI, 43–46.
[45] Proprietors to Governor Tynte, November 3, 1709, ibid., V, 304–305.

through high taxation.[46] The only approach to the dilemma which was politically feasible was to keep the number of slaves within what was judged to be a controllable proportion to the total population, by increasing the rate of white immigration.

Under a law passed in 1712,[47] the Public Receiver was authorized to pay £14 current money to the importers or to owners of "healthy male British" servants between the ages of 12 and 30 as soon as these servants were delivered to the Public Receiver. Servants obtained in this way were to have their terms of service sold to make the greatest profit for the province. Importers were to certify that each servant had not been in jail or produce a certificate from a magistrate in England declaring that the servant was not a criminal. The penalty for importing a servant from Newgate or any other English jail was specified in the statute. Servants were to be sold to serve four years if 16 or older or until 21 years of age if under 13. Only £300 was appropriated to purchase contracts of servants offered to the Public Receiver, though the wording of the statute implied that expected profits from sales would keep a sufficient fund available.

Of course, the basic headright was in effect for all white immigrants who arrived. Thomas Nairne's publicity pamphlet published in 1710 sang the praises of the area.[48] At best, these diverse efforts had limited success. All population statistics indicate only a modest white population growth from all types of immigration between 1705 and 1715. No organized groups arrived to swell the total dramatically, and the province gained new people only in driblets as had been the case for some years.

As a result of the failure to entice large numbers of whites

[46] Cooper and McCord (eds.), *Statutes of S.C.*, II, 280.
[47] Ibid., II, 385–389.
[48] Thomas Nairne, *A Letter From South Carolina.*

and the reluctance to curb slave importations, the slave population became greater than the free populaton during the years from 1708 to 1715. Population statistics for 1715 vary considerably, but the general range is from 6,250 to about 7,500 whites. Several estimates for 1715 indicate 1,400 or 1,500 fighting men, which supports the 6,000 to 7,500 counts, if each fighting man represented four or five others as is commonly estimated. This was a net gain of about 50 per cent for the white population since 1708. On the other hand, the Negro slave population of 4,100 in 1708 had at least doubled to 8,000; one estimate goes as high as 16,000 and another is 10,500. Both seem out of line, since a more trustworthy count in 1720 placed the total number of slaves at 11,828.[49] Slave importations from 1706 through 1714 amounted to at least 1,161.[50] An arbitrary guess would place the total population of South Carolina at about 15,000 by 1715. Probably the 1705–1715 period showed the most sustained population growth the province had yet experienced, the most of the additions were slaves. In 1708, Governor Johnson had placed the ratio of blacks to whites at 1:1; by 1715 that ratio may have been changed to 4:3 or even to 3:2.

The growth and expansion between 1705 and 1715 occurred in the face of the usual catastrophes of the era. In 1711 and 1712 "pleurisies" struck, and 300 or 400 slaves died, along with great numbers of whites.[51] In the fall of 1711 smallpox, fevers, and flux all reported to be raging. Commissary Gideon Johnston judged that 1711 was the worst year for diseases since settlement started.[52] In 1712 an act was passed to control diseases brought from Africa and

[49] For a collection of estimates, see Greene and Harrington, *American Population Before 1790*, 173–174; Table I, Appendix.

[50] *Historical Statistics of United States*, 770 (Series Z 303) .

[51] Waring, *History of Medicine in South Carolina*, 24.

[52] Duffy, "Eighteenth-Century Carolina Health Conditions," *Jour. So. Hist.*, XVIII (1952) , 298–299.

elsewhere by providing for such measures as the inspection of incoming vessels for contagious diseases and the right to confine sick persons to the pest house; these steps doubtless were of only limited effect.[53] The third major hurricane struck in 1713, with the loss of 70 persons by drowning and great damage to buildings. Much of the fury of the storm was experienced in Charles Town and north of the city.[54] Such discouragements were, at most, temporary checks.

While Charles Town itself was growing as the commercial center of the province, much of the area being developed after 1705 was to its south and west, the area designated Colleton County. It figured increasingly in the political alignments, for many of its residents were dissenters. They also were active in support of Thomas Nairne, the first Indian agent, in his fight with Governor Johnson. The surviving land grants show that this county was second only to Berkeley County in the number of grants and total acreage granted between 1705 and 1715. Craven and Granville counties were only gradually starting to draw settlers at this time.[55] While it is not practical to plot the pattern of this growth, the proprietary interest in founding a town on Port Royal in the 1710–1712 period pointed to the rising prominence of this general area. Settlers coming in, however, did not form a large population center, but located widely over the country in search of the best land.

Though over-all growth of the economy was rapid from 1705 to 1715, the deerskin trade continued to be the single most valuable commercial activity. Aided by the regulatory act of 1707 and a fundamental change in its conduct, the Indian trade accelerated during this ten-year span. The

---

[53] Cooper and McCord (eds.), *Statutes of S.C.*, II, 382–385.
[54] Ludlum, *Early American Hurricanes*, 42–43.
[55] Table II, Appendix.

change was made inevitable by the destruction of the tribes near Charles Town, the pressure of whites for lands near Charles Town, and the necessity of trading with distant tribes to obtain skins. Once, almost any planter lived close to Indians and could participate in this trade as a lucrative sideline. Now anyone trading for deerskins had to go far into the interior, and spend much time among the Indians who killed the deer and dressed the skins. The necessity of making the trek to the interior converted the Indian trade into a specialized form of commerce, a demanding business enterprise which required increasing amounts of capital. A man who was primarily a planter found himself stretched financially to his limit buying land and slaves. Ordinarily, he had no extra money to tie up in trading goods and could not leave his fields for long periods of time.

As the planter was eliminated from participation in the Indian trade, the emerging merchant community was able to seize the opportunities presented. Some of these early important merchants were of local origins, perhaps having started as planters dabbling in the deerskin trade as a sideline. Others came to the province to engage in the growing trade of a growing colony. All of any consequence had to have strong connections in England to dispose of deerskins, rice, naval stores, and other exports; in turn, they had to depend on their English correspondents to keep a steady flow of manufactured goods headed toward Charles Town. Some of the active South Carolina merchant groups at this time included the partnership of Andrew Allen and William Gibbon, the partnership of Benjamin Godin and Benjamin de la Conseillere, Samuel Eveleigh and his associates, Samuel Wragg acting for his uncle who remained in England most of the time, Charles Hill and Company, and Walter Lougher, who appears to have been the only one with Bristol connections.[56] Probably all participated in all export trades, but some concentrated more on one trade than another. Samuel Eveleigh is generally credited with being the leading dealer in deerskins.[57]

If a majority were involved in the deerskin trade, practically none went to the Indian villages to do the actual bartering for skins.[58] Some merchants may never have gone into the backcountry in their entire lives. Instead, with this reorientation or reorganization of the trade, they acted as underwriters for the traders. One common method of doing business was for the merchant to hire traders at wages and supply them with trading goods. In another arrangement, the merchant supplied trading goods on credit to traders, but the traders bartered on their own. Under the latter method, the traders and the merchant settled accounts at the end of the year.

Under either of these general methods of doing business, it was the trader, his helpers, and his assistants, who went to live at an appointed place in the wilderness to barter with a certain tribe or group of tribes. These men, numbering at most 400 in a given year and sometimes as few as 100, took the risks and spent much of their lives in a savage culture. Generally described as being the poorer sort, rough, ready, crude, profane, they were called by adventure but often were lured to death rather than to profits. Yet it was this sort of man who was supposed to treat the Indians fairly and cement their friendship to the South Carolina side in the competition with the Spaniards and French. The expectation that men of this stripe would serve the best interests of

[56] Clowse, "The Charleston Export Trade, 1717–1737," 113–114, 116–126, 280–290; Sirmans, *Colonial South Carolina*, 104–105; Crane, *Southern Frontier*, 120–121.

[57] Crane, *Southern Frontier*, 121–122.

[58] See ibid., particularly 108–136, for a detailed account of the conduct of the trade.

the province seems naive, but a large segment of the province's trade and its safety depended on their conduct.

Common recognition that abuses in the Indian trade were present and that they were dangerous brought on the regulatory act of 1707. Ineffective though this enactment turned out to be, it has been used as the dividing line between an Indian trade conducted informally and a regularized commerce with licenses and standards.[59] While not eliminating abuses, this systematized trade forced the completion of the transition from haphazard bartering carried on by planters and opportunists to a business carried on by professionals. The assignment of posts among the tribes tended to disperse the traders ever more widely and aided South Carolina's backcountry expansion. The form of business relationships worked out at this time shaped the Indian trade until the end of the colonial era.

Having formalized the commerce generally, the South Carolina merchants and Indian traders were able to increase dramatically the volume of skins exported from Charles Town between 1705 and 1715. These new arrangements enabled them to take fuller advantage of the trading link which had been forged to the Creeks in the 1690's. The increase was registered despite Queen Anne's War, skirmishes with their enemies, and even the Spanish invasion of 1706, and despite potentially negative influences, such as the taxes on deerskins exported and competition from Virginia-based traders. In the long run, South Carolinians fought the Virginia traders successfully. As South Carolina's share of the trade increased, Virginia's share declined.[60] Since regulations were ineffective, this booming trade grew in an atmosphere of greed by the whites and resentments among the red men.

[59] Ibid., 120.   [60] Ibid., 154–157.

The total number of deerskins shipped from 1706 through 1715 was an astonishing 587,465, according to one accounting. This would be an average of over 58,000 annually as compared to 45,000 average annual export from 1699 to 1705. In 1707 a record of some sort must have been set when 121,355 skins were shipped. Yet, this quantity is easily accounted for by noting that only 43,243 were shipped in the two previous years. From 1709 to 1715 the trade seems to have reached a sort of plateau, though the 1711–1712 figures show the upsetting effect of the Tuscarora War.[61] Since shipments were up 30 per cent in an average year of the 1706 to 1715 period, as compared to the annual average for the years 1699 to 1705, it must be assumed that the gross value and profits of the trade were up proportionally. The traders, at least some of them, must also have made money from selling Indian slaves since this was a wartime period. The dimensions of the slave trade are unknown. Governor Johnson reported 1,400 Indian slaves in 1708, but only 350 in 1703.[62] Traffic must have been brisk in the intervening years.[63] The exact economic impact of this Indian slave trade is part of the larger riddle of the financial structure of the Indian trade.

It was not, however, the Indian trade which had given the average person in South Carolina hope for a better future after 1705, but the twin opportunities presented by rice and naval stores as marketable commodities. It was production of these two commodities that brought dispersal of settlers seek-

[61] Table III, Appendix; the same figures are also used by Crane, *Southern Frontier*, 328.

[62] Governor Nathaniel Johnson and Council to Proprietors, September 17, 1708, *BPRO-SC*, V, 203–210.

[63] Many references in the records allude to Indian slaves and an Indian slave trade in this period. For example, Cooper and McCord (eds.), *Statutes of S.C.*, II, 634–641. This reference is to a law passed in early 1716 having to do with disposing of Indians taken during the Yamasee War.

ing suitable lands and sole reliance on slavery as the answer to the labor shortage. To buy necessary land and slaves, South Carolinians invested whatever they could scrape together. As settlers for the first time began to generate appreciable amounts of wealth from tilling the soil rather than from the Indian trade, some men could in truth be characterized as large planters, men who owned and worked large plots.

Though production problems persisted, by the early years of the eighteenth century, South Carolinians were successfully planting, growing, harvesting, and preparing rice for market. In rice culture, innovations which might speed threshing, particularly, were still being sought. In a rare reference to economic matters after 1705, the proprietors urged the assembly in 1709 to work for the improvement of "manufactures," especially rice and silk.[64] In 1712 a financial reward was offered by provincial statute to the man who would invent an improved rice mill.[65] Nevertheless, enough years had now elapsed between introduction of the crop and build-up of seed rice, opening of lands, and obtaining and training a slave labor supply to permit expansion of this commerce as rapidly as South Carolina's planters could accomplish it. Statistics prove that hundreds of acres had to be planted in rice by 1705.

Though the records of rice exportation give conflicting evidence on the rapidity of production increase, all sets of figures agree that production accelerated sharply after 1705. All figures have built-in weaknesses. Exports in terms of barrels, compiled by naval officers, are missing until 1717. Even when exports are given in terms of barrels, there is always doubt about how much a barrel contained.[66] The

---

[64] Proprietors to Deputies and Council, April 9, 1709, *BPRO-SC*, V, 271–274.
[65] Cooper and McCord (eds.) , *Statutes of S.C.*, II, 385–389.
[66] See Footnote 93, Chapter V.

Inspector General of Customs kept records of imports into England starting in 1698, but these only record rice imported into England, an unknown fraction of the total exported from Charles Town. Moreover, the Inspector General's books were put together by using set values and rules of thumb which make these figures of questionable worth.[67] As a result of these deficiencies, only the drift of rice production and export can be substantiated by consulting these various compilations.

The fragmentary records available suggest that rice exports jumped from approximately 2,000 barrels in 1700, to over 12,000 barrels in a 12-month span in 1712–1713, to about 15,000 barrels by 1715.[68] The Inspector General's records of imports of rice into Great Britain, based on poundage, convert to no more than 9,000 barrels in 1713, the leading year for imports between 1706 and 1715.[69] This set of records obviously does not reflect all exports from Charles Town. While this pattern indicates South Carolina's growing commitment to rice, the rice industry was in its infancy. By 1715 the province was only exporting perhaps 8 per cent or 10 per cent as much as it was to export 50 or 60 years later, on the eve of the American Revolution.[70] It must be pointed out that export figures do not take into account the amount of rice consumed locally, sometimes estimated to be as much as 10 per cent of the total crop.[71] To reach an approximation

[67] See Footnote 96, Chapter V.

[68] Table III, Appendix. Given the 1712–1713 exports this seems a reasonable estimate.

[69] Computed by dividing gross poundage by an average barrel of 350 pounds. Gross poundage from *Historical Statistics of United States,* 768 (Series Z 274–280).

[70] Even allowing for a gradual increase in the size of rice barrels, this conclusion seems valid. See the Table cited in Footnote 69 above for rice exports for the entire colonial era.

[71] Gray, *History of Agriculture,* I, 287.

of actual production, exports must be increased to some degree.

It is difficult to prove that enumeration had an adverse effect on the rice market before 1715, although South Carolinians thought that it did. No testimony on this point is more eloquent than the law passed in December 1712 which appointed Abel Kettleby as the province's agent in Great Britain. A portion of his pay was set, but the balance would depend on his effectiveness as a lobbyist. If he obtained a continuation of the bounties on naval stores, he would be paid an additional £150 current money; if he got Parliament to lift the prohibition on shipping rice directly to ports south of Cape Finisterre, he would be paid an additional £500.[72] Since the rice market in England had not been oversupplied in view of the quantities of future exports, the only thing that may have been hurt was the price of rice, owing to the loss of a competitive market.

If enumeration did depress the selling price, profits remained high. Despite few quotations, the demand for rice apparently was fairly steady in this period. Governor Robert Johnson in 1721 reported that rice sold for 18s. sterling per hundredweight.[73] Other quotations place rice prices within range of his figure.[74] If the price were fairly consistently at this level, or even quite a bit below, the 12,727 barrels shipped in 1712–1713 could have brought £40,000 sterling or more gross price. Profits were only a fraction of the gross sales figure. Nevertheless, rice continued to be the most important agricultural commodity exported and at least equal

[72] Cooper and McCord (eds.), *Statutes of S.C.*, II, 600–602.
[73] "An Account of the Net Produce of Rice Shipped Off . . . 1721 and 1731," referred to in Governor Johnson's letter, December 16, 1731, BPRO-SC, XV, 69–71.
[74] For example, Francis Yonge to Alured Popple, December 10, 1722, ibid., IX, 170–171. Yonge says that rice had fallen from 25s. per barrel a few years before to 15s. in 1722.

to deerskins in total monetary value in the over-all economy. Rice was, of course, more important to more people than the deerskin trade.

It is fairly safe to assert that the increase in rice culture was mainly responsible for the rapid growth of the slave population up to the year 1715. A "common computation" in the eighteenth century was that each field hand should produce about a ton of marketable rice annually.[75] If this rule of thumb were applicable to the 1715 situation, every five or six barrels of rice exported represented the labor of one field hand. On this basis, a minimum of 3,500 slaves were engaged full-time in rice growing, as opposed to perhaps 500 in 1700. While such figuring must be used cautiously, the demand for slaves for the rice fields had to be sharp since many slaves in this period must have worked primarily to clear and ready new rice lands for cultivation.

With the expansion of rice culture were simultaneous moves by enterprising individuals to take advantage of the bounty act on naval stores. While some naval stores had been prepared in the province since the start of settlement, there were techniques of processing which had to be worked out before commercial production could be undertaken in earnest. The exact nature of these difficulties and their solution have been obscured but probably account for the gradual rise of exports of naval stores rather than any sudden flood of these commodities being shipped to England. Regardless of the sequence of steps taken to overcome manufacturing problems, settlers soon found that tar and pitch making was particularly suited to the South Carolina situation. The area had vast forests of longleaf pine trees. The work which could be done in summer as well as winter was often carried on whenever there was a lull in the rice planting

---

[75] *American Husbandry*, I, 395. This source says that each hand made 4½ barrels of rice with each barrel averaging 400 to 500 pounds.

routine. It was also work which could use many unskilled hands, with any necessary judgments being made by a few trained men.

As it developed in South Carolina, tar and pitch manufacture was a crude process.[76] Necessary facilities were easily and rapidly constructed, requiring few special materials or tools. Tar was made in a kiln where the pine wood was heated to extract the resinous materials from it. The kiln was generally a circular hole in the ground. The center or one end of this kiln was made lower than the rest of the floor, which was graded slightly so that the tar would run to the low spot. From this low spot, a pipe (probably a hollowed log) was extended to an outside pit which was considerably lower than the floor of the kiln. In this lower pit, barrels or other receptacles were placed to receive the tar as it flowed from the kiln.

After the kiln was built, the pine wood was piled on the floor until the stack reached normal ground level. The wood was then covered with dirt except for a small opening left for lighting the fire. After the fire was lit, the wood was supposed to smolder, never bursting into flames. The dirt served as a damper and contained the heat which was driven downward toward the floor of the kiln. It was a simple matter to speed up the burning process by punching holes in the earthen cover with a pole, allowing more air to reach the pit. The heat fried out or tried out the the tar (resinous matter) from the pine wood. The tar dripped to the floor, ran to the low spot, down the pipe, and then to the barrels placed to receive it. If the manufacturer wanted pitch, the tar was distilled by boiling it in a large kettle or by burning it in a round hole

[76] Descriptions of naval stores manufacture are more plentiful than accounts describing rice culture. The generalized account here based on Gray, *History of Agriculture*, I, 151–160; Nairne, *A Letter From South Carolina*, 10–11.

dug in the ground. The residue left after distilling or burning was pitch.

This manufacturing process was to remain a problem for South Carolina and other American colonies. The Royal Navy and English merchants always thought of American-made tar as being inferior, though there is evidence that some of it was as good as its competitor, Swedish tar. At least, South Carolina agents in London consistently found experts from various naval yards who would testify to the Board of Trade that South Carolina tar was comparable to the Swedish product.[77] The complaint voiced against South Carolina tar was that it was too "hot." That is, when applied to a rope as a preservative, the tar tended to scorch the rope, weakening it. This "hot" quality was traced to the way in which American tar was made. In South Carolina, "dead" pine trees (trees which had been downed for some time) were commonly used in the kilns, since such trees had been felled by past storms and could be gathered with a minimum of effort. On the other hand, Swedish tar was extracted from live or standing trees which had been recently cut. The resulting product was known as "green" tar, sometimes called "tar manufactured by the Swedish method." Green tar supposedly had those superior qualities sought by shipbuilders and refitters.

South Carolinians, who always claimed that the Swedish process was too costly for their situation, sometimes protested that they did not know how to manufacture by that method. Francis Yonge argued in 1721 that the additional labor required to fell trees to provide live pine wood for the kilns was so great that profits were reduced drastically on a commodity which was not very profitable even with the bounties. After cutting the trees, green timber yielded only one-third

[77] For example, A certificate by several ropemakers, March 2, 1717, BPRO-SC, VII, 12.

as much tar as dead wood processed by the method tradition-ally followed.[78] As a result of this question about the utility of South Carolina tar, the Royal Navy apparently refused to certify great quantities and thus make it eligible for the bounty.[79]

Other charges against South Carolina tar and pitch were soon voiced after shipments to England began. The Navy and English merchants complained that colonial tar was often full of dross. There is a likelihood that this criticism was true. Given the rough conditions under which processing took place, it seems logical that dirt, leaves, and other for-eign matter got into the barrels. Sometimes it was claimed that the planters put in dirt to bring watery tar up to weight standards required under the bounty act. Complaints were also registered that colonial tar was often packed in irregu-larly sized barrels which did not meet legal limits.[80] Colonial naval stores never completely lived down their reputation for inferiority and fraudulent packing as long as bounty acts were in effect. As the colony leading in the export of naval stores, at least up to the 1730's, South Carolina's agents in London and officials at home did what they could to combat the critics of the bounty, many of whom soon wanted to repeal the subsidies. The nebulous future of the ten-year bounty may have been a factor in the slowness of American colonials to engage extensively in naval stores production. The extension of the bounties in 1714 for another decade may have been responsible for the trade's expansion.[81]

Whatever the reason, the few statistics available point out

[78] For a detailed airing of the quality problem of South Carolina naval stores, see Francis Yonge to Board of Trade, marked received February 5, 1723, ibid., X, 2–11.
[79] Sir William Beveridge, *Prices and Wages in England: From the Twelfth to the Nineteenth Century* (Vol. 1: *Price Tables: Mercantile Era*) (London, 1939), 624–630.
[80] Ibid., 661.   [81] 12 Anne, c. 9.

that the bounty on tar and pitch had a very weak impact on all the American colonies before 1715. Prior to 1705 various proposals had been made to the English government by English merchants to supply American tar and pitch to the Royal Navy on contract. Nothing had come of these negotiations, and in 1704 the total importation of tar and pitch into England from all colonies amounted to 872 barrels. From 1705 through 1714 tar and pitch to England from the colonies varied from 2,346 barrels in 1705 to 11,639 barrels in 1714. For most years the range was 4,000 to 7,000 barrels. In 1715 American tar and pitch imports did exceed 25,000 barrels. For most of this period from 1705 to 1715, England was importing a total of about 40,000 barrels annually from all sources. It appears, with all the questions about the figures, that the American plantations supplied no more than 15 per cent of all tar and pitch imported into England.[82]

South Carolina supplied only a minor fraction of all exports of tar and pitch from the colonies to Britain before 1715. According to the customs records, 334 lasts of tar and pitch were imported into England from the colonies in 1706, less than one-third (about 1,250 barrels) originated in South Carolina.[83] New England seems to have been a more important source this first year the bounties were in effect. It might be noted that, of course, some South Carolina-produced tar and pitch may have been credited to New England, having found its way north in the coasting trade and from there to England. Crown officials noted that the quality of these first shipments was poor, but they decided that the bounty should be paid to encourage the producers.[84] The first isolated fig-

[82] Lord, *Industrial Experiments*, Appendix B.
[83] Treasury 1/101, No. 2 (fol. 3) , Custom House Office report signed by Charles D'Avenant, January 3, 1707. (Copy of BPRO document in North Carolina State Archives, Raleigh, N.C.)
[84] Lord, *Industrial Experiments*, 66.

ures which pertain to South Carolina show that from June 6, 1712, to June 6, 1713, 6,617 barrels of tar and pitch were shipped. This total, incidentally, conflicts with other compilations which list only 10,089 barrels of colonial tar and pitch imported into Britain throughout 1712 and 1713.[85] The discrepancies, however, are not great enough to modify the conclusion that by 1715 South Carolinians had only begun to get into this business in a serious way. Annual exports just before 1715 were only about 15 per cent of what they were to be by the 1717–1720 period.[86]

A number of immediate and short-range factors appear responsible for the slow start of the naval stores trade rather than the more chronic questions regarding quality. A lack of profits despite the bounty seems to have been the root of the problem. In particular, the lower freight rates between Sweden and England prevented South Carolina tar and pitch from being very profitable even with the bounty. For example, in 1709–1710, the cost of freight from Sweden for tar was £3 sterling per ton versus £10 per ton from South Carolina.[87] Thomas Byfield, long associated with projects to produce tar and pitch in America and export them to England, explained the dilemma to the Board of Trade in 1710 by calculating that the cost of tar and pitch manufactured in Carolina plus freight was so great that the market price plus bounty was not sufficient to leave much profit.[88]

Since one of the chief buyers of naval stores was the Royal Navy, we do have better pricing information on naval stores than on any other commodity class for the early period. Ironically, due to wartime circumstances, American tar and

---

[85] Comparison of figures: Table III, Appendix, with Lord, *Industrial Experiments*, Appendix B.

[86] Table III, Appendix.   [87] Gray, *History of Agriculture*, I, 153.

[88] Meeting of Board of Trade, February 8, 1710, *Journal of the Commissioners For Trade and Plantations, 1704–1782* (London, 1920–38), II, 123–124.

pitch sold consistently for higher prices in England from 1706 to 1715 than they did at any other time during the entire colonial period.[89] American tar ranged from 17s. to 27s. sterling per barrel delivered in England from 1706 to 1715. European tar always sold at a few shillings per barrel higher at any given moment owing to its more acceptable quality. American pitch in this period ranged from about 23s. to 35s. per barrel. The highest prices for both commodities were paid in 1710, when the prices of both commodities peaked. The same year, complaints of lack of profits were heard despite the favorable price structure. If these prices are at all accurate, it is apparent that South Carolina's annual shipments, which may never have reached 10,000 barrels in a single year by 1715, grossed £15,000 to £20,000 in England, but profits to the planters may have been small. Most likely, the net value and profits on tar and pitch were considerably less than for either rice or deerskins by 1715.

South Carolinians were interested at various times in the bounties offered on other naval stores besides tar and pitch; however, only turpentine and rosin were ever produced for export. One of the major difficulties with preparing these two commodities was the more complicated manufacturing process, though it was far from a sophisticated one.[90] Both are products derived from the longleaf pine. In this process, growing trees were used. Cuts or channels in the form of a "V" were made in the bark of the tree. The top of the cuts was at about the height of a man, with the two slashes joined near the base of the tree. At the bottom of the "V," boards (or a trough) were placed to receive the turpentine as it dripped down from the wounds on the trunk of the tree. To

[89] Beveridge, *Prices and Wages in England*, I, 673, 675. Beveridge's prices are based on records of the Royal Navy, the largest purchaser of naval stores.
[90] Gray, *History of Agriculture*, 159–160; Nairne, *A Letter From South Carolina*, 10–11.

stimulate flow, the bark was peeled off so that the bare wood of the trunk was exposed to the sun. Slaves gathered the heaped up turpentine on the boards or in the trough about every two weeks until frost. To obtain oil of turpentine, the raw turpentine was distilled in kettles. The residue after the distillate was drawn off was rosin.

Since making turpentine demanded much more constant attention to the work than tar making, it is not surprising that comparatively little turpentine and rosin were produced in colonial South Carolina. The necessary discipline of the labor force added to overhead. More man-hours were necessary than in tar making, always a consideration in a labor-short society. This had to be a specialized business activity which required a special gang of slaves devoted to making only these products, for it was a summertime pursuit carried on during the planting months. Probably labor could be better and more profitably used on rice.

No more than a few hundred barrels of turpentine and rosin were exported in any one year before 1715.[91] After 1715 the top year for export in the entire colonial period was 1735, when over 8,000 barrels were shipped. Most years no more than 2,000 barrels were transported, an annual level not reached until about 1730.[92] Turpentine and rosin had too many drawbacks in a province developing several other commercial activities which seemed to be surer profit makers.

The naval stores businesses, though of modest proportions by 1715, made considerable impact on the pattern of the province's growth. Some lands which had been viewed as of limited worth for growing crops, now became more valuable

[91] This conclusion is conjectural. None of the compilations shows South Carolina exporting much turpentine at any time in the colonial era.

[92] Clowse, "The Charleston Export Trade, 1717–1737," 193; *Historical Statistics of United States,* 770 (Series Z 304–307).

because stands of pine trees grew on them. Some individuals who had too little capital to go into rice growing may have been influenced to search out pine lands which could be worked with a small investment and a few hands. These businesses were further outlets for slave labor and another motivation for buying slaves. Moreover, such activities influenced the dispersal of the population generally. Those who sought out lands with longleaf pines growing needed vast tracts, for forests were used up rapidly owing to the wasteful methods employed. An area would be quickly cleared of its "dead" pine wood which went in the tar kiln. Although there are few careful evaluations of productive methods of the eighteenth century, one estimate made after examining pine forest industries in Florida held that ten workers could exhaust 1,000 acres in a three-year span.[93] In South Carolina, the drive to find pine lands to exploit led some individuals to encroach on lands they they did not own. Sometimes these aggressive spirits got into litigation with other settlers, but most likely they raided ungranted lands. The proprietors, and later the crown, complained from time to time about the indiscriminate practices of some individuals. The influence of the naval stores business was to become much greater after 1715, but the pattern was unfolding between 1705 and 1715.

Despite new and attractive businesses, South Carolinians did not neglect on-going trades after 1705. The provisions trade held its importance, and probably reached its peak in volume between 1705 and 1715. The many references to herds of cattle in frontier areas, Colleton County in particular, seem to point to the largest herds in the history of the province.[94] Once more, we have no way to measure the extent of cattle and hog raising by this time. Perhaps these large herds were the results of a favorable climate which

[93] Gray, *History of Agriculture,* I, 111.
[94] Rivers, *Sketch of History of S.C.,* 241–242.

allowed stock to multiply rapidly and forage for themselves. The presence of large herds does not prove that the activity was particularly profitable. The earliest dependable figures for beef and pork are for 1712–1713. During a span of 12 months, 1,963 barrels of beef and 1,241 barrels of pork were shipped. They must have been shipped to the West Indies. This 3,204-barrel total was much higher than the annual totals for the 1717–1724 period when exports ranged from 1,000 to 1,500 barrels.[95] The 3,204 barrel total (at 190 pounds per barrel net) represented about 600,000 pounds of meat and thousands of cattle and hogs slaughtered. Barreled beef and pork sold for comparatively small amounts, perhaps £2 or £3 current money per barrel, but since its production had a low overhead, and could be shipped short distances on local vessels, it may well have been a deceptively high profit maker. Yet, the provisions trade clearly had fallen far behind rice and naval stores as export commodities long before 1715.

The lumber trade probably increased from 1705 to 1715, but, unlike the provisions trade, it continued to grow after 1715. How much or how rapidly it developed can not be determined from the sources available; however, the assembly passed a law in 1712 which attempted to advance this trade.[96] One of the difficulties of the lumber industry was the flatness of the South Carolina coastal plain, which limited the possibilities of using water power to saw timbers. To overcome this problem, the statute offered a monopoly for eight years to anyone who would "erect a mill to saw with wind or water, so as to bring the same to complete perfection, as in Holland or in other countrys." Samuel Deane and

[95] Clowse, "The Charleston Export Trade, 1717–1737," 193; Report of trade from June 6, 1712 to June 6, 1713, author and date prepared not stated, BPRO-SC, VI, 173–174.
[96] Cooper and McCord (eds.), *Statutes of S.C.*, II, 385–389.

William Wragg, prominent merchants, tried to take advantage of the offer. In the 1730's, they petitioned the Board of Trade for a grant of 6,000 acres of crown lands to cover expenses involved with building sawmills, "raising pot ash," and carrying out other projects in South Carolina in 1713. Their depositions certified that they had paid the transportation of 30 skilled workmen from Holland to South Carolina where these men worked under a two-year contract. When the Indian war struck, the men were finishing one sawmill "to goe by wind which frequently workt with Thirty six Saws at a time." The governor took the men to fight, and this prevented the building of two more mills. As soon as their contracts expired, the men returned home, leaving the project unfinished. Deane and Wragg placed their losses at £1,500 sterling, and they asked for the land grant to cover the deficit.[97] While this particular scheme came to nought, the settlers were still interested in exploiting the natural wealth of hardwood and softwood forests as well as using the pines for naval stores.

The same act encouraging the building of sawmills offered concessions to persons who would start other specific projects.[98] The rationalization in the law stated that "the numbers of the inhabitants being few for so great an extent of land, the erecting of mills of all kinds and other mechanick engines will greatly improve the country itself, and its trade, and navigation." The person who would instruct people in how to make potash would be given a bounty of 40 shillings per ton for the first 500 tons shipped to Great Britain. An additional sum of £50 would be paid to the first two persons who set up potash works. "For advancing a coasting trade to the northern parts of this Province, and the

[97] Hearings on a Petition by Samuel Deane and William Wragg, Meeting of Board of Trade, July 23, 1735, BPRO-SC, XVII, 351–355.
[98] Cooper and McCord (eds.), *Statutes of S.C.*, II, 385–389.

encouragement of sowing wheat and barly . . ." and to supply flour locally and for trade, the first person constructing a wind- or water-driven gristmill would receive monopolistic privileges for five years. Any person who demonstrated an improved rice-beating mill to the specified commisioners, who would then certify that the invention was an improvement, would be given a reward not to exceed £100, depending on the degree of increased speed. The first person to build a "tobacco pipe works" would be given an eight-year monopoly. These special inducements indicate that South Carolinians were not mentally committed to commercial agriculture by 1712, and they still hoped for and were attempting to build a more diverse economy, though the pull of self-interest was working against these objectives.

The assembly's drive for diversity extended to the shipbuilding industry, though in part the subsidies offered may have been intended to undercut the carrying trade dominated by English merchants. A 1711 law authorized money payments from the public treasury to the builder or owner of any ship or vessel in the province. Certain drawbacks were also allowed for stores and supplies used in the building of any vessel in local facilities. This law was renewed in 1714, 1718, and 1720.[99] Whether it had any effect is somewhat conjectural, but the years from about 1712 to 1720 appear to have been the peak period for the South Carolina shipbuilding industry before 1740. Incomplete records reveal that one ship of 120 tons burden was built locally in 1712, and in 1714 at least three vessels more, including one of 90 tons burden.[100] Unfortunately, the exact complement of the locally owned merchant fleet can not be determined before 1717, but the fleet must have been more numerous including

[99] Ibid., II, 365.
[100] Clowse, "The Charleston Export Trade, 1717–1737," 307.

larger vessels in 1715 than the 10- or 12-vessel flotilla owned in the province in 1708.

If one tries to see the changing South Carolina economy as a whole from 1705 to 1715, the same difficulties crop up which face one when examining any single facet. We have no trustworthy balance of trade figures, and those we do have tell more about the general increase in South Carolina trade than they do the balance of trade as such. From present fragmentary data, it is impossible to calculate one. The Inspector General of Customs did determine one, but he used far too many questionable methods to arrive at meaningful figures. His calculations show, for example, that from 1705 to 1715 the book values of exports from Britain to Carolina (North and South) were less than those of imports from Carolina.[101] This seemingly rosy portrait of the circumstances of the South Carolina settlers is misleading, for these calculations do not take into account various amounts that must be subtracted or added to give a full picture. To the book values (generally understated in terms of real value) of exports from Carolina, the gross cost of producing the goods, freight, and other charges must be subtracted to arrive at a profit figure for South Carolinians. To exports from England, one must add the freight and other charges, plus the mark up when sold in South Carolina at retail. Neither export nor import figures reflect the purchases of slaves, probably the single most costly expenditure made in an expansive planter society. There are other variables in this equation, but any trial total reveals that any time before 1715 South Carolinians were importing more than they were exporting in terms of value in sterling.[102] Doubtless this is one of the reasons that some individuals focused on paper

101 *Historical Statistics of United States,* 757 (Series Z 21–34).

102 Historians have long recognized the relatively unfavorable position of the South Carolinians. For example, Rivers, *Sketch of History of S.C.,* 241.

money as a means of scaling down their personal obligations. In 1715 most South Carolinians were still struggling to make their business operations profitable, but the general situation had never looked more favorable. Moreover, the political calm which descended over the province after 1712 predicted even better things to come. The people of the province were steadily gaining control of their own destinies within certain limitations. Sometimes the proprietors interfered, mostly over land and quitrents, but their distant authority had been blunted and weakened and generally could be taken lightly. Even proprietary restrictions on land granting had come so late that the people already had grants to so much land that it would be years before a land shortage would be felt, though the closing of the land office might hurt immigration. The crown could not be defied with as much impunity, but the English government generally ignored South Carolina from 1705 to 1715, not even vetoing the Bank Act. Most crown activity and inactivity, with the exception of the enumeration of rice, had been favorable to South Carolina's interests. Naval stores bounties had been extended for another ten years. Even the crown's intrusion into local affairs had been more helpful than harmful, as when they stopped the Anglican zealots who had wanted a repressive established church and disallowed a potentially disruptive and explosive law. It may well have been the generally light and benevolent hand of the English government in this period which inclined the people to view the crown as a better master than the proprietors who had done little for years to further the province's interests. In 1715 South Carolina was comparatively tranquil. A firm foundation for permanent prosperity and a better life for its people appeared to have been built.

CHAPTER VII

Expansion Checked
1715–1725

O^N GOOD FRIDAY, APRIL 15, 1715, THE TRIBES ON SOUTH Carolina's southern border began a major uprising. The start of this so-called Yamasee War is thought to mark a turning point in the history of the colony. It is generally regarded as the catalyst for a long series of disasters peaking with the overthrow of the proprietary government in 1719 and carrying over into the disastrous 1720's. Although the consequences of this war were severe and should not be belittled, designation of this event as the chief cause of a subsequent chain of economic ills obscures and misleads. The Yamasee War was only one link in the chain, and it had nothing to do with many of the diverse economic problems facing South Carolinians after 1715. What should be emphasized is that the war precipitated a confrontation, which had been long postponed, among the settlers, the proprietary, and the crown (the Board of Trade) over the economic, as well as the political, future of South Carolina. Out of this three-cornered engagement came the decisions which permanently altered the colony's position within the British Empire.

From 1715 to 1725 the settlers suffered as the three forces

interacted because they had the least power and were the vulnerable party. Having boldly, proudly, and repeatedly asserted their right to independent action, they had to call upon both proprietors and crown when the war started. Failing to receive significant help from the proprietary, they inclined more and more toward the crown as the only possible source of protection. They could not hope to dominate crown officials, but by showing that imperial interests and South Carolina's interests were the same, they hoped to influence royal decisions favorable to them. Their approach was through letters, petitions, memorials, and testimony from their agents or sympathetic merchants before the Board of Trade. Since only a fraction of the program they advocated was obtained, this was a frustrating experience for South Carolinians. The gloomy prophecies they wrote during these trying years bear this out.

Pressed by settlers from below and pressured by the crown from above, the proprietary was caught in between. The proprietors' grip on the province had been weakening for years, and now they seemed about to lose it entirely. Yet, even as their hold on South Carolina slipped, the proprietors aroused themselves enough to reassert their prerogatives, and they used their position to the detriment of the colony. When forced out of the government in 1719, the proprietors retained legal rights to the soil. They refused to surrender these rights graciously or gratuitously to the crown. They gave up their claims and accepted a generous cash settlement only after exhausting legal maneuvers. The time lag between the overthrow of the governor and the assumption of all powers by the crown meant that the proprietary held considerable influence over South Carolina for more than ten years after the 1719 political revolt.

After hearing testimony, evaluating evidence, debating, and grinding its administrative mill in leisurely eighteenth-century style, the Board of Trade made its decisions on the primacy of Great Britain's interests. The strategic location of South Carolina and its trade influenced the Board more than abstract concepts of justice, governmental systems, or economic concessions satisfactory to the colonists. Board of Trade decisions were aimed at shaping a mercantile empire to benefit the mother country no matter how much the resulting configuration might warp South Carolina's economy. This may have been a sound approach for the empire, but it weakened South Carolina, already dislocated by internal developments. The Board of Trade's tardiness in reaching decisions and the form its policies finally took had much more economic impact, both immediately and in the long run, than the more eye-catching Yamasee War, whose effect was comparatively short-lived.

Nevertheless, tangible destruction and disruptions as a result of the war were considerable.[1] During the initial fighting, the Indians rapidly took control of everything south of the Edisto River. The two organized parishes of St. Helena (Beaufort) and St. Bartholomew (between the Combahee and Edisto Rivers) were depopulated. Fighting then shifted northward, and, before the militia could gain the upper hand, this northern frontier had been pushed back almost to the long-settled Goose Creek area. By the late summer and fall of 1716 South Carolina consisted of a semicircular area extending 25 or 30 miles into the interior and up and down the coast from Charles Town. Reports in 1717 indicated that half the cultivated land of the province had been abandoned. It was years before reoccupation of much of the frontier area was attempted. Even after peace was made in 1718, many incidents were reported.

It is impossible to calculate the direct cost of the war and

---

[1] For the most complete account of this war see Crane, *Southern Frontier*, 162–186.

difficult even to catalog, much less assess, the intangible impact. At least 400 colonists were killed, buildings were burned, livestock was driven off, and cultivation of crops in some areas was halted for years. The Indian trade was almost completely ruined temporarily and did not recover its pre-1715 vigor until at least 1722.[2] The entrepreneurial drive was bound to fall victim to the general discouragement which hit the people.

As if the war were not enough, pirates became active off the Carolina coast almost simultaneously with Indian hostilities.[3] Piracy had been a problem in the western hemisphere since the end of Queen Anne's War, so South Carolina was not being singled out for special harassment. Nevertheless, by 1717 and 1718, piracy was a serious situation, interfering with the colony's commerce. With a flourishing legitimate trade, the province now had no need to trade for pirate goods and stood to lose a great deal. Outbound vessels carried hard money, rice, naval stores, and deerskins. Inbound vessels brought European-manufactured goods, wines, and slaves. The extent of pirate depredations is impossible to figure, but they may have been considerable in a brief span. The pirate trials indicate that many vessels were captured.[4] The naval lists are blank for outgoing vessels from August 16 to October 9, 1718, except for one small sloop clearing Charles Town.[5] No other stoppages appear in these records; moreover, the total tonnage of vessels clearing during 1718 was greater than the total tonnage clearing in either 1717 or

---

[2] Ibid., 185.

[3] Hughson, *Carolina Pirates*, 58–127. Trial records for the piracies are to be found in South Carolina Admiralty Court Records, I and II (Federal Records Center, East Point, Georgia).

[4] South Carolina Admiralty Court Records, I and II, *passim*.

[5] C. O. 5/508 (British Public Record Office manuscript copy as found on microfilm: A. C. L. S. British Manuscripts Project, PRO 52, available from Library of Congress).

1719.[6] This makes it appear that the pirates had only a temporary negative influence on commerce; however, the South Carolina government was forced once more to call on the proprietors and the crown for assistance. The proprietors did nothing and the crown little despite its continuing efforts to end piracy. The colony eventually did much of the work and bore the expense of eliminating this threat to local commerce.

The Yamasee War and the pirates brought on a financial crisis. To meet the expenses incurred, the assembly turned, as it had regularly since 1703, to paper money issues. Though this method of meeting governmental obligations had caused some economic and political trouble since the passage of the Bank Act in 1712, paper money now became the single most divisive and explosive question facing South Carolina. To some degree, the province's fiscal crisis deepened as a result of the minimal amount of outside help received, but the government would have been in trouble anyway. After the first Indian raids between April and June 1715, an appeal was sent to the proprietors for 500 men and extensive war supplies. Later the South Carolinians would insist that only 150 muskets were sent.[7] Appeals to the crown and to neighboring colonies were also forwarded. Royal aid met only a fraction of the total needs, but the crown helped more than the proprietary did. North Carolina was generous, but Virginia does not seem to have been.[8] Most of the expenses, however, such as paying the militia, would have normally been borne by the provincial government under any circumstances. Besides, the emergency was immediate;

[6] Clowse, "The Charleston Export Trade, 1717–1737," 202.
[7] Council and Assembly to the Crown, February 3, 1720, BPRO-SC, VII, 271–299 .
[8] McCrady, S.C. Under the Proprietary, 545.

military preparations within the colony had to be rushed to meet the attacks.

Four months after the Indians struck, a law was passed authorizing the stamping of £30,000 in bills of credit to give the government a source of funds. The issue was to be retired by taxes collected in April 1717.[9] Expenses kept mounting as hostilities dragged on. More issues were authorized in 1716 and 1717; it was as though the dam of resistance to paper money had burst. After 1717 law after law was passed in confusing succession.[10] It is difficult to pinpoint the total amount of paper money in circulation at any time, since earlier issues were invariably canceled or incorporated into reissues. It is not inconceivable that by 1719 the amount had reached £100,000 or more, as compared with £56,000 following the Bank Act. About 1717 the value of the bills, which fluctuated with the shifting fortunes of the colony, fell to new lows in relation to sterling, perhaps to a 5:1 ratio, whereas it had been 3:1 or 4:1 from 1712 to 1717.[11]

Depreciation of currency, however, was not the sole cause for sharp merchant reactions to the state of the economy. New taxation schedules were passed to make "merchants and inhabitants" of Charles Town bear an increased share of governmental costs. The town was to pay one-sixth of the total tax raised by a levy against real and personal property.[12] Earlier taxes had mostly been raised on land and slaves, and, therefore, mostly paid by the planters. Before 1716 only small duties had been placed on exported deerskins and some other exported and imported commodities. At this juncture, new import and export duties were im-

[9] Cooper and McCord (eds.), *Statutes of S.C.*, II, 627–633.
[10] These laws and amounts issued and information about retirement of issues is in Bull, Sr., "An Account of the Rise and Progress of the Paper Bills of Credit in South Carolina . . ." in ibid., IX, 770–780.
[11] Ibid., IX, 771, 773.   [12] Ibid., II, 662–676.

posed. The minimum placed on any item imported was 5 per cent rated at prime cost, but major imports such as Madeira wine, rum, and sugar were assessed much more heavily. A head tax of £3 current money was laid on slaves brought from Africa and £30 on slaves imported who had lived over five months in any other colony in America. Selected exports, including Indian slaves, cedar timber, and leather, were taxed.[13] While such taxes would normally be passed on to the last buyer, such an extensive set of taxes in an embattled and impoverished society was bound to have a negative effect on business. Reorganization of the Indian trade as a public enterprise in June 1716 temporarily closed to merchants one of the most lucrative branches of commerce.[14] Finally, the merchants were threatened by stiff penalties if they refused to do business using the new currency, for it was legal tender for all debts.[15]

As a result of the unchecked flood of paper money and the financial pressure on them, the merchants, who were just beginning to find their political voices, turned against the proprietors for their inability to control the province. They looked instead to the crown to protect them from the excesses of the assembly. As a new force, and an influential one, they must have been instrumental in weakening the proprietary's position. It is impossible to imagine that the Board of Trade was not swayed by the flood of petitions and testimony directed to them after 1715 from merchants complaining about the state of affairs in South Carolina.

For the settlers, these financial problems were the final blow. They were already disillusioned with living under virtually nonexistent proprietary protection. The new burdens of paying more property taxes than ever before, increases in the cost of living, and an unsettled economy gener-

---

[13] Ibid., II, 649–661.   [14] Ibid., II, 677–680.   [15] Ibid., II, 665–666.

ally were depressing. Physically, their none-too-easy lives
grew harder. In 1716 and 1717 shortages of food due to
wartime interruptions in planting brought near famine conditions,[16] and 1717 and 1718 were years of fever epidemics
and smallpox,[17] developments which did not lift spirits. Such
discouragements, added to the political discontent which
had been brewing for some years, created an explosive
situation.

The economic crisis in the colony placed the proprietors
under fire from settlers, from merchants, and from the Board
of Trade. The South Carolina government and the majority
of people on one side and the merchants on the other, for
obviously different reasons, stepped up agitation against the
proprietary. But in 1716 and 1717 most settlers were probably not yet committed to the idea of making the province
royal. The ever-widening splits in the South Carolina structure and the resulting petitions must have kept the case
constantly before the Board of Trade, who was interested in
excuses for converting proprietaries to royal colonies. After
the assembly's appointment of Joseph Boone and Richard
Beresford as their agents in 1715, these talented men and
their successors were effective in keeping the viewpoint of the
settlers before the Board.[18]

The proprietors were able to hold their own against the
pushing of the assembly and the people until after 1717. In
South Carolina, Nicholas Trott and William Rhett continued to lead a proprietary party which was moribund but
not yet expired.[19] In England, the Board of Trade was critical of the proprietary's handling of the province, but no
open moves were made against the charter. To save the

[16] Abstracts of several letters from S.C., dated in March and April, 1717,
BPRO-SC, VII, 17–21.
[17] Duffy, "Eighteenth-Century Carolina Health Conditions," *Jour. So. Hist.*,
XVIII (1952), 299; Wallace, *History of S.C.*, I, 377–378.
[18] Sirmans, *Colonial South Carolina*, 117.   [19] Ibid., 118–119 .

situation, the proprietary had to stop the deterioration in the colony, but they did not do anything to help. Perhaps they were misinformed by former Governor Craven, Trott, and Rhett. Apparently, they were operating on the assumption after 1716 that the worst of the Yamasee War was over and that complaints from the people were, therefore, largely unjustified.[20] Their appointee to succeed Governor Craven, Robert Daniel, proved inept and unpopular; they were forced to remove him.[21] When they appointed Robert Johnson in 1717, they placed him in an almost impossible position. Son of a former governor, Johnson knew South Carolina and its problems. He conscientiously tried to alleviate conditions in a manner consistent with his instructions from the proprietors. When finally forced to choose between the wishes of the people and his oath to the proprietors, the latter was the only choice his conscience could sanction.[22]

Realizing that they were close to losing their province, the proprietors resolved to reassert themselves. Their instructions to Governor Johnson reflected a new hard-line approach.[23] Besides the customary directives given each appointee to this office, he was ordered to control the assembly and specifically to reduce the amount of paper money in circulation as soon as possible. Though he was at loggerheads with the assembly over certain other instructions, such as increasing the price of land, in December 1717 Johnson did sign a law issuing more bills of credit.[24] The measure did not violate the spirit of his instructions, since the law pur-

[20] For example, Proprietors to Board of Trade, July 27, 1716, BPRO-SC, VI, 230–231.

[21] Sirmans, Colonial South Carolina, 118–119.

[22] For Johnson's early career, see Richard P. Sherman, Robert Johnson Proprietary and Royal Governor of South Carolina (Columbia, 1966), 1–57.

[23] Instructions from Proprietors to Governor Johnson, April 30, 1717, BPRO-SC, VII, 31–35.

[24] Cooper and McCord (eds.), Statutes of S.C., III, 34–38.

ported to reduce the amount in circulation ultimately and to bring order out of the paper money chaos. William Rhett, loyal proprietary adherent, undercut the governor and protested against the law to the proprietors in the name of all merchants, likely a misrepresentation.[25]

Determined to regain the upper hand, the proprietors decided in the summer of 1718 to veto a number of laws. Such was their undoubted right, but employment of the veto, which had not been exercised since 1693, was an inflammatory action. Using it not only threatened political rights, but portended grave economic consequences as well. Among the laws disallowed were the 1716 act which levied taxes on imports and exports, the Indian Trade Act of 1716 creating the public monopoly, and a 1716 law for resettlement of lands vacated by the Yamasee. Veto of the first meant that the planters' land and slaves once more were to bear the greatest tax burdens. To negate the Indian Trade Act would restore the old system of trading which had brought disaster.[26]

Having served notice that governmental arrangements would henceforth be according to their wishes, the proprietors moved against the land system. They forbade the granting of any more land without special proprietary permission, a move interpreted as a measure of their anger over the very limited collection of quitrents and the small profits from land sales.[27] In 1719 they decided that no more land would be granted under any circumstances.[28] Neither old settlers nor new immigrants could obtain lands. The "land office,"

[25] William Rhett to Commissioners of Customs, December 31, 1717, BPRO-SC, VII, 104–106.

[26] Sirmans, *Colonial South Carolina*, 122–124.

[27] Proprietors to Governor and Council, September 12, 1718, BPRO-SC, VII, 159–160.

[28] Proprietors to Governor and Council, September 4, 1719, ibid., VII, 205–206.

as it was commonly called in South Carolina, was to remain closed from 1719 to 1731, a move which scarcely encouraged anyone to settle in the province. That same year, the proprietors reserved all of the Yamasee lands for themselves and divided the area into 15 baronies.[29] They later justified this move by claiming that it provided improved prospects for white immigrants, since each proprietor would have to promote his own land.[30] This policy decision was contrary to the proprietors' often expressed desire to prevent scattered settlements and large blocs of land in the hands of single individuals.

These aggressive actions must have driven most of their few remaining supporters into the opposition. Despite increased signs of active resistance, the proprietors never relented. Governor Johnson's position now became untenable. In a series of events too familiar to recount, he was allowed to retire to his plantation and the government was taken over in November 1719 by men who were technically rebels. Regardless of legal points, it was a popular, bloodless overthrow of a government which had neither met the needs of the people nor merited their continued support.

The crown was unprepared for these events in South Carolina. The Board of Trade did acquiesce, more by lack of reaction than by direct deeds, in the ouster of the proprietary governor. The proprietors, for their part, indicated an unwillingness to give up the province without a legal fight. Nevertheless, English subjects had to be ruled and the southern frontier defended. After months of deliberation, the Board of Trade advised the Privy Council to assume the government of the colony pending a final decision about its

[29] Proprietors to Francis Yonge, Surveyor General, April 17, 1719, ibid., VII, 183.

[30] Petition of Proprietors to the Crown, 1728 (no month or day specified), ibid., XIII, 3–7.

future.[31] Sir Francis Nicholson, an aged public servant of vast colonial experience and an uneven record of effectiveness, was appointed governor in August 1720, but he did not arrive in Charles Town until late May 1721.[32] The proprietors' rights to the soil remained undisturbed, and the land office stayed closed.

This peaceful rebellion tentatively placed the South Carolinians under the crown, a haven some had sought for several years. They anticipated an immediate improvement in their lot, but elimination of the proprietary middlemen did not bring a return to the happy prospects enjoyed before the Yamasee uprising. It was not long, indeed, before the Board of Trade showed that it could have as little appreciation of the settlers' viewpoint as the proprietors had exhibited. Moreover, they proved to be procrastinators when it came to making the substantive decisions which had to be made if the colony were to recover. Yet, once a policy or instruction was set, the Board of Trade could not be defied as easily as the proprietors had been.

Governor Nicholson was under orders to be conciliatory, and he was. He chose a council balanced among Anglicans and dissenters, among merchants and planters, and among former proprietary adherents and anti-proprietary men.[33] These old divisions, however, were no longer as meaningful as they had once been; paper money was now the question. The new governor had orders to return the colony to sounder money policies and to disallow any laws authorizing more bills of credit, a directive which was bound to set the political pot boiling.[34]

Nicholson's inability to satisfy all factions on the money

[31] Sirmans, *Colonial South Carolina*, 129.
[32] For a sketch of his career, see *DNB*, XIV, 457–458.
[33] Sirmans, *Colonial South Carolina*, 137–144.
[34] Instructions for Governor Nicholson from Board of Trade, August 30, 1720, BPRO-SC, VIII, 101–138, 139–165.

question was his undoing in the long run. Since he did not adhere to his hard money position, he became vulnerable to attack from merchants strongly opposing all paper issues and from the Board. His dilemma was not an easy one. The province was in sad shape. Nicholson had no choice but to let stand most of the legislation passed under the interim "rebel" regime of Speaker of the House James Moore (son of the old governor). Some of these laws of 1720 and 1721 reflected the low state of affairs. For example, an act offering relief to debtors mentioned that it was difficult to know the value of the "several sorts" of bills of credit, that interest rates were at 25 per cent and that English goods were selling at 10 or 12 times their prime cost in England. This law allowed payment of some debts in rice, naval stores, and deerskins, since money was scarce.[35] Another law passed in December 1720 levied a tax of 1,200,000 pounds of rice (perhaps 3,000 barrels or one-seventh of an annual crop at this time), one-sixth to be paid by Charles Town residents and five-sixths by rural residents. This rice poundage was to be the backing for rice orders or rice bills, that is, bills of credit backed by rice, in the amount of £18,000 to circulate until 1723.[36] Probably the governor felt that a colony in such a weakened condition could neither retire old bills very rapidly nor cease issuing new bills until internal conditions could be restored to normal. His attempt to bring order brought on a long and stormy debate. During the course of deliberations the assembly put 28 petitioners against paper money in jail until they apologized. In 1721, and again in 1723, laws were passed with Nicholson's assent which to-

---

[35] Cooper and McCord (eds.), *Statutes of S.C.*, III, 105–108. This act is dated February 13, 1719, but is signed by James Moore, which probably means it was passed in 1720 not 1719. Editors' note appended to Act No. 405, ibid., III, 98, applies to this debtor relief act as well.

[36] Ibid., III, 112–115.

gether authorized a total of £120,000 in bills of credit. Of the amount, £80,000 represented old bills not retired and £40,000 (added in 1723) was for governmental expenses.[37]

Some historians have concluded that nearly every merchant now became an opponent of bills of credit.[38] This may be an overstatement, since the opposing camps may have formed long before Nicholson arrived. Nevertheless, there was unquestionably an outpouring of stronger and more numerous objections than previously. Petitions from merchants requesting the Board of Trade to disallow this act and the act of 1720 (issuing rice orders) contained strongly worded attacks on Governor Nicholson.[39] The creditors did have a point. The exchange ratio between bills of credit and sterling widened from 5:1 to 7:1 or 8:1. In other words, debts already contracted declined as much as 40 per cent in real value, a potentially ruinous situation for merchants.[40] This rapid inflation may have been the sharpest increase in a short period of time during the entire colonial era.

The Board of Trade ordered the laws of 1721 and 1723 superseded by corrective legislation despite protests from the commons, the council, and settlers who insisted that the sum was not excessive.[41] The Board of Trade was not moved from its hard money position, which was imperial policy. Some defiance remained in South Carolina. When the new law was passed in 1724 to tidy up the paper system, £61,000 was left "current" indefinitely, a deliberately vague and open-ended

[37] For the political fight over paper money see Sirmans, *Colonial South Carolina*, 145–151; for the laws see Cooper and McCord (eds.), *Statutes of S.C.*, III, 149–157, 188–193; for an explanation of the confusing paper money situation at this time see Bull, Sr., "An Account of the Rise and Progress of the Paper Bills of Credit in South Carolina, . . ." in ibid., IX, 773–776.

[38] For example, see Sirmans, *Colonial South Carolina*, 149.

[39] For examples of merchant petitions and other papers concerning this controversy, see BPRO-SC, X, 87–91, 111–112; ibid., XI, 164–166.

[40] Wallace, *History of S.C.*, I, 315.

[41] Sirmans, *Colonial South Carolina*, 149.

promise. Backing the local consensus once more, Governor Nicholson went along with the law.[42]

Besides his acquiescence in paper money laws, another part of Governor Nicholson's program may have antagonized the merchants. Nicholson was very interested in incorporating Charles Town under a city government similar to those of New York and Philadelphia. He believed that this reform, along with other needed changes, would make commerce more orderly and better regulated.[43] Having his way with the assembly as usual, Nicholson had his law passed in 1722.[44] It changed the name of the town to Charles City and Port, to be ruled by a board of 19 men who would be self-perpetuating, for the remainder would appoint a successor when an incumbent died or retired. The merchants interpreted this as a change by the assembly aimed at controlling them. Their protests to the Board of Trade about this unrepresentative system were sharply worded.[45] That body, acting on legal opinion that the law was oppressive, had it declared null and void.[46]

Whatever allegations merchants made about his motives, Nicholson busily addressed himself to the problems of the province during his tenure. Before paper money absorbed all political attention, he succeeded in obtaining a number of worthwhile pieces of legislation, the most important of which dealt with the Indian trade. He was particularly interested in this matter, partly because he represented imperial authorities who were concerned over the southern frontier.

[42] Cooper and McCord (eds.), *Statutes of S.C.*, III, 219–221.
[43] Sirmans, *Colonial South Carolina*, 143; Wallace, *History of S.C.*, I, 286–287.
[44] Cooper and McCord (eds.), *Statutes of S.C.*, IX, 49–57.
[45] Memorial of Richard Shelton on behalf of Charles Town inhabitants against the Charles City Act, May 24, 1723, BPRO-SC, X, 82–86. For a different interpretation, see Carl Bridenbaugh, *Cities in the Wilderness* (New York, 1938), 304.
[46] Declaration of the Privy Council, June 27, 1723, BPRO-SC, X, 115–116.

He also recognized that South Carolina would never be secure until the Indians were pacified and that a well-conducted trade was the most effective means of binding them to the colony's interest and commercial benefit. The attempt of the planter-dominated assembly in 1716 to turn the trade into a public monopoly had been disallowed by the proprietors. In 1719 the assembly made the trade a partially public and a partially private enterprise, a scheme which was not a success commercially and drew continual complaints from merchants.[47] In 1721, at Nicholson's urging, the trade became completely private enterprise once more, under the close supervision of three commissioners.[48] Further refinements of the system took place in 1724. The assembly was to control policy while a single commissioner administered regulations of the trade and assumed many diplomatic functions as well.[49] The efficiency of this arrangement, not dissimilar to the stipulations of the 1707 law, was responsible for the rapid recovery of the Indian trade. The system of administration lasted with only brief interruptions until 1756.[50]

From the average settler's point of view, regulation of the trade was worthless unless the crown took defensive measures to secure the frontier and prevent a repetition of the Yamasee uprising. Since concern over international competition in the area was one motivation for imperial authorities to assume the government from the proprietors, it is ironical that a comprehensive scheme commended by both colonists and the Board of Trade was eventually rejected. The plan, sometimes loosely designated the township system, was presented to the Board of Trade in August 1720 by Joseph Boone and John Barnwell, the latter an old Indian fighter who likely

[47] For a discussion of the conduct of the trade under these two acts, see Crane, *Southern Frontier*, 193–199.
[48] Cooper and McCord (eds.), *Statutes of S.C.*, III, 141–146.
[49] Ibid., III, 229–232.   [50] Crane, *Southern Frontier*, 200.

conceived it. Essentially, the plan involved a string of frontier forts. These would be manned in time of trouble by
white settlers enticed by special concessions to settle in exposed positions on the frontier. These forts would be located
to form a protective outer ring or perimeter for the colony's
defense. Impressed with Barnwell's strategy, the Board of
Trade rapidly approved the proposal and integrated it into
broad-scale plans for defending the frontier from Canada to
Florida. The Privy Council, who found the design too grand
and the projected expense too great, demurred and approved
only the building and garrisoning of one fort on the Altamaha River. Though Fort King George, as the post was
named, was the start of British defenses against French en-
croachments, South Carolinians recognized that imperial
plans for frontier defense were inadequate.[51]

Governor Nicholson's term proved that as long as the
Board of Trade supervised closely and listened to the merchants, South Carolina controlled its own destiny less than
ever before. About the only actions left to the assembly were
those things which did not infringe on crown policies or on
the sensitivities of the merchants. In response to the rising
tide of protests, the Board summoned Nicholson back to
London to explain his role in the paper money legislation
and in other controversial matters.[52] His departure in 1725
ended another phase of the colony's political history, and,
coincidentally, came at a moment when the export trade
pattern of the colony was undergoing a forced change which
marks 1725 as the end of a phase of the colony's economic
history as well. To understand how and why South Carolina's political and economic histories merge in a pattern of

[51] For a thorough discussion of all the ramifications of this proposed plan,
see *ibid.*, 220–221, 229–234.

[52] Minutes of the Privy Council, August 22, 1724, BPRO-SC, XI, 164–166.

despair, the economic developments since 1715 must be superimposed on the political pattern.

While waiting for the crown to determine their ultimate role in the empire, South Carolinians continued, as they had done for many years, to promote their province. With the proprietors having put a stop to land granting, the local government was unable to initiate a drive to populate the ring of projected townships on the frontier or to offer land for white immigrants generally.[53] This fact not only frustrated attempts to secure the frontier, but it hampered economic recovery after the Yamasee War. Even during the period of fighting, the assembly passed an act encouraging "foreign protestants" to take up vacated Yamasee lands, forming a shield for established areas.[54] Generous concessions were offered, and it is generally recorded that 500 Irish protestants took advantage of these terms before the act was nullified by the proprietors in 1718.[55] The hasty action was a catastrophe for the poor immigrants who could not be given other lands since the land office was closed. It was one of the unpopular vetoes which led to the downfall of the proprietary government.

This abortive plan was probably the most successful attempt between 1715 and 1725 to increase the white population, for other promotional efforts were weak. One act of 1716 offered bounties in current money to importers of white male servants.[56] Though no records indicate that the white indentured population jumped dramatically, the preamble

[53] This was one of the complaints against the proprietors when South Carolinians urged the crown to take over the province. For example, see Memorial of Assembly in answer to Mr. Shelton (Secretary to the Proprietary), May 21, 1726, ibid., XII, 38–50.

[54] Cooper and McCord (eds.), *Statutes of S.C.*, II, 641–646.

[55] Ackerman, "S.C. Colonial Land Policies," 69–71.

[56] Cooper and McCord (eds.), *Statutes of S.C.*, II, 646–649.

of a 1717 law said that great numbers of white servants had lately arrived and that a new regulatory code to govern their behavior was necessary.[57] The plans of individuals and other schemes to find white settlers came to little. The London-Charles Town correspondence of 1716 mentioned that rebel supporters of the Stuarts taken at Preston were being sent to South Carolina. One report indicated that 80 had arrived in August 1716.[58] In 1717 the proprietors negotiated with Sir Robert Montgomery about a grandiose plan to set up the Margravate of Azilia between the Altamaha and Savannah Rivers.[59] Some plans reflected the renewed though belated interest of the proprietors in promoting their lands. Even after losing the government, the proprietors corresponded with several would-be underwriters, including Jean Pierre Purry who eventually did deliver Swiss settlers in the 1730's.[60] Judging from records, white immigration was small from 1715 to 1725.

As a consequence of these unsuccessful promotional efforts, the total white population remained static from 1715 to 1720. The few hundred immigrants barely offset losses from the Yamasee War. In a letter dated in January 1720, the recently deposed Governor Johnson estimated that only 100 more white people lived in the province in 1720 than in 1715.[61] That same month the council and assembly placed the white population at 9,000, with a 2,000-man militia com-

[57] Ibid., III, 14–21.
[58] Proprietors to Governor Craven, May 10, 1716, BPRO-SC, VI, 163; Benjamin Godin to "Sir," August 6, 1716, ibid., VI, 235–243.
[59] Indenture between Proprietors and Sir Robert Montgomery, June 18, 1717, ibid., VII, 56–58; Indenture between Proprietors and Sir Robert Montgomery, June 19, 1717, ibid., VII, 59–67.
[60] Documents dated in 1724 and 1725 having to do with Purry's project are to be found in ibid., XI, 14, 282, 314–315, 320–321.
[61] Governor Robert Johnson to Board of Trade, January 12, 1720, ibid., VII, 233–250.

posed of free men from 16 to 60 years of age.[62] In July 1720 representatives of the proprietors told the Board of Trade that white population had actually decreased in the past few years.[63] In an accounting of taxes, temporary Governor Moore reported in 1721 that 1,305 paid taxes, which might indicate nearer 5,000 than 6,000 whites.[64] Evidence seems weighted toward a total white population of 6,000 to 7,000 in 1720, with only a high birth rate providing any increase after that date. It is difficult to visualize a white population greater than 7,500 by 1725.[65] This lack of growth in the white population might in itself have limited increases in productivity to some degree between 1715 and 1725.

If the increase in the white population was small after 1715, the black population of South Carolina grew rapidly, sustaining a trend already under way before the Yamasee War started. Even in the midst of the fighting when many plantations were nonoperative, more slaves were purchased from abroad, though only 148 were imported during 1715 and 1716. Between 1717 and 1720 at least 500 per year were brought in, and the total for the four years was 2,244. An additional 1,363 were imported from 1721 through 1724.[66] William Hammerton, Charles Town Naval Officer, largely confirmed these figures for the 1720's. In a report to London he counted 1,881 slaves imported between May 30, 1721, and September 29, 1725.[67] At a level of 8,000 to 10,000 in 1715, by

[62] Council and Assembly to Board of Trade, January 29, 1720, ibid., VII, 251–270.

[63] Testimony of representatives of Proprietors before the Board of Trade, July 28, 1720, ibid., VIII, 253–255.

[64] James Moore to "Sir," March 21, 1721, ibid., IX, 22–23.

[65] Table I, Appendix.

[66] Historical Statistics of United States, 770 (Series Z 303).

[67] A compilation of numbers of slaves imported into South Carolina was prepared by William Hammerton, Naval Officer, and enclosed in a letter from Edmund London to "Good Sir," December 30, 1726, BPRO-SC, XII, 180.

1721 the slave total was reported by Governor Moore to be 11,828, a number which probably represents only taxable slaves and excludes the aged and small children.[68] There is every reason to believe that 14,000 or 15,000 slaves were living in the colony by 1725. The total population was divided almost 2:1, black to white.

Despite the growing disparity between the slave and free populations, circumstantial evidence suggests that South Carolinians did not wish to stop buying slaves even if it might be desirable to limit their numbers for reasons of internal security. Rumors of slave intrigues, and occasionally overt action, fed latent fear. After a minor uprising in 1720, 14 slaves were executed and many others severely punished.[69] Yet controls on the flow of slaves to the colony were weak and ineffective, as they had been before 1715. The tactic of encouraging whites to settle in the province was ineffective in these first decades of the eighteenth century. Though comparatively high duties (a minimum of £10 current money) were placed on slaves imported by speculators, these levies were more revenue makers than control measures. A planter importing slaves for his own use paid no duties.[70] Such a differentiation seems to have been the type of assembly action which influenced relations between merchants and planters. The tax did produce some revenue, for £3,905 current money (over one-third of all duties paid) was collected by the Treasurer for slaves imported during 1722 and 1723.[71] Most slaves imported, however, were obviously brought in duty-free by planters. Before 1715 slaves had become so essential in this staple crop colony that regulations to curb importations were only halfhearted.

[68] James Moore to "Sir," March 21, 1721, ibid., IX, 22–23.
[69] Unsigned letter to Mr. Joseph Boone, June 24, 1720, ibid., VIII, 24.
[70] For example, Cooper and McCord (eds.), *Statutes of S.C.*, III, 56–68.
[71] Payments made and income received by the Public Treasurer, 1722–1723, BPRO-SC, XI, 55.

Though very little land was obtained from the proprietors between 1715 and 1725 (and virtually none after 1719), South Carolinians had enough for their needs and for the growing slave population to work. Only 17 grants, representing 19,000 acres, survive from the years 1715 to 1719.[72] Even if these records are incomplete, it is difficult to imagine that much land was taken up during a time when it was dangerous to be on the frontier, much less live and work there. During the 1720's the proprietors made a few special grants from London, and some settlers exercised patents received earlier.[73] Otherwise, no new holdings were parceled out.

Since the assembly had to tax land, tax returns provide some insights into land distribution and the pattern of settlement at the end of the proprietary era. In 1721 more than 1,160,000 acres were taxed.[74] The total is more than twice the amount one can account for in surveying surviving grants dated before 1720.[75] Since this figure was used as the basis for estimating tax revenues from land in 1723–1724,[76] apparently little additional land was conveyed during the next several years. There is disagreement among those who have examined the records as to the acreage involved in the conversion of patents to grants during the 1720's. One historian claimed that 800,000 more acres passed into private hands in this way;[77] a more recent estimate places the total at 290,000 acres added to the tax rolls in the 1720's.[78] Regardless, a million to two million acres is a huge expanse. For perspective, 1,160,000 acres is about 6 per cent of the total land area within the present state of South Carolina.

[72] Table II, Appendix.
[73] Ackerman, "S.C. Colonial Land Policies," 86–93.
[74] James Moore to "Sir," March 21, 1721, BPRO-SC, IX, 22–23.
[75] Table II, Appendix.
[76] Estimate of the Charges of Government from September 29, 1723, to September 29, 1724, BPRO-SC, XI, 48–51.
[77] Wallace, *History of S.C.*, I, 325.
[78] Ackerman, "S.C. Colonial Land Policies," 87.

In 1721 most of the land granted (70 to 80 per cent) was located within parishes closest to Charles Town. This area designated as Berkeley County, included the parishes of St. Philip's (Charles Town), St. Thomas and St. Dennis, Christ Church, St. James Goose Creek, St. Andrews, St. John's Berkeley, and St. George Dorchester. Perhaps 80 to 90 per cent of all whites and blacks lived in these parishes. Among the other four parishes, only St. Paul seems to have had a very large slave population or extensive land grants made. This parish and St. Bartholomew made up Colleton County (the area hit in the Yamasee uprising). St. Helena (the only parish of Granville County) to the far south and St. James Santee (the only parish of Craven County) to the far north were thinly settled, though St. James Santee had enough slaves to indicate either naval stores or rice production in the area. While about half the land taxed was north of the Ashley River and half south, the greater physical size of several parishes to the south supports the frequent contemporary observation about the thinly settled area south of the Edisto River.[79]

By 1720 the inefficient and easily corrupted land system had allowed so much land to be put in private hands that, even without more grants over the next decade, production for export could climb by developing the large tracts already available. This system of larger land units was further strengthened as the economy crumbled, since a buyer needed cash or credit to obtain land from other individuals. This hurt the poor man's chances of purchasing. Aside from the economic and social pressures which the land situation generated, it is apparent that lands granted were sufficient to permit over-all growth for years to come.

After the Yamasee War any hope for a rapid return to a

[79] Material in this paragraph based on letter from James Moore to "Sir," March 21, 1721, BPRO-SC, IX, 22–23.

complacent era of expanding and profitable production hinged, however, on the role South Carolina was to play in a mercantilistic empire. After 1715, as before, the Board of Trade had the power to support or weaken the economy as it willed. Its policies kept the economy weak; in turn, this kept the government weak and ineffective even after changing it to royal status, and made the 1720's a disastrous decade. South Carolinians learned that the ability and willingness to produce ever greater quantities of commodities were of no advantage if that increased production could not be marketed profitably under imperial rules.

The Indian trade was the branch of commerce least molested by the crown. After suffering almost complete disruption in the 1715–1717 period, this trade gradually recovered as South Carolinians were able to make peace with the various tribes and put the trade back in order. In 1716 fewer than 5,000 skins were shipped, and from 1717 through 1719, the years of public trade and remaining tensions in the wilderness, the range was from 17,000 to 24,000 annually, not half the pre-1715 yearly volume. In 1720 and 1721, when the trading system was partially public and partially private enterprise, 35,171 skins were shipped the first year and 33,939 the next. With the return to licensed private traders supervised by government officials, volume moved to the 60,000 to 65,000 level annually.[80]

Lack of pricing information makes it almost impossible to do more than guess at losses suffered by merchants and traders due to the disruption of the deerskin business. It is obvious that vindictive regulations originating in the planter-dominated assembly retarded recovery before the early 1720's. If profit per skin shipped was only a few shillings, which seems likely, total profits annually ran to thousands of

[80] Crane, *Southern Frontier,* 329.

pounds sterling, perhaps £10,000 to £20,000 in a year when 60,000 skins were shipped.[81] Nearly all such profits were lost to merchants between 1715 and 1722, a fact which did not improve merchant sensibilities during this period. Since the trade benefited merchants and Indian traders alone, the major return for the colony as a whole remained the duties collected on exported skins. Even these sums were modest. For example, for 1722 and 1723 combined, the Public Treasurer's books show over £11,000 current money collected from duties on exports and imports. Of this total, only £1,500 was accounted for by duties on deerskins.[82]

The Yamasee War seems to have hurt the naval stores business least among the agricultural export trades. While many of the tar works were on the edge of settlement, they could be easily restored to working order once the threat of attack was past. As a result, during the time of this war, naval stores production actually increased several times above pre-1715 levels of export. Some planters whose rice fields were not safe to work may have turned to naval stores as an outlet for their slave labor. It is possible that this contributed to the rapid increase in production in these years. Although there are no figures for 1715 and 1716, by 1717 a total of 43,957 barrels of tar and pitch was shipped from Charles Town. This total contrasts markedly with the 6,617 barrels transported in a 12-month span in 1712–1713. In 1718 exports reached 52,215 barrels, only to drop to 42,984 barrels in 1719.[83]

In simplest terms, this South Carolina shipping pattern suggests that the planters had been so encouraged by renewal of the bounties for at least another ten years and by local

[81] Pricing data are contradictory, and there is very little information on profits. Therefore, these are at best tentative estimates.

[82] Payments made and income received by the Public Treasurer, 1722–1723, BPRO-SC, XI, 55.

[83] Table III, Appendix.

motivations to manufacture so much tar and pitch that after 1715, they gradually glutted and then broke the British market by 1719. Colonial tar sold to the navy for 19s. sterling per barrel in 1715. In 1716, the price had fallen to 18s.; in 1717, to 17½s.; in 1718, to 14s. In 1719 and 1720, when the bottom had fallen out, the price per barrel declined to 9½s.[84] Much of this excess tar and pitch had to be re-exported to continental markets, mostly Holland.[85] This break in the market bore more heavily on South Carolina than any other American colony. Until 1715 only a small fraction of all tar and pitch imported into England came from America. After 1715, through 1725, over half of all tar and pitch imported into England came from America, and South Carolina supplied most of the American share.[86]

The tremendous quantities of colonial tar and pitch appearing on the British market brought a reappraisal among royal officials about the future of tar and pitch bounties. From about 1717 through 1719 the correspondence to and from Charles Town began to question whether the bounties would be extended beyond September 29, 1724. Parliament passed a law in 1718, doubtless at the request of imperial officials, that after September 29, 1719, no certificates would be issued for tar and pitch which was not free of adulteration and dross.[87] More distressing than the perpetual problem of irregular packing was a navy report which showed just how badly wasted the expenditures for bounties were. In the years 1713 through 1717 the navy had purchased only 4,438

[84] Computed from the last price as determined by Beveridge, *Prices and Wages in England,* 673, 675.

[85] Gray, *History of Agriculture,* I, 155.

[86] Computed by comparing South Carolina export figures as found in Table III, Appendix, against total imports of tar and pitch into England as found in the compilations by Schumpeter, *English Overseas Trade Statistics,* 52–55, and Lord, *Industrial Experiments,* Appendix B.

[87] 5 George I, c. 11. See Lord, *Industrial Experiments,* 75, for further consideration of this change in the law.

barrels of tar and 2,398 barrels of pitch imported from the colonies. None at all had been bought in 1713 and 1714 and only 75 barrels of pitch in 1716. Yet, the navy had paid out over £90,544 sterling in bounties during those five years.[88] Clearly, only a fraction of the bounty money had been paid on naval stores purchased by the navy. Still the Board of Trade and other officials were reluctant to allow bounties to expire as long as Sweden was fighting Russia, Denmark, and Saxony (a prolonged conflict which had started in 1701 and was to drag on until 1721).[89] The year after that war ended, Parliament enacted another general naval stores act which, among its many clauses, served notice that after September 29, 1724, only tar manufactured by the Swedish method would be certified for bounty.[90]

In the meantime, South Carolina's trade in tar and pitch fell as colonial naval stores came under market, administrative, and legislative pressure in England. In harvest year 1721 only 23,501 barrels were shipped, less than half the 1718 total, though by 1723 exports were rising again. The greatest amounts of the colonial era were shipped from Charles Town in 1724 and 1725 before the bounty system was reshaped to favor tar manufactured by the Swedish process. The 1725 total of over 60,000 barrels was the pinnacle, as planters rushed to unload what they had on hand.[91] This outburst may also reflect the desire to denude pine lands, since such lands would be of little value if the new stipulations on tar manufacture were to go into effect.

The margin on tar sales after 1719 must have remained considerably below those of earlier years. From the low point of 9½s. per barrel in 1719 and 1720, prices rallied briefly in

---

[88] Lord, *Industrial Experiments*, 74, 81–82.   [89] Ibid., 75.
[90] 8 George I, c. 12. See Lord, *Industrial Experiments*, 77–78, for further considerations of this alteration in the system.
[91] Table III, Appendix.

1721 to 13s. per barrel, fell sharply in 1722 to 8½s., and then rose again in 1723 and 1724 to the 13s. level.[92] South Carolina correspondents generally confirm the latter-day compilations of prices, though naturally no two sets of quotations agree completely. For example, in 1724 Governor Nicholson quoted a 6s. per barrel price for the recent past (probably 1722) but noted that the price of tar had risen to 13s. or 14s.[93] From 1715 to 1725 Swedish tar was being purchased by the navy yards for 22s. to 26s. per barrel and was never lower than 16½s. In any given year, the navy was paying several shillings per barrel premium for Swedish tar as opposed to the offering price for colonial tar.[94]

Despite a number of other problems concerning colonial naval stores, the future of the bounties really hinged on improving the quality of colonial tar to equal the Swedish product. Since the navy was reluctant to buy colonial tar, one of the major purposes for having a tar bounty had been defeated. If colonial tar could be brought up to the standards set by Swedish tar makers, then the bounties could be adjusted downward to bring the supply nearer England's actual demand. Because the navy, shipbuilders, and fitters generally needed thousands of barrels of tar annually but only a few barrels of pitch, tar was the key. This was ironical because the navy never found fault with the qualities of colonial pitch. In fact, from 1720 to 1756 colonial pitch was used almost exclusively in navy yards though the amounts purchased were quite small. From 1660 to 1755, in peacetime years, between 4 and 50 lasts (48 to 600 barrels) were bought by the navy; during war years, between 40 and 150 lasts (480 to 1,500 barrels).[95] Compared to the thousands of

[92] Beveridge, *Prices and Wages in England*, 673, 675.
[93] Governor Nicholson and Council to Board of Trade, September 4, 1724, BPRO-SC, XI, 203–209.
[94] Beveridge, *Prices and Wages in England*, 673, 675.   [95] Ibid., 666.

barrels of pitch South Carolina alone sent to England annually between 1715 and 1725, these were mere driblets.

Negative assessments of colonial tar and the navy's preference for Swedish tar when available began to affect the South Carolina tar and pitch export pattern by 1720. Until that year, the colony shipped much more tar than pitch. From 1717 through 1719, 60 per cent was tar and 40 per cent pitch. In 1720 with total shipments of both commodities cut due to the oversupply on the market, pitch made up 70 per cent of the total. The trend appears to have been reversed in 1721 and 1722, harvest years when slightly more than half of all shipments was tar (prices of tar rallied in these years). Yet, by 1723 two-thirds was pitch. In 1724 and 1725 about 95 per cent of 60,000 barrels was pitch.[96] Though definitive reasons for this shift are lacking, possibly the navy stopped certifying much of the colonial tar offered for sale after the 1722 law was passed. At the least, the switch from tar to pitch by South Carolina exporters indicates that the tar market was virtually shut down for them. Probably this huge amount of pitch was re-exported from England to the continent, as excess naval stores had been for years past. From the planters' vantage point, this development was a portent of the eventual complete destruction of the naval stores business. Pitch was considerably lower in price than tar, nearly always selling for several shillings per barrel less than tar at any given time. For example, in 1724 when the navy offered 13s. or 14s. per barrel for tar, the price of pitch was only about 7½s. per barrel.[97] We must assume that profits on pitch were, therefore, considerably less than those on tar.

About 1718 or 1719 the South Carolina government, settlers, and merchants launched a campaign to save the bounties. Success depended on effective lobbying in London to

[96] Computed from the exports as found on Table III, Appendix.
[97] Computed from Beveridge, *Prices and Wages in England*, 673, 675.

convince the Board of Trade, the Royal Navy, and the Parliament that continuing them was advantageous to the empire. One tactic was to insist, as lobbyists had done since before 1705, that Carolina tar was as good or better than Swedish tar. The Board of Trade always responded to such presentations that it wanted definitive proof that colonial tar was preferred to Swedish tar in navy yards. This put the South Carolina agents and merchants in an impossible position, since the navy always insisted that the Swedish tar had more utility than colonial tar. In rebuttal, sometimes the argument was advanced that the question of quality arose from conspiracies to discredit South Carolina tar. One group of villains singled out was comprised of certain navy yard personnel who claimed colonial naval stores were inferior in order to keep their price low compared to the Swedish product.[98] A more likely charge was that some merchants trading to Sweden and the Baltic area vilified colonial naval stores in order to protect their own businesses. Governor Robert Johnson expressed these sentiments strongly when he once wrote that he was "satisfied it is mostly Owing to ye intrest the East Country merchants have with ye Ropemakers who being obliged to buy there hemp of them will not lett them have it without they will give them their price for their Tarr also and oblige them to give it a good name & decry ours. . . ."[99] This may not have been a farfetched evaluation of the situation, since the navy awarded all contracts on a bid basis with jobbery and bribery an accepted part of the procedure.[100] South Carolina may have even hoped to fight this alliance of tar and hemp suppliers by passing a law in 1722 to encourage the growing of hemp in

[98] Testimony of Joseph Boone and Richard Beresford before Board of Trade, February 25, 1718, BPRO-SC, VII, 79–80.

[99] Governor Robert Johnson to Board of Trade, January 12, 1720, ibid., VII, 233–250.

[100] Beveridge, *Prices and Wages in England,* 621.

the colony.[101] But hemp never did become an export item and must be listed as just another of the many crop possibilities tried.

Since English opponents of plantation tar could not be converted, more and more the campaign centered on arguments to stress the mercantilist advantages in continuing these subsidies. Without the bounty, it was frequently pointed out, the Swedes would return to their monopolistic position, would raise prices, and drain the nation of specie. One advocate said that competition from colonial tar had forced the Swedes to lower their per barrel price from 50s. before 1705 to 11s. or 12s. at the present time (early 1720's). Another argument stressed that South Carolina and the colonies generally had the resources to expand naval stores production indefinitely and almost infinitely without fear of foreign interference. Colonial naval stores required a large merchant marine to carry such bulky commodities, thus giving training and employment to sailors and shipbuilders supplying the fleet. Moreover, colonial naval stores manufacture would stimulate shipbuilding in America and the West Indies.[102]

English governmental officials were quite aware at all times of the need to protect the nation's tar supply. The problem by the early 1720's had become one of cutting the cost of the bounty system or abandoning it. The initial attempt at reform was written into the naval stores act of 1722, which notified colonial producers that after September 29, 1724, only tar manufactured by the Swedish method would qualify for the subsidy. This was only a tentative change, for the clause in the 1722 law pertaining to tar was

---

[101] Cooper and McCord (eds.), *Statutes of S.C.*, III, 184.

[102] Documents relating to efforts to save the naval stores bounty are many, including those in BPRO-SC, VII, 5–8, 12, 13–14, 79–80, 222, 233–250; X, 2–11; XI, 203–209, 364–366.

really only an amendment to the current bounty system which would itself cease on September 29, 1724, unless renewed by Parliament. To colonials, a new threat had been added. Not only was the bounty system in doubt, even if it were kept, only tar produced by the Swedish method and certified by close surveillance of the manufacturer would draw the bounty.

The American, particularly the South Carolinian, reaction to this new drift in imperial tar policy was predictably negative. They continued their efforts to have the bounty system perpetuated, but after 1722 much effort was concentrated on showing the impracticalities of the Swedish method of making tar for South Carolina planters. Francis Yonge catalogued these objections in a petition to the Board of Trade. He said that South Carolinians did not know how to select the trees for stripping as described in the 1722 act. Of 20 cut, no more than two trees would be fit for the kiln. This lack of understanding of the method was, therefore, most destructive of the forests. Moreover, using equal amounts of wood (amount unspecified), the old or deadwood method would produce 600 barrels of tar and a profit of £150 sterling for the planter, while the green wood or Swedish method would result in 200 barrels of tar and a net profit of only £37 10s. To follow this method, a planter would have to employ his labor in naval stores manufacture the year round, not just in the winter, the usual practice in South Carolina. Since rice would now be more profitable to export, this would tend to limit tar and pitch making. The extra labor necessary to make tar by the new method turned a marginally profitable commodity into an even less attractive investment. Labor costs in South Carolina were four times greater than labor costs in Sweden. Also, freight from South Carolina to England was four times greater than freight from Sweden to England. In the end, Yonge admitted that South Carolinians could follow the Swedish method, but the obstacles to profit were so many and so great that they would not.[103]

Despite the aggressive lobbying efforts by South Carolinians, other colonials, and some merchants, the Board of Trade and Parliament were not moved. The matter of the Swedish method of making tar became academic after it was decided to let the bounty law lapse. Perhaps the constant barrage of testimony that Americans would never manufacture tar by this complicated and time-consuming process convinced imperial officials that bounties could not force or induce Americans to alter their method of making tar. A system built up to meet certain imperial needs had seemingly outrun its usefulness and should be terminated. In dropping the bounty system, officials were not concerned with the reverberations of their action in South Carolina, but its demise can be easily related to the economic and political troubles of the colony.

What did the tar and pitch trades mean financially to South Carolina? While there is adequate pricing information for the English market, we have little testimony on the profits for planters. Yonge's estimates are probably conservative, since he was trying to prove a point, but he claimed that by 1723 and 1724 profit on tar was only 3s. 6d. or 4s. per barrel, even with the bounty.[104] Pitch, with its lower price per barrel, probably brought an even smaller return. Using Yonge's figures, profits on the 45,000 barrels shipped in 1724 might have been in the £5,000 to £10,000 sterling range. Since we know that prices dropped for 1725, the 60,000 barrels (95 per cent pitch) probably did not bring any greater profits.[105] Even if this projected profit is low, it is

[103] Francis Yonge to Board of Trade, marked received February 5, 1723, ibid., X, 2–11.

[104] Ibid.

[105] Though it is clear from statements made in correspondence that by 1724 South Carolinians had reconciled themselves to the death of the bounties, it

almost inconceivable that total profits exceeded £15,000 sterling annually after 1718, though profits may have been higher from 1715 through 1718. Wiping out this profit would have gone hard on a struggling colony any time, but it was a disaster at this particular juncture when, as we shall see, no trades which planters depended on were doing very well.

It should be added that the foreseeable demise of the tar and pitch trades did not drive the planters or anyone else in South Carolina to produce and ship turpentine and rosin, though the bounties still applied. In the peak year between 1715 and 1725 only 1,245 barrels of turpentine were shipped, and the total for most years was considerably below that level. After 1720 amounts exported declined rather than grew. In 1724 only 469 barrels were shipped. Rosin exports continued to be negligible.[106]

Nor did the great drive to manufacture tar and pitch after 1715 lead to the neglect of rice culture. Considering the actual physical disruptions within the colony, it is remarkable that so much rice was grown from 1715 through 1718.

---

is difficult to determine whether the great amounts of tar and pitch shipped from late 1724 through 1727 received the subsidy. A number of possibilities may be noted. These shipments may have been certified since the renewal of the bounty act in 1713 (12 Anne, c. 9) specified that the continuation would be to September 29, 1724, and from that date to the first session of the next Parliament. The first session of the Seventh Parliament of Great Britain did not meet until January 23, 1728. The many complaints from South Carolina seem to support the conclusion that payments stopped long before early 1728. Of course, the Royal Navy could have ceased paying at any time merely by refusing to certify naval stores, which, in effect, would have ended the bounties. Yet, Francis Yonge's many calculations showed that without the bounties it was impossible to ship naval stores from South Carolina to England at a profit (gross prices, and presumably profits, were already very low by 1724). It hardly seems likely that the South Carolinians shipped the great quantities of 1724 to 1726 only to take a loss. The best chance for a full answer to this riddle might come to light if surviving navy accounts contain full information about when and to whom bounties were paid.

[106] Table III, Appendix.

The explanation may be that abandoned frontier areas produced little or no rice. Reduced crops resulted more from the conversion of planters into Indian fighters. A planter who was unavailable to supervise cultivation was not likely to have a good yield. Since rice was much more profitable than tar and pitch by 1715, rice planters were eager to resume expansion as soon as possible, as the records of shipments attest.

After peace came, rice exports gradually regained the level of pre-1715 annual shipments. On the basis of questionable data, the year 1715 seems to have been the low spot, and 1716 was better.[107] In 1717 only 8,289 barrels were shipped, about two-thirds as much as was transported five years earlier. By 1718, the year of the last formal peace treaty, shipments reached 13,749 barrels or about 1,000 barrels more than had been sent out in 1712–1713 over a 12-month span. After 1718 the tendency was toward a steadily increasing export total, though shipments were affected from year to year by the prevailing weather and other cultivation factors. The 1719 total was almost 15,000 barrels, and in harvest year 1720 over 20,000 barrels, the largest crop to date, left Charles Town wharves.[108] This accomplishment came despite the worst drought in the colony's history, when it did not rain for five months.[109] After 1722, when exports reached 23,559 barrels, the total shipped annually fell back to about 20,000 barrels for the years 1723–1725.[110] After 1720 South Carolina obviously was capable of consistently growing and shipping more than 20,000 barrels annually. Why did it not until after 1725?

An analysis of this trade suggests that saturation of rice

---

[107] *Historical Statistics of United States,* 768 (Series Z 274–280) . The figures in this table came from the highly questionable customs records.
[108] Table III, Appendix.
[109] Richard Splatt to Samuel Barons, July 20, 1720, BPRO-SC, VIII, 34–35.
[110] Table III, Appendix.

markets legally open to South Carolinians was the restraint on the expansion of rice cultivation between 1720 and 1725. Since 1705, when enumeration went into effect, at least 70 to 80 per cent of all rice exported had gone to England.[111] But the English market was limited, and much of the rice was re-exported to the continent. A Board of Trade paper dated 1721 calculated that about 70 per cent of the rice imported into England for the five years 1713 through 1717 was re-exported to northern European ports (mostly Holland and Germany), 10 per cent was re-exported to southern Europe (mostly Spain and Portugal), and 20 per cent was consumed at home.[112] Yet, it was commonly held that southern Europe potentially was the largest market of the three. Rice was in great demand in these Roman Catholic countries during Lent when it was served in place of meat. Thus, it was essential that rice destined for southern Europe reach there in early spring to be on sale during the season of greatest demand. But South Carolina rice was largely barred from this market, for under enumeration it took too long to ship the fall's harvest to England and then transship it to Spain and Portugal.[113]

Virtual loss of the southern European market was not too damaging until the English market and the northern European market had been fully supplied. Francis Yonge once calculated the normal yearly demand for these two markets at 10,000 to 12,000 barrels.[114] Although South Carolina reached that level of exportation about 1712, demand had not yet been satisfied, since 20 to 30 per cent of the exported

[111] This conclusion based on an analysis of the naval lists from the 1717 to 1720 period; it is probable that the situation was the same from 1705 to 1717. Clowse, "The Charleston Export Trade, 1717–1737," 212.

[112] Board of Trade to His Majesty, September 8, 1721, BPRO-SC, IX, 65–76.

[113] Memorial from Joseph Boone to Board of Trade, November 22, 1721, ibid., IX, 41–42.

[114] Francis Yonge to Board of Trade, marked received February 5, 1723, ibid., X, 2–11.

rice normally went to the northern colonies and the West Indies.[115] Some of the latter may have subsequently been shipped to England, but much of it was consumed in these colonies. The Yamasee War inhibited any rapid increase of production for export until about 1718 or 1719, but by 1720 and 1721 the harvests in South Carolina were too great for the English and northern European markets to absorb at high prices. It is precisely at this point that Yonge pinpointed a 25 per cent decline in rice prices from 21s. sterling per hundredweight delivered in England in 1719 to 16s. in 1721.[116]

Limitation of the rice market under imperial laws had always been irksome to South Carolinians who felt that enumeration in 1705 had ruined a budding trade with Spain and Portugal. Nevertheless, they had soft-pedalled the rice question as long as the naval stores bounty matter was unresolved. They were seeking to hold onto something they had rather than putting energy into a cause which, though desirable, was not as pressing. By 1720, however, facing the prospect of losing the tar and pitch bounties, they had to agitate and lobby for modification of the law pertaining to rice shipping. Increasingly, spokesmen emphasized the advantages to empire and colony if rice were allowed a free market. Joseph Boone calculated that loss of the southern European market cost the empire £20,000 sterling annually plus the benefits of employing more sailors and vessels.[117]

Various proposals were advanced to collect the crown duties in South Carolina, since imperial officials were con-

---

[115] Clowse, "The Charleston Export Trade, 1717–1737," 213–214. This conclusion holds true at least through 1720.

[116] Francis Yonge to Board of Trade, marked received February 5, 1723, BPRO-SC, X, 2–11.

[117] Memorial from Joseph Boone to Board of Trade, November 22, 1721, ibid., IX, 41–42.

cerned that these would be lost if enumeration were ended.[118] Advocates of the reform even insisted that, with rice off the enumerated list, the crown would actually be adding to its revenues. A ton of rice was often exchanged for a ton of wine. Each ton of wine brought into Britain carried a duty of £22 while a ton of rice imported only bore 11s. 8d. customs duty.[119] By 1724 the governor and the council resorted to scare tactics, as they reported that the French were growing rice at Mobile and feeding it to their troops. Once they had learned cultivation techniques, it was feared that they would supply Roman Catholic countries.[120] As in the case of naval stores, the Board was not moved to alleviate South Carolina's marketing problem for rice.

Though the prices of rice are not as certain as those of naval stores, it is reasonably clear that they continued to decline from 1720 to 1725. Governor Robert Johnson placed the price at 18s. sterling per hundredweight in 1721, 2s. more than Yonge's price.[121] Yonge set the 1722 average price at 15s., indicating a further weakening of the market. Deducting duty and freight, commissions, warehouse costs, cooperage costs, and petty charges, he calculated that planter profits were down to 2s. 6d. per hundredweight, or 10s. sterling per 400-pound barrel.[122] If Yonge is to be believed, the approximately 20,000 barrels exported annually in the early 1720's netted between £10,000 and £20,000 sterling.[123] This would

[118] For example, ibid.
[119] H. Walpole to Alured Popple, September 28, 1722, ibid., IX, 140–145.
[120] Governor and Council to Board of Trade, September 4, 1724, ibid., XI, 203–209.
[121] "An Account of the Net Produce of Rice Shipped . . . 1721 and 1731," conveyed with a letter from Governor Johnson to Board of Trade, December 16, 1731, ibid., XV, 69–71; Francis Yonge to Board of Trade, marked received February 5, 1723, ibid., X, 2–11.
[122] Francis Yonge to Alured Popple, December 10, 1722, ibid., IX, 170–171.
[123] Yonge calculated profit from the 1719 crop at £21,263 19s. 7d. and from the 1721 crop at £17,092 19s. 5d. in his letter to the Board of Trade, marked received February 5, 1723, ibid., X, 2–11

make total annual profits as much as or slightly more than the profits on naval stores in the same years.

Tracing the path to oblivion for tar and pitch bounties and the downward trend for rice profits explains much of the planters' anger and the general discontent of 1719 and the desperate 1720's. It is not entirely coincidental, though more data are needed for an unequivocal conclusion, that the political revolution occurred in late 1719, the same year that tar and pitch prices dropped sharply and the rice market began to show signs of being oversupplied. Planter attitudes on currency and finance become clearer, since it is apparent that they were in straits almost as bad as they claimed they were. They wanted to manipulate something in their own favor! If the profit on naval stores, rice, and the minor trades was at least £30,000 to £40,000 sterling annually in about 1720 (and perhaps under £20,000 annually by 1725), the people were not able to offset their current obligations. They were buying at least £20,000 to £30,000 of manufactured goods from England and an average of over 500 slaves annually (£10,000, at £20 each slave on the average).[124] Moreover, the planters were buying land when possible, paying high taxes on land and slaves, and, in many cases, paying off old debts and replacing war losses. No wonder the mood was one of desperation.

Nor did any of the established minor trades offer any hope for expansion to take up the financial slack being left by the demise of the naval stores trade and the weakened market position of rice. Of these minor trades, provisions had always been the most important. Exports of beef and pork actually declined from 3,204 barrels shipped in 1712–1713 to a level

[124] There are many conflicting sets of figures for the value of total imports and exports. For example, see *Historical Statistics of United States*, 757 (Series Z 21–34). This table gives higher values for "Carolina" exports to, and imports from, England than the figures used above.

of 1,000 to 1,500 barrels annually in the 1715–1725 period.[125] This decline is traceable directly, in the short run, to the Yamasee War. Settlers driven from the frontier areas of the colony were forced to stop herding, a business which was often carried on until more sophisticated types of agriculture could be introduced after land was cleared and prepared for cultivation.

In the long run, however, herding failed to recover. Yonge pointed out that though curtailment of this trade hurt, it had never been "very Beneficial" owing to its profit structure.[126] While pricing data are scanty, items sold in barrels (flour, peas, corn, biscuit, bread, and other foods, as well as beef and pork) did not sell for more than a few pounds current money per unit. This low profit trade might have developed strength and importance through high volume, but the more northerly colonies, particularly Pennsylvania and New York, were efficient competitors and prevented South Carolinians from building this part of their commerce. A provisions trade was not an adequate replacement for naval stores and not a supplement to rice.

To help themselves, South Carolinians were interested in new schemes for commercial crops and revived old ones between 1715 and 1725. In 1716 Stephen Godin testified before the Board of Trade that Carolina-produced silk was as fine as Piedmont silk. Further, he said that he had sold several bales of South Carolina silk for 33s. per pound. Coffee and other "drugs" should be tried in the colony, he suggested. He was particularly interested in cochineal. This insect, bred under prickly pear leaves growing near the ground, was "wild" in South Carolina. As a result, the insects did not grow as large and flat as the variety the Span-

---

[125] Table III, Appendix.
[126] Francis Yonge to Board of Trade, marked received February 5, 1723, BPRO-SC, X, 2–11.

iards were able to produce through cultivation and improvement in gardens. He said, nevertheless, that, pound for
pound, South Carolina cochineal was as good as the Mexican
product.[127] At a later meeting of the Board, he showed some
scarlet cloth, one piece dyed with Spanish cochineal and
another piece with cochineal gathered in South Carolina.
Under questioning, he admitted that it took three times as
much South Carolina cochineal to give the same color in-
tensity as achieved with Spanish cochineal.[128] Whatever
hopes and dreams were held for these and similar projects do
not seem to have been realized, and no new commercial
staples were developed at this time, when they might have
been welcomed and certainly were needed.

In the midst of all their difficulties after 1715, the South
Carolina assembly continued to try to promote shipbuilding
and a carrying trade dominated by local men. Some of their
inducements were clearly aimed at English merchants, and
the stratagem was quickly spotted by hurt parties. A March
1719 law levying import-export duties allowed goods imported on locally owned and locally built vessels to enter at
sharply reduced rates of taxation. Some stipulations were
openly geared to favor local merchants. A South Carolina
merchant importing goods on his own vessel, not necessarily
built in the province, was entitled to half rates on his imports. This did not encourage shipbuilding; it gave the competitive edge to local merchants. The English merchants and
the proprietors saw through the ruse and other inconsisten-
cies in the law, and it was speedily disallowed in July 1719.[129]
This minor skirmish offers an additional bit of proof of the
growing tensions between the planters, represented by the

[127] Journal of the Board of Trade, June 28, 1716, ibid., VI, 286–288.
[128] Journal of the Board of Trade, July 25, 1716, ibid., VI, 289–290.
[129] Cooper and McCord (eds.), *Statutes of S.C.*, III, 56–69.

lower house of the assembly, and the merchants, particularly the English merchants.

Other laws were not devious in purpose. A 1711 enactment, renewed in 1718 and 1720, continued subsidies of 7s. 6d. current money per ton for vessels built in the province, although the law apparently was not reinstated after it expired in 1722.[130] This subsidy may have helped keep local shipbuilders active from 1715 through 1719, the last period of comparative boom in South Carolina vessel construction. Indeed, the peak of shipbuilding and vessel ownership until after 1740 came during these years of economic trouble. From 1715 through 1719 at least 27 vessels were launched in the province. Of these, 21 were very small coasting vessels, ranging in size from 6 to 30 tons burden. Most were classified as sloops. Five were between 50 and 80 tons. Only one was over 100-tons burden, the size ship usually employed to sail from Charles Town to England. This was the ship *Princess Carolina*, 150 tons burden.[131] Benjamin Austin, the man who built her, was her first master. He, his apprentice, and 14 other men including 11 shipwrights, a sawyer, a caulker and a joiner were protected from being pressed into military service by order of the proprietors in 1716.[132] They were regarded as too valuable to the province to risk in an Indian war. After 1720, incomplete naval lists substantiate to a reasonable degree of certainty that shipbuilding declined. These available naval lists indicate only four vessels being built from 1720 through 1724.[133] Doubtless others were built, but shipbuilding activity seems to have declined sharply starting about 1720.

[130] Ibid., II, 365; III, 84–86; III, 117.
[131] Clowse, "The Charleston Export Trade, 1717–1737," 149–152, 307–308.
[132] Proprietors to Governor, February 23, 1716, BPRO-SC, VI, 148.
[133] Clowse, "The Charleston Export Trade, 1717–1737," 307–308.

Vessel ownership in the colony closely correlates with local shipbuilding activity. In 1717 the Charles Town-based fleet had 33 craft totaling 1,143 tons burden, approximately three times as many vessels as Governor Nathaniel Johnson had listed in 1708. While the size of this little merchant fleet varied considerably from year to year, in an average year during the 1717–1720 period, 25 vessels aggregating 942 tons burden were held by South Carolinians. The mean size of these vessels was in the range of 35 to 40 tons burden, not much larger than the average size of vessels reported in 1697–1698. Three to five vessels capable of sailing to England were always included in the total. After 1720, when the fleet had diminished to 20 vessels, fewer larger vessels were owned locally. By 1724 Charles Town's merchant fleet consisted of ten vessels, only two of which were of sufficient size to brave the voyage to England.[134] This index reflects the growing strain on the local mercantile community in a colony where nearly all trades were declining in profits if not in volume.

From this anatomization of the economy in the years between 1715 and 1725, two major conclusions seem inescapable. First, the crown was responsible for South Carolina's steadily weakening fiscal foundation. Second, the deepening economic crisis was the single most important underlying cause for the political rebellion in 1719 and the constant tensions over money and finances after 1715. The proprietors, the crown, the Yamasee and their allies, the pirates, and even the merchants and planters may be blamed for conditions, but only the crown had the power to correct the fundamental structural weaknesses in the colony's economy and, thus, give the South Carolinians a chance to solve their other problems. In particular, the decision to terminate tar

[134] Ibid., 144–145, 305–309.

and pitch bounties after 20 years and the refusal to open continental rice markets were disastrous judgments for the colony. A favorable change of policy in either or both matters would have most surely gone a long way toward correcting the economic and political ills which accumulated during these ten years.

By 1725 South Carolina was in the midst of a serious depression. Remedies were beyond the reach of the colonists. They could only wait for relief from London. Sometime in the 1720's, these South Carolinians must have come to recognize that exchanging their proprietary masters for a royal one was no sure cure for their ills. Insensitivity of the crown may well have kindled the idea that only local control of government and economy could insure a people's future. Already the Commons House of Assembly was the voice of the people, and it was to become more strident and abrasive rather than less so in pursuit of this self-interest. Governor Francis Nicholson, alert guardian of the crown's prerogatives, may have detected this nascent feeling of alienation. The year before he departed the colony, he wrote that "the Spirit of Comon Wealth Principles both in Church and State increase here dayly . . . ," though he ascribed this disturbing drift to the influence of the variable South Carolina climate and the New Englanders among the people.[135] When he sailed, he did leave settlers with blighted hopes and an uncertain future.

[135] Governor Nicholson to Board of Trade, June 18, 1724, BPRO-SC, XI, 134.

CHAPTER VIII

An Era Ends
1725–1730

Between 1725 and 1730 the proprietary era dragged through its concluding phase. Although any South Carolinian in 1725 knew that these were terrible times, few could have foreseen the nadir reached before a rebound would begin. From 1725 to 1729, while the Board of Trade continued its procrastinating evaluations of the situation in process since at least 1719, the South Carolina caretaker government became impotent, and the economy crumbled further. Then, during 1729 the Board of Trade formulated a number of policies and started to implement them. In December 1730, when the first royal governor with full powers and this authorized program assumed office in Charles Town, an era ended and another began.

During these years, the colony and its people were adversely affected by the economy's weakness. The deterioration of every major trade, except deerskins, during this period eroded the economic gains which had been made. Though total productivity could have been expanded after 1725, this increased capacity was of little use as long as imperial regulations and low market prices made increased exportation an unprofitable or low-profit exercise. The bleak outlook made individuals insecure. While some doubtless clung to their positions in society, others were so devastated by the conditions that they were forced lower on the economic and social ladder. Those striving to rise found it difficult or impossible to do so. It is little wonder that from 1725 to 1730, this was a surly society in constant turmoil and flux.

For the first time in the colony's history, the problem of the economy had come to overshadow all purely political issues. Settlers, merchants, local governmental officials, and imperial officials alike gradually came to the realization that South Carolina could never regain stability in both government and economy unless something were done to bolster the weakened market position of the colony. In the final analysis, the recommendations of the Board of Trade mattered most. Before 1725, for imperial considerations, Board of Trade policies had undermined the economic foundation it had helped build some 20 years before; by 1729, finding some of South Carolina's needs consistent with imperial needs, the Board had decided that policy revisions necessary to aid the empire would also revive the colony.

To understand how and why events occurred as they did in Charles Town and in London, the colony's trade and general business health must be examined first, since the all-important imperial policies were designed as cures for specific ills. Unfortunately, this is a difficult task. Most aspects of the economy between 1725 and the early 1730's have a certain amount of mystery about them. In nearly every significant series of records, there are major omissions. Some series, such as the naval lists, disappeared entirely and are not now known to exist, if they were ever sent to London. Correspondence between Charles Town and London is less full, and therefore less revealing, than the multitudinous dispatches surviving from the period before 1725 or after 1730.

One suspects a causal relationship between the disintegration of the local government and the scarcity of surviving records. Any view of the period must, accordingly, be atomistic; the missing links must be filled by hypotheses, conjectures, and interpolations. Nevertheless, worsening conditions after 1725 have continuity with the train of events unleashed in 1715 and, despite qualifications, an economic configuration may be constructed from piecing together the fragmented sources.

Total population growth between 1725 and 1730 was considerable but can be attributed mainly to importations of slaves. White immigration continued to be negligible, as it had been for years. Perhaps a few Swiss reached the colony,[1] but not many others from any source. The high birth rate was chiefly responsible for enlarging the white population. As usual, the various estimates conflict, and they range from a low of 8,000 whites to a high of 16,000 for the late 1720's and early 1730's. Governor George Burrington of North Carolina estimated that there were 2,000 adult white males in 1729.[2] This would justify an estimate of 8,000, if each white male tithable represented four others. The weight of evidence seems strongest for no more than 10,000 whites in the colony by 1730, possibly an increase of about 2,500 to 3,000 since 1720.[3] None of the population compilations from this period separate white indentured servants from the general white population, though it is generally assumed that there were comparatively few servants by this time.

On the other hand, Negro population growth outstripped the white increase. The slave population may have doubled between 1720 and 1730 despite all the economic woes. Con-

[1] John Vat to His Majesty, "after January 1726/7," BPRO-SC, XII, 190–192. This letter seems to indicate that 24 Swiss had arrived in the colony.

[2] Governor Burrington to Board of Trade, July 28, 1729, ibid., XIII, 373–374.

[3] Table I, Appendix.

siderable increase would have come from the high birth rate, commonly reckoned to be 10 per cent annually; however, importation remained the chief means of rapidly adding to the slave total. From 1726 through 1730 over 7,000 slaves were brought into the colony. This was a far greater number imported than for any previous five-year span. Even during the worst years for commercial exports, 1728–1729, the buying pace did not slacken appreciably.[4] Strong circumstantial evidence for an augmented slave trade may be found in the expanding rice trade of the 1725–1730 period, for rice was one staple grown and harvested almost exclusively with black labor. Governor Burrington placed the slave population at 20,000 tithables in 1729;[5] Governor Robert Johnson used the same figure in 1731.[6] Other estimates fall close to this one. In absolute terms, there were 8,000 to 10,000 more slaves in South Carolina in 1730 than there had been in 1720.[7] The proportion of blacks to whites remained two to one. Few mentions of Indian slaves are made in documents from this period, and it must be assumed that they no longer formed a significant part of the slave population.

The 10,000 to 12,000 increase in population in the 1720's did not accompany an extension in the area occupied. The land office remained shut, as it had been since 1719. As long as they retained rights to the soil, the proprietors continued to authorize some grants; but the total acreage was meager, and most such grants were probably not laid out at this time. Of necessity, the process of consolidation which had been

[4] Based on data from the contemporary broadside, "Account of Importations and Exportations at the Port of Charles-Town, South Carolina, from 1724 to 1735" (Charles-Town, 1736).

[5] Governor Burrington to Board of Trade, July 28, 1729, BPRO-SC, XIII, 373–374.

[6] "An Account of the Net Produce of Rice Shipped . . . 1721 and 1731," conveyed with a letter from Governor Johnson to Board of Trade, December 16, 1731, ibid., XV, 69–71.

[7] Table I, Appendix.

going on since the end of the Yamasee War continued after 1725. While the inability to obtain headrights for slaves imported must have contributed to discontent among the planters, it is inconceivable that, even with the growth, the total population was too great for the amount of land already privately owned.

One meaningful trend after 1725 was the rapid decline in tar and pitch exportation and the shift to rice, the only profitable commodity left. Yet, even after the bounties were supposedly dropped, tar and pitch shipments in 1726 and 1727 were not insignificant. From the 1725 peak of 60,000 barrels, in 1726 the total exported fell to 38,000 barrels; in 1727, to 25,000 barrels; in 1728 the bottom was reached when only slightly more than 5,000 barrels left Charles Town. The sharp break between 1727 and 1728 suggests either that some or all shipments in 1726 and 1727 received the bounty or that South Carolinians were testing to see if they could continue to sell these commodities at a profit without the subsidy.[8] After 1728 shipments increased slightly for the next three years, amounting to 20 per cent of the 1725 level of annual exports.[9]

The lack of profits without the bounty destroyed the naval stores trade. Without the government price supplement, the thin profits of 1725 became thinner or disappeared. Tar and pitch prices in Britain remained low from 1726 through 1730. Swedish tar was purchased by the Royal Navy for between 13s. and 15s. per barrel in this five-year period. These were the lowest prices since the 1680's. Since the compilers list no prices for American tar in 1725, 1727, 1728, and 1729, because little or none was purchased by the navy,

[8] Table III, Appendix. On the question of profits, see note 105 in Chapter VII.

[9] Shipments and computations in the above paragraph based on *Historical Statistics of United States*, 770 (Series Z 304–307).

we can not be sure of its price. If past experience held true, it was doubtless several shillings per barrel cheaper than Swedish tar on the open market. To give these prices fuller meaning, it should be recalled that American tar sold for as much as 26s. or 27s. sterling per barrel (plus bounty) during the favorable 1705–1717 period. Moreover, only about one-third of all tar and pitch exports from Charles Town between 1726 and 1730 was tar.[10] The other two-thirds, pitch, sold at an even lower price, generally about 8s. or 9s., though pitch prices were slightly higher from 1726 to 1730 than they had been from 1720 to 1725.[11] In 1726 the reduction in the volume of exports, the low prices, and the loss of bounties combined to lower total profits from tar and pitch for planters of the colony to £5,000 sterling or less. By the 1728 low point, profits were practically nothing.[12]

As naval stores became a low-profit item, rice received ever greater emphasis. Every harvest from 1725 through 1730 was larger than the year before. In 1725 more than 17,000 barrels were shipped; in 1726, about 23,000; in 1727, almost 27,000; in 1728, about 30,000; in 1729, more than 32,000; and in 1730, more than 48,000 barrels. Despite some reservations about this compilation, it does affirm that rice exports were going ahead by leaps and bounds from 1725 to 1730; by 1730 they were more than double what they had been in 1725.[13]

While pricing data for rice are weak, Governor Johnson in 1731 wrote that in 1721 rice had sold for 17s. sterling per hundredweight (£3 12s. per 400-pound barrel). He calcu-

[10] Table III, Appendix.

[11] Beveridge, *Prices and Wages in England*, 673, 675.

[12] It is assumed that profits in 1726 and 1727 would be about the same as from 1720 to 1725 if the tar and pitch received bounties; profits would have been small or nil without bounties.

[13] C. J. Gayle, "The Nature and Volume of Exports from Charleston, 1724–1774," *The Proceedings of the South Carolina Historical Association, 1937,* 30; Table III, Appendix.

lated that the 22,000 barrels shipped made a net profit for the planters of £28,661 sterling or about £1 6s. sterling per barrel. By 1731, rice prices had dropped about 20 per cent to 14s. 6d. per hundredweight (£2 18s. per 400-pound barrel). He figured that the 50,000 barrels exported made a net profit of £33,333 sterling or about 13s. or 14s. per barrel (about half the profit per unit shipped when compared to 1721). He pointed out that it took double the capital investment in slaves (10,000 in 1721 versus 20,000 in 1731 at £20 sterling each) and three times the amount of land for the increased crop.[14] Again, we have many unanswered questions, but the trend is beyond dispute. Nor did rice prices improve in the 1730's, generally fluctuating between 5s. and 12s. sterling per hundredweight.[15] No one ever summarized the long-term problem of American agriculture better than Governor Johnson when he explained that "Rice is at present the staple but by reason of the great quantitys made and the confined market" the price had fallen and "the planter will be ruined by his own industry." [16]

This forced shift away from naval stores to rice had important social implications as well as economic impact. The rice planter was the only large operator deriving wealth from the soil after 1725. Rice lands became the only lands of any great value. Anyone owning such lands was not going to sell them. Though the rice planter was hurting financially because of limited markets, the man who had depended on tar and pitch to make wealth was ruined, whereas the rice planter had the means to survive in the late 1720's. He most likely

[14] "An Account of the Net Produce of Rice Shipped . . . 1721 and 1731," conveyed with a letter from Governor Johnson to Board of Trade, December 16, 1731, BPRO-SC, XV, 69–71.

[15] Arthur H. Cole, *Wholesale Commodity Prices in the United States, 1700–1861: Statistical Supplement Actual Wholesale Prices of Various Commodities* (Cambridge, Massachusetts, 1938), 15–21.

[16] Governor Johnson to Board of Trade, marked received January 26, 1732, ibid., XV, 87–89.

already had vast reserves of land and many slaves. He had room to maneuver, to adapt to the reorientation of the economy in progress.

The smaller planter owning few or no slaves was hit the hardest. He most likely owned poorer lands, including pine lands, and might have once depended on naval stores as the chief item of production. After the bounties lapsed, this yeoman farmer lost his export trade and even his pine lands fell in value since their potential was gone. The yeoman planters saw a major access route to wealth blocked. In a debt-ridden society with monetary troubles, credit was non-existent or very expensive. Loans without valuable land or slaves for collateral were most likely unobtainable. The cleavage between the rice-planting elite and the rest of the whites widened and deepened in the late 1720's. This South Carolina experience parallels to some degree the Virginia experience of the eighteenth century when narrowing tobacco profits squeezed out the little planters. In both colonies, only the big operators who owned suitable lands and a large pool of slave labor could hope to hold on under adverse marketing conditions.

To analyze how these changes in the fortunes and opportunities for individuals affected political alignments and contributed to the political instability of the period is difficult. There is no body of data which allows us to establish that a given man or group of men took the political stand they did as a result of alterations in economic and social position. Yet, it is inconceivable that the discontent, the threatened violence, and the governmental disintegration are not related to the economic changes. This is one of the mysteries that political historians must delve into if they are going to explain more completely why events happened as they did during the 1720's.

The lack of complete records interferes somewhat, but the

minor trades seem to have made no advances from 1725 to 1730. By looking ahead to the 1730's, it appears safe to assert that all these trades lacked vitality after 1725. In fact, most slipped in importance despite market weaknesses in what had been the major export commodities. The provisions trade in barreled beef and pork did not recover, and in the late 1720's totaled between 400 and 700 barrels annually. By the 1730's its volume was less than it had been in 1724 and about half of what it had been in 1717–1720. The 1730's records show more flour, bread, peas, and corn exported than in the 1717–1720 period, but total volume remained very small. Lumber exports continued to increase, but even in the 1730's only limited amounts of shingles, boards, staves, and similar products were shipped.[17]

Considering the depressed condition of the colony, it is doubtful that the merchant community built more vessels in South Carolina after 1725 than previously. The naval lists for 1731 and 1732 indicate local shipowning at about the level it had been in 1724. In 1731, the number of locally held vessels was 11, and in 1732 the total was 13.[18] Nothing points toward any established business endeavors expanding to replace naval stores.

Nor do records of the time hint that any new product emerged. Thomas Lowndes, a South Carolina official, wrote two letters in 1730 in which he advocated potash and sesame seed as appropriate products. He sent a sample of sesame seed to the Royal Society. He thought that sesame would grow well on the pine lands of South Carolina with each acre producing 20 to 25 bushels of seed which would press out to

[17] Clowse, "The Charleston Export Trade, 1717–1737," 193–194; the broadside, "Account of Importations and Exportations at the Port of Charles-Town, South Carolina, from 1724 to 1735," has export data which support the basic conclusions offered in this paragraph.
[18] Clowse, "The Charleston Export Trade, 1717–1737," 301–304.

11 quarts of oil usable in woolen manufacture.[19] In recommending a scheme for making saltpeter, a Mr. Slater promised the Board of Trade to make 200 tons a year for each 10 men employed. The Board was unimpressed with his presentation and refused to subsidize a pilot project.[20] Hemp was often mentioned in the records of the 1720's, but it never caught on. Richard Hall, who in the 1730's had gone to Holland to obtain hemp seed, put his finger on the problem of trying to turn this rice-oriented society toward new crops when he wrote that ". . . the planters are so much attached to following Rice being a commodity most contracted for paying merchants and factors for Negros &c. and most of the inhabitants are so much in Debt that they are fearful of entering new projects till they are further convinced of the difference between Hemp and Rice. . . ." [21]

The deerskin trade was the single exception to this generally dismal story. If total exports are a valid index, only Indian traders and some merchants were prosperous after 1725. Nothing seems to have interfered with the trade, though the flare-up with the Yamasee in 1727–1728 gave the whole colony some anxious moments. An average annual export level of about 80,000 deerskins was reached in the 1726–1730 period. This was about one-third more than in the 1720–1725 years when the trade was recovering from the Yamasee War.[22] In all the tumult and debate over finance, comparatively little attention was paid to the deerskin trade except to be sure that it was supervised and taxed. Though profits are difficult to calculate, 80,000 deerskins may well

[19] Thomas Lowndes to Board of Trade, May 19, 1730, BPRO-SC, XIV, 132–133; Thomas Lowndes to Board of Trade, August 26, 1730, ibid., XIV, 261–262.

[20] Minutes of Board of Trade, November 30, 1731, ibid., XV, 3–4.

[21] Richard Hall to Board of Trade, May 8, 1735, ibid., XV, 313–315.

[22] Crane, *Southern Frontier*, 330.

have drawn a profit to the colony of £20,000 to £30,000 sterling.[23] Certainly, the trade was second only to rice in total value. Yet, while it flourished when most trades languished, the deerskin trade supported some traders and merchants and did not help the majority.

Within this context of economic stagnation and deterioration, South Carolina's government had to function. Soon after Governor Nicholson departed in May 1725, the troubles started. He left Arthur Middleton, President of the Council, at the head of a caretaker government.[24] Middleton was instructed to veto any radical legislation passed, a shackling restriction in a society with a large public debt, paper money problems, defense problems, a stagnated economy, and a discouraged people, who, nevertheless, had developed a strong political sense of their right to legislate for their own benefit. It was not long before Middleton, the Council, and a few merchants were pitted against the Commons, representing a majority of the settlers, in a deadlocked fight over fiscal policies. Middleton had become a hard money man since he had to follow orders, though previously he was reckoned a moderate on the question. The Commons wanted more bills of credit. Each side stymied the other, but until 1727 cooperation was sufficient to pass necessary legislation. In 1727 government virtually broke down when the two factions became so divided that compromises were no longer possible. The demise coincided with the more obvious manifestations of a troubled economy, as reflected by the export figures. It will be recalled that the 1727 shipments of tar and pitch were 40 per cent of what they had been in 1725, and these were the last which could possibly have received any

[23] Estimated profit. The figures are not based on enough firm pricing data to be completely trustworthy.

[24] The account of politics in this paragraph follows Sirmans, *Colonial South Carolina*, 151–163.

bounty protection. In 1728 tar and pitch exports dropped to under 10 per cent of the 1725 level of exportation. In 1727 and 1728 rice exports appear to have spurted ahead to 150 per cent of the shipments in 1725, with a suspected concurrent fall in sale prices. To add to these woes, a major hurricane struck in August 1728, destroying 2,000 barrels of rice and damaging or destroying 23 ships.[25] A serious yellow fever epidemic struck during the same year.[26]

As the depression deepened, passions of those advocating paper money as a cure for the colony's economic ills rose. All settlers were touched, but those who were hit hardest (probably the debt-ridden and devastated yeoman planters) organized in early 1727 to act. Mob violence threatened another political revolution, but renewed aggression by the Yamasee drove all factions together temporarily. Both houses and Middleton agreed to suspend the sinking act and emit thousands of pounds of new bills.[27] An expedition under Colonel John Palmer was sent out and drove the Yamasee all the way to St. Augustine in 1728.[28] Once the threat was past, the factional political fighting was resumed; the government lapsed into a state of paralysis.

From 1728 to 1731 the assembly occasionally sat, but no business could be transacted. Indeed, from March 1727 until August 1731 only a few statutes were enacted.[29] No tax bills were passed and no legal provision was made for paying government expenses. The court system functioned imperfectly all the time and sometimes not at all. The situation

[25] Ludlum, *Early American Hurricanes*, 43–44.

[26] Waring, *History of Medicine in S.C.*, 34–35.

[27] Cooper and McCord (eds.), *Statutes of S.C.*, III, 273 (title only is listed); Bull, Sr., "An Account of the Rise and Progress of the Paper Bills of Credit in South Carolina . . . ," ibid., IX, 776.

[28] For a detailed account, see Crane, *Southern Frontier*, 249–251.

[29] The titles of all acts passed during this period are listed on one page in Cooper and McCord (eds.), *Statutes of S.C.*, III, 273.

has aptly been described as "a state of near anarchy." [30]
While local partisanship and passions were largely responsible for the situation, much of what happened was the result
of the frustrations accumulated since 1715, and the economic
depths reached by 1727–1728.

While the South Carolina situation deteriorated after
1725, the Board of Trade did not hurry to any quick decisions to improve the situation. The Board worked from
evidence and advice. In South Carolina's case, the conflicting
testimony after 1725 must have been confusing. Where Francis Yonge had been effective in presenting a single view of
the colony's questions in the early 1720's, now the Commons'
agent, Samuel Wragg, and the Council's agent, Stephen
Godin, carried on the local fight in London.[31] Former Governor Robert Johnson was in London after 1724 soliciting his
own affairs and was frequently called before the Board for
his opinions. As long as he lived, Governor Nicholson was
espousing views in defense of his own conduct. And then
there were the ever-present merchants, generally pushing
views favorable to their own interests. Various crown officials
also had opinions which were heard. Not the least among the
babel of confusing voices from the various interest groups
was that of the proprietors, who had to be reckoned with as
long as they owned the soil of Carolina.

If the Board's position was difficult, many of its actions
after 1725 are inexplicable, and some are indefensible.
Though it might not have anticipated that Nicholson's leaving the colony would bring chaos—since governors frequently were given leave to come home without any great
problems emerging—the failure to relieve Nicholson and
put another in his place in late 1726 or 1727 after reports of
the colony's deteriorating government circulated in London

[30] Sirmans, *Colonial South Carolina*, 158.   [31] Ibid., 160.

is not easily explained. Even more surprising is the failure to make an appointment after Nicholson's death in early 1728. It was, in fact, late 1729 before the Board did appoint a governor, and another year elapsed before that governor arrived in the colony. Forceful leadership, particularly from 1727 to 1730, might have relieved some of the worst aspects of the deepening crisis, though it is difficult to see how even a strong governor could have done more than kept the government functioning. Positive policies were required to reinforce the underlying weakness of the economy, which would in turn strengthen the government. Why the Board moved so slowly to make those decisions is the largest part of the riddle, especially since it did not always act in such a desultory fashion. Possibly the complexity of deciding exactly where imperial interests lay caused the delays.

The initial step toward aiding South Carolina came when the proprietors were eliminated. Though such an agreement between crown and proprietors was not formalized until 1729, it was a foregone conclusion after 1727. The resurrected interest of the proprietors after 1725 received no encouragement from crown officials. In 1726 the proprietors' nomination of Colonel Samuel Horsey as governor and their requests to have the South Carolina government collect quitrents drew strong protests from the settlers.[32] After the Board of Trade showed little inclination to aid the proprietors or to pay attention to their advice, it must have become obvious to them that Carolina was lost. In May 1727, after years of sparring, they offered to sell their shares to the crown.[33] Negotiations were slow, since the proprietors wanted compensation for the lost quitrents and the sover-

---

[32] On this see Sirmans, *Colonial South Carolina*, 153–154.

[33] The earliest indication in the records that the proprietors agreed formally to divest themselves of Carolina seems to be a letter from Proprietors to His Majesty, May 31, 1727, BPRO-SC, XII, 217.

eignty they were surrendering. They settled, because they had to, for a cash payment of £2,500 to each proprietor and a total of £5,000 for the estimated arrears in quitrents.[34] Lord Carteret, one of the eight shareholders, took land in lieu of his cash payment and subsequently received a special crown grant in North Carolina. Considering that none of the final shareholders had expended much, and the original proprietors had expended most, those who sold in 1729 received more than they deserved. Since the proprietary had been formed in 1663, it probably had not spent much more than the £25,000 it was awarded when accounts were settled with the crown. The Board finally had one major restriction on its freedom of action removed; the settlers were rid of an irksome connection which had not aided them much for many years and of late had been mostly a hindrance to the colony's development and stability.

After the crown was committed to take over the complete supervision of South Carolina, the Board of Trade came to grips with the problems of the colony. Much of its concern centered on the economic weaknesses, always viewed, of course, within the context of the best interest of the empire. The old arguments over tar and pitch production in America versus supply from the Baltic were dusted off and rehashed. While the Board saw the advantages accruing to South Carolina if the bounties were reinstated, the argument pointing out the vulnerability of the Baltic trade in wartime seems to have been the most telling one. Parliament, acting on the recommendation of the Board of Trade and other officials, passed a new and comprehensive naval stores law in 1729, which was aimed at fulfilling Royal Navy needs from within the empire. Framers of the law, however, took into

[34] The proprietors claimed that they were actually owed £9,500 in past due quitrents. Proprietors to Privy Council, (no month or day) 1728, ibid., XIII, 8–9.

account that the first bounty system had brough
tar and pitch. The new bounties were accordir
to meet the anticipated demand of the navy
Regular tar, the product made from deadwood
premium of £2 4s. per ton (as opposed to £4 per ion
tar, as specified in the original bounty act). The preferred
"green" tar, made by the Swedish method from green or live
trees, was to have a subsidy of £4 per ton (a 2s. per barrel
advantage over tar manufactured from deadwood). The law
clearly and carefully described the Swedish process and how
certificates were to be made specifying that a given shipment
of tar had been made from green wood. Pitch, in much less
demand than tar, was to have a £1 per ton premium (as
opposed to £4 per ton in the original act). The turpentine
bounty was cut to £1 10s. per ton (from £3 per ton provided
by the first act). Rosin was dropped from the list of naval
stores subsidized. Further, merchants who re-exported colonial naval stores from Britain to the continent had to repay
the bounty money.[35] While this new system offered a possible
chance for South Carolina to regain its tar and pitch trade, it
remained to be seen how beneficial these subsidies would
be.[36]

The Board of Trade also was interested throughout the
1720's in the marketing problems of the South Carolina rice
growers. In many ways, this was not as thorny an issue as that
of tar and pitch. South Carolinians, many merchants, and
even the Board of Trade had long recognized that direct
shipments of rice to Spain and Portugal would expand the
market. The major problem was how to collect crown duties
on rice should this exception to enumeration be allowed.

[35] 2 George II, c. 35.
[36] For a convenient summary of the Board of Trade viewpoint, see their
report to Parliament presented April 8, 1730, as found in Leo F. Stock (ed.),
*Proceedings and Debates of the British Parliaments Respecting North Amer-
ica*, (Washington, 1924–1941) IV, 67–71.

Francis Yonge was instructed to make an alteration of this law one of his objectives.[37] In 1725 a bill to that end was introduced in the Commons, but it was never acted upon.[38] By the late 1720's the Board was ready to recommend a revision of the law restricting rice exports to points within the empire. In early 1730 the proposal was being considered seriously for the first time by Parliament. Many of the merchant petitions originally sent to the Board were now exhibited for the benefit of the lawmakers.[39] After a thorough airing in both Commons and Lords, a law was passed in May, 1730, which was to be effective after September 29, 1730. Under the statute's clauses, the shipment of rice directly from South Carolina to ports south of Cape Finisterre was permitted. Thus, in effect, the rice markets in Spain and Portugal were opened up. Under this amendment to the existing laws, vessels carrying rice only could participate in this trade after obtaining a special license. After completing the voyage, each vessel had to sail to England where one-half the duty which would have been paid on the rice had it been landed in England first and then re-exported was paid.[40] The most convincing argument offered in the Parliamentary debates seems to have been that, despite the lower tax rate on rice, the losses would be recouped by the increase in trade generally and by an expansion of rice markets. There can be little doubt that South Carolina would not have received what appeared to be a benefit unless imperial interests could be protected.

While devoting attention to the colony's economic underpinning, the Board of Trade was simultaneously engaged in a search for a governor and was trying to determine policies

[37] Instructions for Francis Yonge and John Lloyd, agents for South Carolina, no exact date but must have been drawn up in 1721, BPRO-SC, IX, 121–131.
[38] Stock (ed.), *Debates of British Parliaments*, II, 480.
[39] Ibid., III, 57–58, 60–62.   [40] 3 George II, c. 28.

which would stop the internal disarray. As it consulted the various interested parties, the Board deferred more and more to the counsel of former Governor Robert Johnson, who generally was ably seconded by Samuel Wragg.[41] As early as 1727 or 1728 some members of the Board may have leaned toward Johnson as the most likely and best candidate for governor. But he was not officially appointed until November 22, 1729, over a year and a half after Governor Nicholson died.[42] The appointment was controversial, for the old proprietors so hated Johnson, whom they blamed for their 1719 troubles, that they petitioned against him even after they had agreed to sell Carolina.[43] Most modern historians, however, have felt that he was the best man available for the job. He had, of course, the great advantage of long experience in the affairs of the colony, and a number of years in England to understand the imperial viewpoint of the colony's position. He also had a program which he insisted would overcome South Carolina's difficulties. Indeed, his program may have won the appointment of governor for him. By 1729 Johnson's and Wragg's recommendations were being followed by the Board of Trade, while Stephen Godin, the agent of the Council, saw his influence eclipsed.

Once Robert Johnson had been named governor, the Board's task became one of writing comprehensive instructions to aid him in restoring political order and pacifying the people. It was essential that Governor Johnson understand the Board's policies fully. The problems were knotty, and correspondence was slow. At the same time, the Board obviously attempted to take into consideration South Caroli-

---

[41] Sirmans, *Colonial South Carolina*, 160–161.

[42] Minutes of Board of Trade, December 2, 1729, BPRO-SC, XIII, 245–246. Johnson was apparently delayed a year awaiting his instructions.

[43] Five Proprietors to His Majesty, October 12, 1727, Ibid., XII, 253–256. Among other flaws, the proprietors note that Johnson had failed to pay his own quitrents.

na's needs and desires. While it might be argued that the set of instructions finally drafted was ten years late, the resulting program is impressive in its grasp of the essential issues facing the settlers and their government.

The most pressing matter the new governor had to face was the paper money controversy with all its political and economic ramifications. For years the Board of Trade had received solicited and unsolicited advice about the question. Most had advocated an all or nothing approach, either a strictly hard money policy or a lenient philosophy favoring only loose restrictions on paper issues. By 1729, however, a number of realists began to offer compromises as the only way out of the colony's dire predicament. Governor Burrington of North Carolina testified that £90,000 currency was not excessive, considering the volume of the colony's trade. He defended South Carolina by noting that it had had to spend four times as much as any other mainland colony on war and preparations for war. He did not believe that the colony was financially capable of sinking the bills rapidly. As a matter of practical politics, he thought that any governor appointed with the authority to allow a reasonable sum of paper money in circulation would be readily accepted and be a more effective executive.[44]

In early 1730 a group of British merchants, in an almost complete reversal of previous statements by this interest group, supported much the same general position. Yet, a close scrutiny of the 21 signers has revealed that at least 12 of these British merchants owned land in South Carolina.[45] Again, this is support for the conclusion that merchants with a stake in the colony other than trade were more sympathetic to local viewpoints and tended to take a middle of the road

[44] Governor Burrington to Board of Trade, July 28, 1729, BPRO-SC, XIII, 373–374.
[45] Wallace, *History of S.C.*, I, 334–335.

stand on the paper money controversy. At this juncture, these men calculated that the colony's trade was worth £100,000 sterling annually (there is no indication how they arrived at this figure), so £100,000 of bills of credit (approximately the amount then outstanding) worth £15,000 sterling (about a 7:1 ratio, currency to sterling) was a reasonable amount to leave in circulation. They advocated that the sinking of bills, which in effect would contract the supply of paper money, be suspended for seven years. Taxes normally expended to retire bills should be allocated toward bringing in poor protestants to increase the white population.[46]

This ingenious package was soon being considered in conjunction with Johnson's favorite proposal to implement the frontier township scheme first seriously considered in the early 1720's.[47] When details were ironed out, Governor Johnson's instructions permitted him to allow the assembly to keep £106,000 in bills of credit in circulation; a seven-year moratorium on sinking bills would be in effect; and poor protestants (it was anticipated that these would be mostly Palatines) would be settled in townships reserved for them on the frontier.[48] In one fell swoop, an officially sanctioned approach had been mapped to solve some of the colony's most pressing political, economic, demographic, and defense problems.

This move left the Board and Governor Johnson with the task of forming a new land system. Decisions had to be made as to how land would be granted in the future, the status of doubtful grants and patents left from the proprietary era,

[46] Minutes of Board of Trade, February 4, 1730, BPRO-SC, XIV, 2; Minutes of Board of Trade, March 12, 1730, ibid., XIV, 3; Petition to Board of Trade, marked rec'd February 4, 1730, ibid., XIV, 32-33.

[47] Johnson wrote to the Board several times on this plan. For example, Governor Johnson to Board of Trade, April 30, 1730, ibid., XIV, 89-91.

[48] Instructions for Governor Johnson from Board of Trade, June 10, 1730, ibid., XIV, 147-214.

quitrents, and a number of other questions. Johnson had ideas about these questions, not all of which were acceptable to the crown. For example, based on his long experience in the colony, he felt that settlers should be allowed to take deadwood from the crown lands to make tar and pitch. He argued that this would make it unnecessary to grant huge tracts of pine lands which were only valuable for tar making. Such a policy would forestall escheating exhausted pine lands back to the crown rather than paying quitrents on worthless acreage.[49] While this advice was not incorporated into his instructions, he was given reasonable guidelines. The assembly was to pass a law which would require persons claiming land under any form of conveyance to re-register it. Quitrents were to be four shillings per 100 acres with an adequate collection system instituted for the first time. A 50-acre headright for each immigrant or slave arriving was to be the rule. At the same time, Governor Johnson was to have considerable latitude to use his own judgment in handling unanticipated circumstances as he put together a workable land system.[50]

Besides the laws of Parliament and the policies of the Board of Trade aimed at improving the colony's posture, Colonel Palmer's expedition and an unexpected diplomatic triumph left the southern frontier more peaceful than it had been in years. A reduction of defense spending and quiet borderlands boded well for Governor Johnson as he undertook his job. Palmer's victories calmed the Yamasee and the Creeks to the south by force of arms. The Cherokee to the west had been charmed by Sir Alexander Cuming, a Scot with peculiar quirks of personality and a myriad of odd

[49] Governor Johnson to "Sir" (probably Board of Trade), January 2, 1730, ibid., 29–31.

[50] Instructions for Governor Johnson from Board of Trade, June 10, 1730, ibid., XIV, 147–214.

interests and unlikely projects. Having arrived in the colony to find unusual native species, Cuming soon appointed himself arbiter when he learned of strained relations between the colony and the tribe. For some reason best known to them, the Cherokee accepted this eccentric wanderer at his own value. Ending up with all sorts of pledges of friendship from them, Cuming took seven chiefs back to England with him. In London, the chieftains were wined and dined, but they also appeared frequently in front of the Board of Trade. Before being sent back to America on the same vessel carrying Governor Johnson, they signed a treaty giving Cherokee allegiance to England and promising England all their trade. South Carolina's frontiers appeared secure in 1730.[51]

Within the context of South Carolina's economic history, the arrival of Governor Robert Johnson at Charles Town in early December 1730 marks the end of one era and the beginning of another. If Governor Johnson's appearance signaled the finish of the proprietary period, he brought no miraculous cures for the colony's ills. Despite his abilities and the respect the settlers had for him, his term had both successes and failures. His blueprint for ending political strife and reviving commerce was imperfect.

He succeeded in restoring political tranquillity in great measure, though dissident voices were never completely stilled. The new land system soon revealed flaws which were bothersome for years thereafter, but it allowed the colony to go into an era of unprecedented expansion. During the 1720's, in the midst of their troubles, colonists had penetrated north of the Santee River searching for good land. About 1729, George Town was founded on Winyah Bay as the center of this growing area. The township system and inducements offered to potential immigrants lured consider-

[51] For details of this diplomacy, see Crane, *Southern Frontier*, 276–280.

able numbers of European settlers, the first such large influx of whites in several decades. In addition to the frontier fortresses, security was buttressed by the start of the settlement of Georgia in 1733, a development not foreseen in 1730. But the economy remained weak, and many established settlers failed to achieve prosperity. The paper money controversy did not die out altogether, though the total amount of bills of credit in circulation was pegged and financial stability was restored. With the new bounty structure inadequate for profitable production, tar and pitch never regained their earlier value to the total economy. The legal modification which allowed rice to be shipped directly to the Iberian Peninsula did not prove to be the panacea its advocates had envisioned. Planters continued to grow and harvest rice beyond market demand, resulting in low prices and low profits.

Nevertheless, in 1730 South Carolinians, unable to discern the pitfalls ahead, could only view the future with optimism. Doubtless they wanted to forget the past as they started anew; however, the battles waged for 60 years against nature, the Indians, the Spaniards, the French, the proprietors, the crown, and each other, had left a legacy which would influence any future which might unfold. Not the least important aspect of this past had been learning how to cope with their environment, how to live in it, and how to use its gifts and potentialities. Despite their troubled progress since 1670, the hard fact of the people's existence had been their limited control of their government and economy, and imperial authorities would continue to be the most powerful shaping force in South Carolina's political and economic future just as they had been in its past.

APPENDIX

TABLE I
SOME POPULATION ESTIMATES, 1670–1730

Sources: As Noted.

Explanatory Note: This compilation includes only those contemporary counts the author thinks trustworthy plus his own estimates of the population at 10-year intervals. None of the early figures give separate totals for whites and blacks though it has generally been assumed that the colony had few slaves until after 1690. For more population data, some of them conflicting with the sampling presented here, see the works cited under Demography in the Bibliographical Essay.

Year	Whites	Blacks	Total	Source of Estimate and Commentary
1670	200	— *	— *	Author's estimate.
1671	200	— *	— *	*Shaftesbury Papers*, 300–307.
1672	400	— *	— *	Ibid., 376–383, 387.
1675	500 to 600	— *	— *	Ibid., 466–468.
1680	1,000	— *	— *	Author's estimate.
1680	1,000 to 1,200	— *	— *	Ashe, *Carolina*
1682	2,000 to 2,500	— *	— *	Ibid.
1690	3,500 to 4,000	— *	— *	Author's estimate.
1700	— *	— *	5,000 or 6,000	Greene and Harrington, *Population*, 172.
1700	— *	— *	6,000	Author's estimate.

251

Year	Whites	Blacks	Total	Source of Estimate and Commentary
1703	3,800	3,000	6,800	*BPRO-SC*, V, 203–210 (plus 350 Indian slaves).
1708	4,080	4,100	8,180	Ibid. (plus 1,400 Indian slaves).
1710	4,500	5,500	10,000	Author's estimate.
1715	6,250	10,500	16,750	Greene and Harrington, *Population*, 173 (other estimates on same page).
1720	9,000	12,000	21,000	Ibid., 174 (other estimates on same page).
1720	7,000	12,000	19,000	Author's estimate.
1721	5,000 to 6,000	11,828	17,000 to 18,000	BPRO-SC, IX, 22–23.
1729	10,000 #	20,000	30,000	Ibid., XIII, 373–374; ibid., XV, 69–71.
1730	10,000	20,000	30,000	Author's estimate.

* No figure.
# This source listed 2,000 white adult males, each of whom probably represented four or five persons on average.

TABLE II

LANDS GRANTED ANNUALLY BY COUNTY: 1670–1719

Source: Compiled by the author from an index to surviving land grants used in the Search Room, South Carolina Archives, Columbia, S.C., with the exception noted.

Explanatory Note: Records of land grants are known to be incomplete for the period before 1730 and thus very little has been written on the general subject. However, an attempt to assess the impact of land policies on economic development seemed germane to this study. No claim can be made that this table includes all surviving land grants, since the index itself is doubtless incomplete. Based on lands taxed in the 1720's, it apparently represents about half the acreage actually conveyed before 1719, when the land office was closed. Questionable though this table may be, it is included here because its figures do support certain conclusions reached in the text and no alternative source of data was available.

Year	Berkeley No. G.ª	Berkeley Acreage	Colleton No. G.ª	Colleton Acreage	Craven No. G.ª	Craven Acreage	Granville No. G.ª	Granville Acreage	Undesignated No. G.ª	Undesignated Acreage	TOTALS No. G.ª	TOTALS Acreage
1670											—	—
1671											—	—
1672											—	—
1673											—	—
1674	1	1,070									1	1,070
1675	7	13,103									7	13,103
1676	18	5,971									18	5,971
1677	14	3,973									14	3,973
1678	9	13,880									9	13,880
1679	15	10,553									15	10,553
1680	15	11,386									15	11,386
1681	30	26,397									30	26,397

TABLE II (Continued)

Year	Berkeley No. G.[a]	Berkeley Acreage	Colleton No. G.[a]	Colleton Acreage	Craven No. G.[a]	Craven Acreage	Granville No. G.[a]	Granville Acreage	Undesignated No. G.[a]	Undesignated Acreage	TOTALS No. G.[a]	TOTALS Acreage
1682	12	9,860									12	9,860
1683	1	400									1	400
1684											—	—
1685	1	12,000									1	12,000
1686											—	—
1687											—	—
1688	4	13,009			2	400					6	13,409
1689											—	—
1690	2	2,900									2	2,900
1691											—	—
1692	3	630									3	630
1693	7	1,310							3	600	10	1,910
1694	38	8,833	14	7,058	1	100			34	5,297	87	21,288
1695	18	4,368	15	6,917					25	4,468	58	15,753
1696	50	25,775	18	10,484	2	500			41	13,467	111	50,226
1697	23	10,608	12	8,000							35	18,608
1698	8	4,945	3	1,036	1	2,800					12	8,781
1699	8	1,870	1	140	4	800					13	2,810
1700	9	2,618	15	13,362					3	2,318	27	18,298
1701	8	3,175	2	640	2	400					12	4,215
1702	4	2,595	1	6,000	3	550			4	1,982	12	11,127
1703	6	2,200	1	300	1	500			4	2,842	12	5,842

Year	No.[a]	Acres	No.[a]	Acres	No.[a]	Acres	No.[a]	Acres	No.[a]	Acres	No.[a]	Acres
1704	31	15,053	5	2,303	2	1,200			3	526	41	19,082
1705	23	16,823	7	3,280	10	3,021	1	500	1	600	42	24,224
1706	19	8,927			3	1,300			2	2,080	24	12,307
1707	5	1,890	4	1,926	1	500	2	1,044	1	1,000	13	6,360
1708	7	2,356	1	400	1	500	1	200			10	3,456
1709	35	40,863	19	6,601	8	3,054	7	3,500			69	54,018
1710	39	15,929	16	6,740	6	2,500	5	2,103			66	27,272
1711	85	33,679	58	21,175	27	9,309	15	6,550			185	70,713
1712	2	1,526			1	50	1	500			4	2,076
1713	1	346							1	500	2	846
1714	19	6,692	20	8,114	7	3,400	5	2,200			51	20,406
1715	1	170					1	468	1	100	3	738
1716	2	826	1	165							3	991
1717	4	13,092	1	500			3	1,550			8	15,142
1718	1	1,869					2	600			3	2,469
1719												—
Totals:	585	353,470	214	105,141	82	30,884	43	19,215	123	35,780	1,047	544,490
1720[b]		775,693		218,535		117,274		51,817				1,163,319

Undesignated and undated: 15 / 8,361

Grand total: 1,062 / 552,851

[a] Number of Grants. Blank spaces mean no grants listed in the index for that year.

[b] James Moore to "Sir," March 21, 1721, BPRO-SC, IX, 22–23. The total acreage taxed is listed in this document as 1,163,239¼ acres; however, the amounts of land credited to each parish total to the figure shown on the table. Whether this small error was made by Moore or by someone copying the original is impossible to determine without the original in hand. The amount of land being taxed is confirmed by an S. P. G. document, quoted by Wallace, *History of S.C.*, I, 309–310. He indicates that it shows 1,163,817 acres taxed in January 1722.

TABLE III

EXPORTS FROM CHARLES TOWN, 1699–1735

Source: Compiled from Charles Town naval lists (British Public Record Office designation: C. O. 5/508 and 5/509) by the author, with the exceptions noted. For a detailed explanation of processing methods followed in handling the naval lists, see his "The Charleston Export Trade, 1717–1737," cited in the Bibliographical Essay, which also includes other works containing trade statistics.

Explanatory note: All export units on this table are barrels except for deerskins and leather. While deerskins were reported on the naval lists in chests, barrels, boxes, etc., other data have been used here since actual skin counts provide a more meaningful measure. Blanks represent a lack of information.

Year	Rice C. Y.[a]	Rice H. Y.[b]	Tar C. Y.[a]	Pitch C. Y.[a]	Total C. Y.[a]	Tar H. Y.[b]	Pitch H. Y.[b]	Total H. Y.[b]	Deer- skins[c]
1699		2,000[d]							64,488
1700									22,133
1701									51,086
1702									49,646
1703									57,881
1704									61,541
1705									10,289
1706									32,954
1707									121,355
1708									31,939
1709									52,014
1710									68,432
1711									33,409
1712		12,727 •				2,037 •	4,580 •	6,617 •	80,324
1713									60,451

Top table (years 1717–1735; column headings not present in this crop):

Year									
1717	10,849	8,289	29,594	14,363	43,957				21,713
1718	8,309	13,749	32,007	20,208	52,215				17,073
1719	14,010	14,821	25,495	17,489	42,984				24,355
1720	14,584	21,741	10,025	24,453	34,478	9,535	15,189	24,724	35,171
1721		23,559				12,288	11,213	23,501	33,939
1722		20,078				17,434	13,536	30,970	59,827
1723		20,372				13,603	28,609	42,212	64,315
1724	20,165	17,285	12,220	32,720	44,940	3,591	55,277	58,868	61,124
1725	17,227	17,734 [f]	3,058	57,277	60,335				79,753
1726		23,031 [f]	8,322 [g]	29,776 [g]	38,098 [g]				79,753
1727		26,884 [f]	10,950 [g]	13,654 [g]	24,604 [g]				79,753
1728		29,965 [f]	2,269 [g]	3,186 [g]	5,455 [g]				79,753
1729		32,384 [f]	3,441 [g]	8,377 [g]	11,818 [g]				79,753
1730		48,155 [h]	2,014 [g]	10,825 [g]	12,839 [g]	1,895	16,602	18,497	79,753
1731	48,238		2,242	20,898	23,140				86,771
1732									74,483
1733									96,523
1734	37,126	45,960	7,368	28,143	35,511				84,958
1735	44,356	49,656	4,910	23,091	28,001				81,017

Bottom table:

Year	Turpentine	Rosin	Pork	Beef	Flour	Peas	Corn	Sides of Leather
1712			1,241 [e]	1,963 [e]				1,965 [e]
1717	669	1	347	444	1,245	63	41	2,463
1718	605	16	255	715	321	8	0	2,600
1719	1,245	5	407	1,052	325	256	43	3,654
1720	75	43	304	676	615	345	232	1,288
1721								
1722								
1723								

TABLE III (Continued)

Year	Turpentine	Rosin	Pork	Beef	Flour	Peas	Corn	Sides of Leather
1724	469	4	333	625	58	172	28	1,966
1725	133 ᵍ							
1726	715 ᵍ							
1727	1,252 ᵍ							
1728	1,232 ᵍ							
1729	1,913 ᵍ							
1730	1,073 ᵍ							
1731	2,967	182	326	28	303	232	964	1,659
1732								
1733								
1734	4,758	47	356	39	193	638	823	4,919
1735	8,676	69	321	104	1,396	541	1,418	2,300

ᵃ Calendar year. Naval lists were quarterly reports, with the autumn quarter ending December 24. As a result, by using the records as prepared, they can be divided into a close approximation of the modern calendar year.

ᵇ Harvest year. This ran from September 29 to September 28 of the following year. A very meaningful division of shipments since it shows the actual amounts shipped from annual crops, such as rice, exported from late fall to the next spring.

ᶜ Deerskin shipments are actual counts or estimated counts from the following sources:

1699–1715: BPRO-SC, VI, 135–136. The same figures are in Crane, *Southern Frontier*, 328. Since Crane's figures vary some from the report cited above, his figures have been used where there are discrepancies. He took his data from the original. 1716–1724: Crane, ibid., 329.

1726–1735: Crane, ibid., 330. In some instances these figures are not for a calendar year, but for a 12-month period. His 1726–1730 figure is an annual average for the period. His 1731–1735 figures represent a year which started on March 25.

ᵈ E. Randolph to Board of Trade, May 27, 1700, *BPRO-SC*, IV, 189–190. He reported that 330 tons of rice had been shipped "this year" which probably means 2,000 to 2,200 barrels from the 1699 crop.

ᵉ Report based on naval lists, but no indication of author or addressee, ibid., VI, 173–174. Goods were shipped in a 12-month period between June 6, 1712, and June 6, 1713, approximately a harvest year.

ᶠ Gayle, "Exports from Charleston, 1724–1774," *Proc. S.C. Hist. Assn., 1937*, 25–33; apparently Gayle took his data for 1724–1735 from "Account of Importations and Exportations at the Port of Charles-Town, South Carolina, from 1724 to 1735." Exports included in the latter compilation were on the basis of a 12-month period (November 1 to November 1, approximately a harvest year).

ᵍ *Historical Statistics of United States*, 770 (Series Z 304–307).

BIBLIOGRAPHICAL ESSAY

This study drew upon sources of varying importance in developing the central theme, and, given limited space, I have been rather selective in choosing items to include in this essay. General works and bibliographical aids commonly consulted in doing research on any aspect of colonial America have been omitted, as have some materials cited which are only peripherally significant in investigating this subject. Primary sources and secondary works which pertain most directly to the economic history of South Carolina during this period, including some materials cited only occasionally or not at all, have been emphasized. Using this format, I have been able both to describe materials and suggest some of the research difficulties encountered; the latter point sometimes, of necessity, has been alluded to in the text.

A. General Guides to Research Materials

There is no bibliographical compilation which comprehensively lists primary sources pertinent to the colonial history of South Carolina, but the place to start finding printed materials relating to any phase of the colony's or state's history remains J. H. Easterby (ed.), *Guide to the Study and Reading of South Carolina History: A General Classified Bibliography* (Columbia, 1950). It proved indispensable in isolating the widely scattered publications dealing with the early agricultural development of the colony. A more recent work contains much found in Easterby's volume along with more leads to primary sources, though it is limited to materials found in repositories in the state: John Hammond Moore (ed.), *Research Materials in South Carolina, A Guide Compiled and Edited for the South Carolina State Library Board* (Columbia, 1967).

B. Primary Source Materials

British Records. By far the most valuable collection of official documents for the study of South Carolina colonial history is the series: Records in the British Public Record Office Relating to South Carolina, 1663–1782, 36 volumes in facsimile, available in the South Carolina Archives, Columbia, S.C., or on microfilm from the Archives. These volumes were prepared from the original documents by W. Noel Sainsbury and his assistants in the 1890's, hence are sometimes cited as the "Sainsbury Transcripts." The first five volumes were published in their facsimile form (Atlanta and Columbia, 1928–1947). Basically, these records contain the official correspondence between the Charles Town officials and the crown functionaries in London, though some letters to and from the proprietors, some private correspondence, minutes of both the Board of Trade and Privy Council pertaining to South Carolina, and various miscellaneous papers are included. This series contains the bulk of official records in the British Public Record Office relating to the colony except that certain enclosures to letters, such as detailed reports and naval lists, were not copied. Most of the documents included are also in the official British calendar series: *Journal of the Commissioners for Trade and Plantations, 1704–1782,* 14 vols. (London, 1920–1938); W. Noel Sainsbury and others (eds.), *Calendar of State Papers, Colonial Series, America and West Indies, 1574– —,* 43 vols. so date (London, 1862– —); W. L. Grant and James Munro (eds.), *Acts of the Privy Council of England, Colonial Series, 1613–1783,* 6 vols. (Hereford and London, 1908–1912). A few important references to South Carolina commerce, not included by Sainsbury in the BPRO-SC series, will be found in Joseph Redlington (ed.), *Calendar of Treasury Papers, 1557–1728,* 6 vols. (London, 1868–1889); William A. Shaw (ed.),

Calendar of Treasury Books and Papers, 1729–1745, 5 vols. (London, 1897–1903).

Fortunately for American scholars, most of the omissions and missing enclosures in the BPRO-SC series, as well as a wide range of other British official and semiofficial documents are now available on microfilm. In particular, the naval lists of shipping entering and clearing Charles Town (C. O. 5/508–5/511 which include the surviving records, 1717–1767) obtained from the Library of Congress proved to be invaluable in understanding shipping patterns and were a source of some information unobtainable elsewhere.

Some insights into vital issues affecting South Carolina are in the compilation edited by Leo F. Stock, *Proceedings and Debates of the British Parliaments Respecting North America, 1542–1754,* 5 vols. (Washington, 1924–1941). Since verbatim accounts of debates were not kept, Stock's explanatory footnotes and introductory essays in the front of each volume are often extremely helpful. The various acts of trade and navigation which affected South Carolina should be read for details sometimes ignored by historians.

South Carolina Records. To capture the flavor of everyday life in early colonial South Carolina, there is no substitute for leafing the many volumes of records found in the South Carolina Archives. Those documents most helpful in coming to an understanding of the conduct of business in the colony are loosely designated "Wills, Inventories and Miscellaneous Records." These run to many volumes and survive almost from the start of settlement. The series is bound and labeled with various titles. Many of the earlier records are neither segregated by type, nor indexed. In these many thousands of pages, the historian can run across prices of commodities, slave manumissions, money exchanges, and a myriad of documents illustrating various facets of commerce.

Of legal proceedings, the Records of the Court of Common Pleas in the South Carolina Archives are extremely valuable. The earliest documents are dated 1704. Since this was a civil court, actions for debts, suits involving merchants, and so forth, have left a body of materials little used by historians. The Records of the Admiralty Court of South Carolina, which start in 1716 and are on deposit at the Federal Record Center, East Point, Georgia, also contain many references to trade. Only fragments of South Carolina's legislative journals survive from the early period, but they are far more complete for sessions after 1720. These records offer some insight into local opinions and the positions of individuals on certain economic questions, though the transcripts are summaries of proceedings. Most petitions sent by the assembly to London will be found in the BPRO-SC series and represent the official position finally taken. Some of the early legislative records have been published by Alexander S. Salley (ed.), *Journal of the Commons House of Assembly, 1692–1735* (title varies slightly), 21 vols. (Columbia, 1907–1946). For a complete accounting of surviving records of both houses and where these records are located, the extremely valuable series of articles by Charles E. Lee and Ruth S. Green should be consulted: "A Guide to the Upper House Journals of South Carolina General Assembly, 1721–1775," *South Carolina Historical Magazine,* LXVII (1966), 187–202; "A Guide to South Carolina Council Journals, 1671–1775," ibid., LXVIII (1967), 1–13; "A Guide to the Commons House Journals of South Carolina General Assembly, 1692–1721," ibid., LXVIII (1967), 85–96; "A Guide to the Commons House Journals of the South Carolina General Assembly, 1721–1775," ibid., LXVIII (1967), 165–183.

Though there are some omissions in this compilation (and the texts of some laws have permanently disappeared), Thomas Cooper and David J. McCord (eds.), *The Statutes at Large of South Carolina,* 10 vols. (Columbia, 1836–1841), is the standard reference for enactments of the colonial period.

Private Papers. The chief stumbling block to writing a fuller and more satisfactory economic history of South Carolina before 1730 is the almost complete lack of private papers after 1675. For the first five years of settlement, *The Shaftesbury Papers and Other Records Relating to Carolina and the First Settlement on Ashley River Prior to the Year 1676,* edited by Langdon Cheves, and published in the *Collections of the South Carolina Historical*

Society, V (Charleston, 1897), provides the largest, and almost the only, body of private correspondence surviving from the first 60 years of the colony's existence. After 1675, only occasional items written by private individuals are to be found in widely scattered places. This lack poses a particular problem to the historian who wants information about such topics as methods of rice culture, the processes of naval stores manufacture, how slaves were employed, and profits in the various trades.

With few private papers to rely on, contemporary writings often designated as narratives or chronicles must be used. Most were written to influence European readers to believe the best about opportunities in South Carolina or were slanted for other reasons. Some were intended for immediate publication and others for private circulation. Despite questions about the objectivity of the reporters, these writings have been and will be used extensively because they provide the only sources for answers to some questions. The most complete collection of early works was compiled by Alexander S. Salley (ed.), *Narratives of Early Carolina, 1650–1708,* in J. Franklin Jameson (ed.), *Original Narratives of Early American History* series (New York, 1911). Much of the same material found in the Salley volume and narratives written after 1708 are in two nineteenth century compilations: Bartholomew R. Carroll (ed.), *Historical Collections of South Carolina . . . ,* 2 vols. (New York, 1836), and P. G. J. Weston, *Documents Connected with the History of South Carolina* (London, 1856). Because of his known experience in the colony, the most authoritative promotional pamphlet may have been written by Thomas Nairne, *A Letter From South Carolina* (London, 1710). Francis Yonge, *A View of the Trade of South-Carolina with Proposals Humbly Offered for Improving the Same* (London, 1722?) also is trustworthy, but Yonge had been expressing his views for some years in official correspondence (in the BPRO-SC series) before this pamphlet appeared.

C. Secondary Sources

General Histories. Since there is no economic history of colonial South Carolina, the general histories have been an important source for over-all interpretations, though their writers have been most concerned with political events and often least concerned with the economy, trade, and agriculture. Alexander Hewatt, *An Historical Account of the Rise and Progress of the Colonies of South Carolina and Georgia,* 2 vols. (London, 1779), was alive during some of the era he wrote about, used much hearsay evidence, and has much material which is difficult to substantiate today. Despite his antiquated frame of reference and his failures to answer many questions more modern historians would have asked, his evaluations continue to be worth noting. David Ramsay, *The History of South Carolina, From Its First Settlement in 1670, to the Year 1808,* 2 vols. (Charleston, 1809), was much inclined to copy Hewatt and added little to an understanding of economic development. William J. Rivers, *A Sketch of the History of South Carolina to the Close of the Proprietary Government by the Revolution in 1719* (Charleston, 1856) made only passing mention of the economy, though this is still a useful work for understanding politics. Rivers' work has an extensive appendix of British documents which should not be ignored, for they must be used to supplement the BPRO-SC series. Despite the length and depth of the volumes by Edward McCrady, *The History of South Carolina under the Proprietary Government, 1670–1719* (New York, 1897) and *The History of South Carolina under the Royal Government, 1719–1776* (New York, 1899), he concentrated on political history, giving some emphasis to legal aspects of government but little space to economic history.

The most recent multivolume history by David D. Wallace, *The History of South Carolina,* 4 vols. (New York, 1934), has many virtues that earlier detailed works do not have. Wallace tried for a much more balanced and complete coverage of all sides of the colony's and state's history, including attention to the economy and its obvious relationship to the political situation at a given time. It remains in many ways the best over-all account of the colonial era. Substantially the same text without the extensive footnotes was published as *South Carolina: A Short History, 1530–1948* (Chapel Hill, 1951).

Important Narrower Studies. Most of the other secondary sources have been placed under the following headings which represent the major topics dealt with in this study. A few monographs and other works, however, do not belong in these confines and should be treated separately.

Political history to the eve of the American Revolution has been ably covered by M. Eugene Sirmans, *Colonial South Carolina: A Political History, 1663–1763* (Chapel Hill, 1966). A work of much merit representing a tremendous amount of research, it is weak in correlating the pattern of economic development to political events. The book has some factual errors involving commerce and trade statistics. Had Dr. Sirmans lived longer, more than likely he would have caught these mistakes and would have corrected his copy. His bibliographical essay should not be overlooked by anyone interested in South Carolina colonial history. It includes many items omitted here because of their limited use in preparing this study.

Early attempts at settlement have been summarized briefly by Paul Quattlebaum, *The Land Called Chicora: The Carolinas Under Spanish Rule with French Intrusions, 1520–1670* (Gainesville, 1956). The first English attempts to settle the Carolina coast have been thoroughly covered by Lawrence Lee, *The Lower Cape Fear in Colonial Days* (Chapel Hill, 1965). The standard work on pirates and piracy is by Shirley C. Hughson, *The Carolina Pirates and Colonial Commerce, 1670–1740* (Herbert B. Adams (ed.), *Johns Hopkins University Studies in Historical and Political Science*, Twelfth Series, VII) (Baltimore, 1894), though this work leaves many questions unanswered.

Since few private papers survive, it is not surprising that few biographies, either short or more detailed, have been written about persons associated with the colony during these early years. Two have been published fairly recently, though neither is particularly enlightening about South Carolina economic matters:

Michael G. Hall, *Edward Randolph and the American Colonies, 1676–1703* (Chapel Hill, 1960), and Richard P. Sherman, *Robert Johnson: Proprietary and Royal Governor of South Carolina* (Columbia, 1967). Randolph's vast correspondence has been published, Robert N. Toppan (ed.), *Edward Randolph: Including His Letters and Official Papers . . . 1676–1703* (Publications of the Prince Society, XXIV–XXVIII, XXX–XXXI [7 vols.]) (Boston, 1898–1907). Most of the items pertaining to South Carolina are in the BPRO-SC series.

Two works, Robert L. Meriwether, *The Expansion of South Carolina, 1729–1865* (Kingsport, 1940) and George C. Rogers, Jr., *Charleston in the Age of the Pinckneys* (Norman, 1969), start at the approximate point this study ends, and some of their chapters continue themes developed in this study.

The Proprietary and the Proprietors. No published work has explored the relationship of the proprietary to Carolina or examined how the proprietary functioned internally. The most complete and searching view is by Herbert R. Paschal, Jr., "Proprietary North Carolina: A Study in Colonial Government" (unpublished Ph.D. dissertation, University of North Carolina, 1961). Hope Frances Kane, "Colonial Promotion and Promotion Literature of Carolina, 1660–1700" (unpublished Ph.D. dissertation, Brown University, 1930), probes the proprietary's early attempts to publicize its lands.

The most meaningful assessments of the proprietary's first years come from Shaftesbury's papers. His biographer, Louise Fargo Brown, *The First Earl of Shaftesbury* (New York, 1933), devotes considerable attention to his ideas about colonies in general and Carolina in particular. Her views should be compared to those expressed by Edwin Ernest Rich, "The First Earl of Shaftesbury's Colonial Policy," *Royal Historical Society Transactions,* 5th Series, vol. 7 (1957), 47–70. Maurice W. Cranston, *John Locke: A Biography* (New York, 1957), assesses Locke's contribution to the project, but the latest word on the Shaftesbury-Locke relationship is in Peter Laslett's introductory essay to his edition of Locke's *Two Treatises of Government* (Cambridge, England, 1960). All but one of the original proprietors and many of the later ones are sketched in Leslie Stephens and Sidney Lee (eds.), *Dictionary of National Biography From Earliest Times to 1900*, reprint edition, 22 vols. (London, 1921–1922), but little is known about their roles in the proprietary. All holders of proprietary shares are identified by William S. Powell, *The Proprietors of Carolina* (Raleigh, 1963). The minutes of proprietary meetings found in the BPRO-SC series and in the John Locke Manuscripts, "Papers Relating to the Colonies," Shelf Mark c. 6, Bodleian Library, Oxford (Microfilm M-3691, Southern Historical Collection, University of North Carolina, Chapel Hill) are so brief as to be of little use in trying to understand proprietary actions. Most information about proprietary policies must come from their correspondence found in the BPRO-SC series after 1675.

Geography, Climate, Health, and Related Considerations. A comprehension of how the settlers adjusted to the area, its soils, its climate, and its health problems is necessary to appreciate fully the problems of economic development.

Basic works by geographers with historical orientations, such as those by Ralph H. Brown, *Historical Geography of the United States* (New York, 1948) or George F. Carter, *Man and the Land* (New York, 1964), help to put the environmental challenge in perspective. The suggestive article by W. P. Cumming, "Geographical Misconceptions of the Southeast in the Cartography of the Seventeenth and Eighteenth Centuries," *Journal of Southern History*, IV (1938), 476–492, delineates the rudimentary understanding which contemporaries had of the area. Among the multivolume histories, Wallace's work is superior for recognizing the influence of geography on South Carolina history.

Several U.S. Government publications provide convenient sources of basic information about soils and climate: *Soils and Men: Yearbook of Agriculture, 1938* (Washington, 1938); *Climate and Man: Yearbook of Agriculture, 1941* (Washington, 1941); *Atlas of American Agriculture* (Washington, 1936). Basic books on climatology, such as those by Glenn T. Trewartha, *An Introduction to Climate*, 3rd. ed. (New York, 1954) and W. G. Kendrew, *The Climate of the Continents*, 5th ed. (Oxford, 1961), also relate data on climate to soil conditions. A monograph by David M. Ludlum, *Early American Hurricanes, 1492–1870* (Boston, 1963), traces the courses and assesses the damage done by these feared and disruptive storms.

Many of the works listed above take into account the interconnection of climate and health conditions, a fact also recognized by contemporaries. Ramsey's second volume has a section on this matter, and Lionel Chalmers, *An Account of the Weather and Diseases of South Carolina* (London, 1776) is still worth examination. The most detailed modern study of conditions in this colony is by Joseph I. Waring, *A History of Medicine in South Carolina, 1670–1825* (Charleston, 1964), but the more general work by John Duffy, *Epidemics in Colonial America* (Baton Rouge, 1953), is more complete in its descriptions of treatments prescribed in colonial America. Two other studies of South Carolina show that death-causing and disabling diseases were factors in the settlement process: St. Julien R. Childs, *Malaria and Colonization in the Carolina Low Country* (Baltimore, 1940) and John Duffy, "Eighteenth-Century Carolina Health Conditions," *Journal of Southern History*, XVIII (1952), 289–302.

Demography. Those who have searched for population figures for colonial South Carolina have been limited to the same sources, so estimates found in the various compilations generally duplicate one another. The standard reference for raw figures is E. B. Greene and Virginia D. Harrington, *American Population Before the Federal Census of 1790* (New York, 1932). Stella H. Sutherland, *Population Distribution in Colonial America* (New York, 1936), emphasizes the pattern of settlement, as does Julian J. Petty, *The Growth and Distribution of Population in South Carolina* (Columbia, 1943).

Few contemporaries thought it necessary to include meaningful anatomizations of the origins, composition, or social stratification of the settlers. This has handicapped historians. Two articles shed some light on who the Barbadians in South Carolina were and their influence in the colony: Richard S. Dunn, "The Barbados Census of 1680: Profile of the Richest Colony in English America," *William and Mary Quarterly*, 3rd Series, XXVI

(1969), 3–30, and John P. Thomas, Jr., "The Barbadians in Early South Carolina," *South Carolina Historical Magazine,* XXXI (1930), 75–92. For a more detailed study of the Barbadian migration, see Vincent T. Harlow, *A History of Barbados, 1625–1685* (Oxford, 1926). French Protestant settlers in the colony are the subject of a book by Arthur H. Hirsch, *The Huguenots of South Carolina* (Durham, 1928).

The matter of indentured servants is another neglected subject. While Warren B. Smith, *White Servitude in Colonial South Carolina* (Columbia, 1961), listed many examples of the presence of servants in the colony, he did not answer the basic questions of total numbers and their importance to the economy at any one time, if indeed such questions can be answered considering the source material limitations. Nor did he refute those who hold that slave labor early became far more important than indentured labor in the colony. A more complete and more systematic examination of this labor system, including some consideration of South Carolina, will be found in Abbot E. Smith, *Colonists in Bondage: White Servitude and Convict Labor in America, 1607–1776* (Chapel Hill, 1947).

Many facets of the over-all topic of slavery remain unexplored. This is especially true of the earliest years of the colony. No study gives more than cursory attention to slave importations before 1730, except for references to the colony which might be found in general studies or statistical compilations. Some of the most useful articles dealing with aspects of the slave system in the first decades follow: M. Eugene Sirmans, "The Legal Status of the Slave in South Carolina, 1670–1740," *Journal of Southern History,* XXVIII (1962), 462–473; Ulrich B. Phillips, "The Slave Labor Problem in the Charleston District," *Political Science Quarterly,* XXII (1907), 416–439; Edward McCrady, "Slavery in the Province of South Carolina, 1670–1770," *American Historical Association Reports, 1895,* 629–673. Though Frank J. Klingberg, *An Appraisal of the Negro in Colonial South Carolina* (Washington, 1941) is of some value, it does not deal with the early years of the colony in any detail.

There were many Indian slaves in the South Carolina settlement at least into the 1720's, but their numbers and how they were used by settlers remain unknown. Careful perusal of the colony's records discloses scarcely any mentions of these slaves, obviously accounting for the lack of studies about this class of labor. The most important work remains the time-honored examination by Almon W. Lauber, *Indian Slavery in Colonial Times Within the Present United States (Columbia University Studies in History, Economics and Public Law*, LIV, No. 3, 118–210) (New York, 1913). Many references to Indian slavery, without any systematic consideration of the subject, will be found in the works mentioned below under the category, *Indians and the Indian Trade.*

Land Policy and Land Distribution. The process whereby land was put into the hands of the settlers, how much they received, and the location of land grants are integral parts of the story of economic development. Many of the more apparent questions are still unanswered. General studies, such as that by Marshall Harris, *Origin of the Land Tenure System in the United States* (Ames, 1953), explain the legal bases for landholding in colonial America, but they do not deal specifically with South Carolina. The quitrent has been explained by Beverley W. Bond, Jr., *The Quit-Rent System in the American Colonies* (New Haven, 1919). For South Carolina, the only comprehensive study is by Robert K. Ackerman, "South Carolina Colonial Land Policies" (unpublished Ph.D. dissertation, University of South Carolina, 1965). Professor Ackerman is preparing the substance of this careful and important work for publication in this series.

Money and Monetary Questions. South Carolina's currency problems are most carefully explained by Curtis P. Nettels, *The Money Supply of the American Colonies Before 1720 (University of Wisconsin Studies in the Social Sciences and History,* Number 20) (Madison, 1934), though Richard M. Jellison, "Paper Currency in Colonial South Carolina, 1703–1764" (unpublished Ph.D. dissertation, Indiana University, 1953), has more details about the South Carolina situation. Much of Jellison's work is summarized in his two articles: "Antecedents of the South Carolina Currency Acts of 1736 and 1746," *William and Mary Quarterly*, 3rd Series, XVI (1959), 556–567; "Paper Currency in Colonial South Carolina: A Reappraisal," *South Carolina Historical Magazine*, LXII (1961), 134–147. Contemporary writings are important, for all secondary accounts are based to some degree on these narratives. One is generally credited to William Bull, Sr., "An Account of the Rise and Progress of the Paper Bills of Credit in South Carolina" (probably published in 1739), in Cooper and McCord (eds.), *Statutes of S.C.*, IX, 766–780; and another is *An Essay on Currency, Written in August 1732* (Charleston, 1734).

Trade Statistics. Export and import data are the best indicators of the commerce of the colony. These trade statistics have nearly all been drawn from documents on deposit in the British Public Record Office in London. Since all compilations come from the same sources, they tend to substantiate one another. Differences in totals for figures taken from the same documents most often come from difficulty in interpreting numbers or from errors in copying or computation. Before using any of these figures, it is important to read cautionary explanations of the pitfalls built into these statistics. A very short but pertinent explanation of the questions inherent in these figures is the introductory essay by T. S. Ashton to a compilation prepared by Elizabeth Boody Schumpeter, *English Overseas Trade Statistics, 1697–1808* (Oxford, 1960). A more detailed evaluation of the sources of trade data is by George N. Clark, *Guide to English Commercial Statistics, 1696–1782* (London, 1938).

Besides the Schumpeter book cited above, there are several other useful collections of trade figures. General ones include *Historical Statistics of the United States: Colonial Times to 1957* (Washington, 1960), which also includes evaluative commentary by Lawrence H. Harper on the information incorporated into the tables. A compilation of figures often used by others is C. J. Gayle, "The Nature and Volume of Exports From Charleston, 1724–1774," *The Proceedings of the South Carolina Historical Association*, 1937, 25–33. Gayle's data for 1724 to 1735 appear to be based on a contemporary broadside, "Account of Importations and Exportations at the Port of Charles-Town, South Carolina, From 1724 to 1735" (Charles-Town, 1736).

Volume of trade has limited meaning unless some monetary values can be established for exports and imports. Unfortunately, the contemporary values placed on commerce by the customs service and others are riddled with questions. Moreover, the lack of market prices for commodities before 1730 makes it difficult to establish even an approximate balance of trade. The most useful set of prices for South Carolina commodities selling in England was compiled under Sir William Beveridge, *Prices and Wages in England: From the Twelfth to the Nineteenth Century* (vol. I: *Price Tables: Mercantile Era*) (London, 1939), but his figures are best for naval stores. It should be pointed out that several compilations of prices start in the 1730's because researchers have had the *South Carolina Gazette,* which began publication in 1732, as a source. In this study, projections have been based largely on prices gleaned from such sources as inventories, business papers, and official correspondence. This tedious procedure is seemingly one of the few avenues open for trying to obtain enough data to attempt to calculate the value of crops, the profits in a given trade, or an over-all balance of trade.

General Agriculture. The most complete and authoritative consideration of colonial South Carolina's agriculture lies within the monumental volumes by Lewis C. Gray, *History of Agriculture in the Southern United States to 1860,* 2 vols. (Washington, 1933). Gray not only has excellent descriptions of rice cultivation and naval stores manufacturing, but he dealt with the minor trades, changes and shifts in productive emphases, and other factors, making his volumes a comprehensive view. A few early accounts of agriculture should be consulted, including the pamphlet by Nairne previously mentioned, Ramsay's general history, and *American Husbandry, Containing an Account of the Soil, Climate, Production and Agriculture of the British Colonies in North America and the West Indies,* 2 vols. (London, 1775). Of course, Gray used these sources and many others in preparing his work.

Rice. Most writers on rice growing have not left much detail about the early days when the crop was grown in regular fields and inland swamps. The explanation of culture by Thomas Nairne is the most complete among early eighteenth-century narratives. Besides Gray, other books and articles used in the preparation of this study include: Robert F. W. Allston, *Memoir on the Introduction and Planting of Rice* (Charleston, 1843), and *Essay on Sea Coast Crops* (Charleston, 1854); Amory Austin, *Rice: Its Cultivation, Production and Distribution* (U.S. Department of Agriculture, Division of Statistics, Miscellaneous Series, Report No. 6) (Washington, 1893); Duncan C. Heyward, *Seed From Madagascar* (Chapel Hill, 1937). General studies, such as that by D. H. Grist, *Rice,* fourth edition (London, 1965), puts the South Carolina rice-growing experience into world-wide historical perspective.

Naval Stores. Unlike rice, naval stores could be and were produced in all mainland colonies. Thus, a much more extensive body of materials is available. Among secondary works, the following were most useful explanations of naval stores production and trade: Robert G. Albion, *Forests and Sea Power: The Timber Problem of the Royal Navy, 1652–1862* (Cambridge, Massachusetts, 1926); H. Roy Merrens, *Colonial North Carolina in the Eighteenth Century: A Study in Historical Geography* (Chapel Hill, 1964); Joseph J. Malone, *Pine Trees and Politics: The Naval Stores and Forest Policy in Colonial New England, 1691–1775* (Seattle, 1964); Eleanor L. Lord, *Industrial Experiments in the British Colonies of North America* (Herbert B. Adams (ed.), *Johns Hopkins University Studies in Historical and Political Science,* extra volume XVII) (Baltimore, 1898); Justin Williams, "English Mercantilism and Carolina Naval Stores, 1705–1776," *Journal of Southern History,* I (1935), 169–185. Since naval stores were tied to the bounty and the Royal Navy, the explanatory material in Beveridge (cited above under *Trade Statistics*) helps clarify navy purchasing policies.

Indians and the Indian Trade. The most authoritative work on backcountry involvement continues to be the study by Verner W. Crane, *The Southern Frontier, 1670–1732* (Durham, 1928).

Crane's main purpose, however, was not to describe or evaluate the economic impact of this trade, a story not yet adequately examined. While assessing the Indian trade within both the imperial and the South Carolina context, he did supply much information about the trade, the various tribes, and the Indian way of life. Chapman J. Milling, *Red Carolinians* (Chapel Hill, 1940) is a much more complete study of the tribes indigenous to the area. John R. Swanton, *The Indians of the Southeastern United States* (U.S. Bureau of American Ethnology, Bulletin 137) (Washington, 1946) provides even more detailed coverage of the tribal structures and cultures than Milling does.

Other Commercial Activities. Many books and articles, as well as occasional references in the sources, touch on the minor trades such as provisions and lumber, but these trades have never been evaluated thoroughly by historians. Very little work has been done to determine the extent of South Carolina shipbuilding and vessel ownership. As a result, the author has been forced to do his own digging through primary and secondary sources to find information about these and other commercial activities. Many of the conclusions and views woven into this study have been taken from his dissertation, "The Charleston Export Trade, 1717–1737," (unpublished Ph.D. dissertation, Northwestern University, 1963).

INDEX

Admiralty, 132–33
"Adventurers about Cape Fayre," 9
Albemarle County (N.C.), 11–13
Albemarle, Duke of, 7, 13
Allen, Andrew, 153–54, 163
Almonds, 8, 59
Anglican Church. *See* Church of England
Archdale, John, 71; governorship of, 96–101
Archdale's Laws, 97–101
Ashe, Thomas, 72, 81
Ashley, Lord: agricultural experiments of, 59–60; Fundamental Constitutions and, 18; hopes of, for S.C., 48, 51; Indian policy of, 64–65; John Locke and, 16–17; leadership of, 14–15; obtaining proprietary share by, 7; promotion activities of, 72–73; role of, as Palatine, 44–45; views of, about colonies and empire, 15–16; *passim*
Ashley River: first settlement on, 24, 66–67; obtaining land on, 50; present Charles Town located on, 78–79; settlements of 1680 on, 80
Assembly: Archdale's reforms and, 95–101; Board of Trade over, 114; division of, 19, 101; growing independence of, 101–2; proprietors attempt control of, 192; *passim. See also* Commons House of Assembly; Council; South Carolina, Government of

Barbadian Adventurers, 9–11
Barbadians: early interest of, in S.C., 4–6; influence of, on S.C. slave code, 107; rice culture and, 124; some Indian slave traders were, 66; some settlers were, 51, 53–54
Barbados: colonial history of, 4–5
Barbados Concessions, 10
Barnwell, John, 199–200
Barter. *See* Money
Beaufort, 159, 162
Beef, barreled. *See* Provisions
Beresford, Richard, 191
Berkeley County: creation of, 77; population of, 103, 132, 162, 206
Berkeley, Lord John, 7, 13
Berkeley, Sir William, 7, 12, 26
Bills of credit. *See* Money
Bishop of Durham clause, 8
Board of Trade: Charles Town incorporation law and, 198; creation of, 114–15; duties of, 114–15; impact of, on S.C., 115–16, 183–86, 194–95, 200–201, 206–7, 226–29, 240–50; Indian and southern frontier policies of, 110, 116, 199–200, 207, 247–50; instructions from, to Governor Robert Johnson, 245–48; instructions from, to Governor Sir Francis Nicholson, 197–200; naval stores bounties and, 132–34, 172–75, 209–10, 212–16, 242–43; policies of, in 1720's, 240–48; proprietors' relationship to, 110, 191, 194–95, 241–42; rice

275